FORGETTING CHILDREN BORN OF WAR

FORGETTING CHILDREN BORN OF WAR

Setting the Human Rights Agenda in Bosnia and Beyond

R. CHARLI CARPENTER   *Columbia University Press   New York*

COLUMBIA UNIVERSITY PRESS
PUBLISHERS SINCE 1893
NEW YORK   CHICHESTER, WEST SUSSEX

Copyright © 2010 Columbia University Press

Library of Congress Cataloging-in-Publication Data

Carpenter, R. Charli.
   Forgetting children born of war : setting the human rights agenda in Bosnia and beyond /
R. Charli Carpenter.
      p.   cm.
   Includes bibliographical references and index.
   ISBN 978-0-231-15130-6 (alk. paper) — ISBN 978-0-231-52230-4 (ebook)
   1. Children and war—Bosnia and Hercegovina.   2. Children's rights—Bosnia and Hercegovina.
I. Title.
   HQ784.W3C38 2010
   362.87—dc22

                                                                    2010006615

∞

Columbia University Press books are printed on permanent and durable acid-free paper.

This book is printed on paper with recycled content.
Printed in the United States of America
c 10 9 8 7 6 5 4 3 2 1

References to Internet Web sites (URLs) were accurate at the time of writing. Neither the author
nor Columbia University Press is responsible for URLs that may have expired or changed since the
manuscript was prepared.

To all my children

I am a war baby.

—Ryan Badol, Bengali-Canadian.

Who will save the war child, baby?

Who controls the key?

The web we weave is thick and sordid, fine by me.

War child, victim of political pride.

Plant the seed, territorial greed.

Mind the war child, we should mind the war child.

—"War Child," The Cranberries

CONTENTS

IN 2004 I TRAVELED to Bosnia-Herzegovina to try to determine what had happened to the children born of the mass rapes that occurred during the war. I had been drawn to this topic by terrible news stories written by Westerners during and after the war, stories of infanticide, stigma, children languishing in institutions. Yet I approached the subject with a certain amount of skepticism. What did Bosnians themselves think about this these "war babies"? Was the truth more complex than the story told by war journalists? Most important, if the children were so vulnerable, why did organizations tasked with protecting children in conflict zones know next to nothing about them?

On my fifth day in Bosnia-Herzegovina, I sat down over cigarettes with a human rights activist at the Association of Concentration Camp Survivors in Sarajevo and asked for permission to collect her insights about the children of the rapes: what had happened to them, how they were faring, whether they faced problems in postwar society, what the policy response had been. Without even missing a beat, the woman nodded and said, "I will tell you a story."

I then heard an elaborate tale of a friend who had seen a little boy climbing on the rocks by the Drina River near Goražde, in the southeast of the Muslim–Croat Federation of Bosnia-Herzegovina. Her friend was not sure what the boy was doing and feared the worst, and so he went over to investigate. The child said he planned to throw himself into the river. "Why?" her friend asked. "Because I am 'Mirka,'" answered the boy. As my informant explained, the boy was referencing a recent German feature film called *Mirka*, documenting the life of a child conceived as a result of war rape during World War II and searching for his birth mother in the aftermath.

This boy, I was told, had learned of his conception by rape in the Bosnian war when his classmates began to call him "Mirka" after the release of the film. Profoundly disturbed, never having realized he was adopted, he sought to contact his birth mother, but, now living abroad and remarried, she refused to acknowledge him. Shocked, rejected, and socially ostracized, the boy had decided to kill himself. My informant's friend coaxed the child off the rocks and befriended him.

So the story went.

The man in my informant's story was a film director who later created a documentary film about this child's life, released with a fair amount of controversy at the 2004 Sarajevo Film Festival. When I asked him in a later interview about this woman's story of the day he met Alen Muhić, Semsudin Gegić smiled and told me, "That's not quite how it happened." Gegić did not describe Alen as suicidal or their friendship as based on a chance meeting. He told me not of personal trauma but of personal strength and national reconciliation. In his view, not only did Alen need to tell his story, but postwar Bosnia and Serbia needed to hear it in order to atone for and move beyond the atrocities of recent history.

I interviewed dozens of civil society activists during that summer and into the next year. Many knew of Gegić and his film; most opposed his work. They argued that Alen was being exploited, that the film was sensationalist and nationalist, insufficiently feminist. They said it did not accurately capture the experiences of Bosnia's war rape victims. Others were concerned for Alen's welfare. They said that the best thing for a child born of war rape was to stay safely anonymous in postwar society, to stay silent.

Yet my conversations with Alen suggest he draws strength from his adopted family, and his outlook on life is positive. His own story—and his decision to air it in the controversial 2004 documentary *Boy from a War Movie*—does not square with the image of such children as traumatized victims of unmitigated ostracism or as needing protection from the truth of their origins.

I share this set of anecdotes not to suggest that Alen's experiences or strengths are generalizable, for his circumstances, strengths, and perspective are unique to him. I share it in order to suggest that although the children of Bosnia's war were difficult or impossible to find, stories about them were everywhere. The adults I spoke to told stories about Alen, based on their particular perspectives, and from this they generalized to the needs and rights of children born of Bosnia's war and other conflicts. Yet few knew Alen or his family or even a single war child; these stories weren't really about him or other children like him. Like the narratives of Western journalists, they were about *notions* of what children need and about the political wrongs that resulted in these children's birth.

In this book, I argue that these kinds of narratives helped explain the puzzle that had originally drawn me to this topic: the fact that human rights scholars and activists weren't writing, thinking, or talking about children born of war, some of whom clearly *are* very vulnerable—to abandonment, stigma, and identity issues—in conflict and postconflict zones.

Indeed, parts of my informant's original story were true. Alen Muhić was born in a Goražde hospital in February 1993 to a survivor of the infamous rape camps in Foča, which later became the subject of the first-ever war crime prosecution to convict soldiers solely on the basis of sexual assaults against women. Unable to face the prospect of motherhood under such circumstances, his birth mother surrendered him at the hospital, where he captured the heart of Muharem Muhić, a local hospital employee, and his wife and teenage daughters. In the midst of a war zone, they adopted him. Although most of the community loved and accepted Alen, nationalist elements in Goražde during the siege stigmatized the family for adopting someone they called a "little Chetnik," and Alen's adopted mother once narrowly escaped an attempt on her life. Throughout childhood, Alen was teased mercilessly by at least one boy at school, and when his parents confirmed what children at school had told him—that he was adopted—it was "the hardest thing for me."[1]

Moreover, many children born of Bosnia's war fared even worse. Out of countless women raped during the conflict, an estimated several hundred children were born in Bosnia-Herzegovina. Some were killed at birth. Many were never adopted like Alen but are growing up institutionalized or housed in the shadow of their birth mothers' trauma. Each child's story is different; but many face troubling questions about their origins in a society still shaken by the circumstances under which they were born. All need, but few have, a space to openly acknowledge their place in the world and their value as human beings, rights guaranteed to all children under the 1989 Convention on the Rights of the Child.

The particular human rights issues that arise from these social dynamics have been given far too little lip service by transnational actors charged with implementing and promoting children's rights. More interesting than the myriad stories about war babies in the press, war crimes literature, and interviews with civil society organizations is the *absence* of such narratives—or serious consideration of these children's human rights—in the global discourse on children and armed conflict that emerged during the same period.

Bosnia's children born of war are but a small number of the 500,000 people worldwide estimated to have resulted from wartime rape or sexual exploitation in conflict zones. Yet in the early 1990s organizations in the international network around children's human rights concluded that stigma and abuse against children born as a result of wartime sexual violence were nonissues from a human rights perspective. Therefore, rather than gathering accurate data, establishing programs to address specific needs, and creating rights-based stories to counter misinformed sensationalism about the topic, organizations promoting children's human rights chose silence, a silence that is only very tentatively being broken today, nearly twenty years later.

This book is about why.

Scholars writing on untouched or difficult subjects are often asked why they were drawn to a particular topic. I've answered this question with platitudes for years as I've researched and lectured, but here I take more seriously the responsibility to situate this project in its own social and intellectual context. Critical theorists argue that much is explained by underlying social structures and chance events that channel people into certain geospatial and institutional locations at particular times with particular sets of resources, capacities, and sensitivities, and James Rosenau argues that researchers should explicitly account for these factors in presenting their projects to the academic community. In truth, this book evolved over many years from a set of interwoven theoretical, axiological, structural, and personal trajectories; moreover, I found myself much more inside my own subject matter on this project than in my earlier work. So I note here a few of the most important factors that led me to this topic and shaped my understanding.

An unorthodox upbringing instilled in me a belief in children's right to participate, to exercise choice, and to speak for themselves. When I was fourteen, this right was enshrined in international law with the entry into force of the Convention on the Rights of the Child. Yet it was apparent to me as a youth that even the great country in which I lived fell far short of the lofty goals articulated in instruments such as these: My fate, and that of my brothers and sisters, was in the hands of adults and of a state that despite its best efforts often misunderstood our needs and capacities. In a nation that valorizes human rights, democracy, and diversity, children then and now endure discrimination, disenfranchisement, and openly sanctioned violence, often understood to be in their best interest.

Such contradictions fascinated me as a child and led me to broader questions about the human capacity not just for committing but also for justifying social exclusion and violence. A grandchild of the Holocaust, my stepmother indulged me, spending spring afternoons home-schooling us not just in math, music, and science but also in the histories of slavery, genocide, and the Inquisition. I was stunned that Nazi generals could love Mozart; that Hitler had most wanted to be an artist. With my older brother, I pored over *The Rise and Fall of the Third Reich* and studied the history of air warfare in the Pacific, marveling at the ease with which kamikaze pilots committed suicide for honor. As a young adult I abandoned my elders' advice to seek a law or business degree and threw myself into the formal study of international affairs. I wanted to understand the machinery and sociology of war and peace.

On the U.S.–Mexico border, Yosef Lapid helped me understand the arbitrariness of political boundaries while I cut my teeth on the analytical tools of realism, liberalism, and constructivism. I watched the Rwandan genocide and the war in Bosnia-Herzegovina unfold on television. I read news stories about mass rape with the sorrow and helplessness felt by so many American women at that time. For a long time I thought about what motherhood meant for the women and girls detained, violated, tortured, and then abandoned by their families and their nation. I identified with the strategies they adopted to maintain their sanity, but even more so with their children. I sensed connections between the vulnerabilities of those children and of the possibility for a peace settlement. Yet I saw no space to raise such concerns in my classes on international negotiation, political terrorism, and national security.

A year after the Dayton Accords were signed, I began to raise a child myself. Her father, constrained by obligations to his government, eventually returned to his own country, and for our daughter's sake I chose not to follow him. I was a graduate student of international relations (IR), and my formal education was supplemented by lessons in the international political economy of single motherhood. I observed how international legal norms placed barriers between my ex-partner's ability to visit our daughter and her ability to enjoy her right to know her parents. Conscious of the connections between our day-to-day lives and the high politics of international security, I was drawn to feminist IR theory.

But much of that discourse, lumping together women and children, as it did then, struck me as too simplistic to account for the power relations *within* families that I knew firsthand and saw as fundamental to the story of international politics. Rather than recast or extend feminist IR, I started off critiquing its limitations. But mainstream IR theories were equally unhelpful in providing a framework for understanding contradictions in international law and their practical implications for people. And I was helpfully discouraged from pursuing a high-risk topic such as children born of war by those responsible for socializing me into the discipline of political science. Instead I chose another dissertation project on civilian protection policy. I married a Canadian-American of Scottish and Jewish descent, had a son, and noticed my daughter begin to think of herself as white.

Bosnia's children of war haunted me. As I worked on other projects, I continued to wonder about that war and the society that had reconstituted itself in the aftermath. Watching my son's fascination with soldiering in a post-9/11 world, I continued to think about children, gender, and nationalism. Watching my daughter negotiate an identity as a citizen of a state that sees people through ethnic categories, I continued to think about liminality, national identity, children's bodies, and the relationship between human rights and social exclusion.

In my first year at University of Oregon, I had written a paper for an independent study on nationalism that was quickly published in *Human Rights Quarterly*. Back then, when my ideas were still forming, I argued that human rights activists were missing something by treating children of genocidal rape as tools of genocide rather than human beings in their own right. I'd hoped naively that this article might change things, but by the time I finished graduate school and was ready to start answering questions about my "post-dissertation project" on the job circuit, there was still no sign of attention to these children in the human rights network. I blurted out once that year, in a conversation that probably lost me a job offer, that my next book might be about children of war. A famous political scientist coolly asked me why was this theoretically significant. It took years for a persuasive answer to that question to materialize.

It was only with the help and encouragement of many individuals and organizations that I was finally able to write this book. Mostly, I was lucky to a have a few influential people place faith in the project at key junctures, to counteract the social and professional pressures urging me in more conventional directions. These include Robert Darst, who spoke in my defense at my first brown bag presentation on this topic; Bert Lockwood, who published my first paper on children of war and provided encouragement and friendship in the years since; Julie Mertus, a mentor in every sense of the word; my patient and engaging editor, Anne Routon, and her colleagues at Columbia University Press, who helped usher this manuscript from draft to polished product; and Philip Schrodt, who went out on a limb by funding my International Studies Association workshop in 2004. This event enabled me to bring together a small community of researchers asking similar questions, without whose rapport and friendship I would have found myself substantively and emotionally impoverished as I pursued this work. Special thanks to Patricia Weitsman, Megan MacKenzie, and Giulia Baldi for their many contributions as friends and colleagues.

Additional funding for archival research, focus group research, and field-work was provided by the MacArthur Foundation, the National Science Foundation, and the University of Pittsburgh's Central Research Development Fund, University Center for International Studies, Graduate School for Public and International Affairs, and Ford Institute of Human Security. I am particularly grateful to the institutions willing to allow me to build childcare expenses into travel budgets, without which the fieldwork for this project would have fallen short. (May more funders follow their lead so that scholars unwilling to be parted from their children for long periods can travel to gather the data on which social inquiry depends.)

The University of Geneva and Columbia University were kind enough to provide facilities for off-site focus groups. Drake University housed me as a postgraduate while I began the initial research for this study, and I'm grateful for the collegiality of the faculty and students at the Department of Politics and International Relations, especially Debra DeLaet, David Skidmore, Marc Riser, and Rachel Caufield. Early on in the research process, I left Drake and accepted a teaching position at the University of Pittsburgh's Graduate School of Public and International Affairs. There, I flourished in the most nurturing environment possible for a junior scholar working outside the box. Special thanks are due to David Bearce, Karen Chervenick, Michael Goodhart, Emily Huisman, Betcy Jose-Thota, Sandra Monteverde, Marianne Nichols, Justin Reed, Simon Reich, Robyn Wheeler, Abbie Zahler, and the director and staff at the University of Pittsburgh's Qualitative Data Analysis Program. But I am most indebted for the research assistance of Vanja Lundell, who not only assisted with coding, copyediting, and translation but also accompanied me to Bosnia-Herzegovina and contributed greatly to my thinking on this topic. After transferring to the University of Massachusetts in 2008, I continued to benefit from the encouragement and mentorship of John Hird, M. J. Peterson, and Peter Haas and from the very rich questions Roberto Alejandro asked about my relationship to my subject matter. Several students and staff also provided invaluable research and copyediting assistance; thank you, Minako Koike, Rachel Ostrowski, and Michelle Goncalves.

In Bosnia-Herzegovina, my field research would not have been possible without the support, guidance, and professional assistance of Jasna Balorda, who began as my interpreter and became my great friend; and of Sanja Barić,

Mirza Hadžimešić, and Ognjen Jelecanović. The professionals at Medica Zenica provided interviews, advice, data, feedback, and, most importantly, inspiration. I'm particularly grateful to Marijana Senjak, Duska Andrić-Ružičić, and Mirha Pojskić. I am also indebted to all the professionals within global civil society who shared their time and insights with me as part of this project, and especially to those at the United Nations Children's Emergency Fund for allowing me to follow the development of the organization's policy so closely yet without losing my critical edge. Special thanks to Jens Matthes, Kerry Neal, Pamela Shifman, and a colleague who must remain unnamed for enthusiasm and encouragement and for reviewing drafts as this project developed.

Numerous colleagues, friends, and family members provided similar support. I am very grateful to the intellectual community of the International Association of Genocide Scholars and to those who provided feedback at Yale University's Genocide Studies Seminar and the University of Pennsylvania's War, Gender and Militarism conference, especially Adam Jones and Laura Sjoberg. Also, many thanks to Edward Carpenter, who shared a morbid day with me in Potocari and helps keep alive my intellectual curiosity about political violence; my father, Dr. Carey Carpenter, for teaching me to communicate through the written word and for making me a child rights activist; Ashley Ciera Smith, for lending insight about the dynamics of adoption reunions; James Ron, for mentorship on applied research in the human rights sector; Patrick Jackson, for ripping apart my drafts and for long conversations about the relationship between theory and practice; and Daniel Drezner, for teaching me how to shut up, stop thinking, and get on with writing.

I would have been unable to undertake this study without a very patient husband, Stuart Shulman, who held down the fort when I was away in the field, shouldered much of the emotional burden this project imposed on our family, and was a constant source of logistical, methodological, and technical advice. And I am so thankful to my children, Haley and Liam, for putting up with the role this project has played in our lives for most of their childhoods. They have allowed me to disappear repeatedly, to drag them into the field, and to fill the bookshelves of our house with grim and forbidding titles while cultivating a sense of humor about it all that would make Bosnians proud. Most importantly, they have kept me healthy by always reminding me that adults, too, have a right (and responsibility) to play.

Finally, deepest thanks to Alen Muhić and his parents for sharing with me parts of their story. I hope this book helps open minds and begin conversations.

ABBREVIATIONS

BiH: Bosnia and Herzegovina
BSA: Bosnian Serb Army
CARE: Committee for Aid and Relief Everywhere
CIDA: Canadian International Development Agency
CRC: Convention on the Rights of the Child
DCI: Defense for Children International
DPA: Dayton Peace Accord
GBV: gender-based violence
HRW: Human Rights Watch
ICC: International Criminal Court
ICRC: International Committee of the Red Cross
ICTR: International Criminal Tribunal for Rwanda
ICTY: International Criminal Tribunal for the Former Yugoslavia
ICVA: International Council on Voluntary Associations
IDP: internally displaced person
IO: international organization
IPTF: International Police Task Force
IR: international relations
JNA: Yugoslav National Army
KM: *konvertible mark*

MSF: Médecins Sans Frontières (Doctors Without Borders)
NATO: North American Treaty Organization
NGO: nongovernment organization
OHR: Office of the High Representative
OSCE: Organization for Security and Cooperation in Europe
OSRSG: Office of the Special Representative of the Secretary General
OXFAM: Oxford Committee for Famine Relief
RS: Republika Srpska
SDA: Party of Democratic Action
UN: United Nations
UNHCR: United Nations High Commissioner for Refugees
UNICEF: United Nations Children's Emergency Fund
UNIFEM: United Nations Development Fund for Women
UNMIBH: United Nations Mission in Bosnia-Herzegovina
USAID: United States Agency for International Development
WCIP: War and Children Identity Project
WHO: World Health Organization

FORGETTING CHILDREN BORN OF WAR

1.
THEORIZING CHILD RIGHTS IN INTERNATIONAL RELATIONS

The birth of a child is a political event.
—Handwerker, *Births and Power*, 1.

AFTER THE DISINTEGRATION of Yugoslavia in the early 1990s, an uncounted number of children, conceived as a result of wartime rape, were born to traumatized mothers.[1] Many did not want them. Children of refugee mothers in neighboring Croatia were initially denied citizenship and education rights.[2] Local and international actors contested the babies' ethnic identities and citizenship rights. Inside Bosnia, there were reports of ostracism and abandonment; some were killed.[3]

At the time I began to gather research for this book, almost nothing was known outside the former Yugoslavia about what had become of these babies, how to protect their human rights, or how issues around their security and identity were being constructed and reconstructed in postwar Bosnia, Croatia, and Serbia and in the various diasporic communities spawned by the conflict. More interestingly to me, no one outside Bosnia seemed to be asking. What I learned on arriving in the region in early 2004 was that few people inside Bosnia were asking either. These children were invisible to the children's rights network, overlooked by the government, and described by women's rights and nationalist organizations in ways not necessarily conducive to securing much-needed attention to their needs as many of them entered puberty.

This book explores why children born of wartime rape have received so little systematic attention from the international actors charged with protecting and promoting children's human rights in conflict situations, both in Bosnia and in similar contexts globally, despite widespread media attention, and it uses this single case as a jumping off point for asking bigger questions about the human rights regime. Aside from being of arguable normative importance for human rights scholars and practitioners, this policy and advocacy gap represents a fascinating puzzle theoretically for international relations (IR) scholars. The literature on transnational advocacy networks suggests that issue networks are most likely to mobilize around precisely populations such as these, where bodily harm or discrimination affects people traditionally seen as vulnerable or innocent,[4] where the harms fall easily within existing human rights law or are easily grafted onto existing advocacy space,[5] where the media and the political economy of activism exert agenda-setting effects,[6] and where issue "entrepreneurs" push for the development of a robust response.[7]

If theory suggests that children born of war should be an obvious subject of human rights concern and they have not, this begs the question of what additional factors account for the shape of the human rights agenda in international society and why certain categories fall through the cracks. The answer to this puzzle can tell us something about advocacy networks in world affairs more broadly and about the social construction of children's human rights as it relates to conceptions of international order and justice.

In the following pages, I draw attention to what both local and international human rights advocates in Bosnia-Herzegovina and in the broader transnational children's rights network repeatedly call "the problematique" of addressing war babies as a focus of human rights concern.[8] My overall argument is that the process of casting blame for one set of atrocities can draw attention away from other harms on which human rights advocates focus their attention. Blaming in one context affects framing in another. Although an interrelated set of factors accounts for the silence of the human rights community on this particular issue, central to all of them is the tension between this issue and other claims already pressed by the human rights community, particularly claims on behalf of female rape victims, claims on behalf of aggrieved minority groups, and broader claims about what constitutes civilized or barbaric international conduct. In short, in conflict zones the social construction of rights claims is contingent partly on the social construction of wrongs.

I will demonstrate how the advocacy network around children and armed conflict was conditioned in the 1990s to accept that children born of war are a side effect of war rape rather than a population of concern for children's advocates in their own right. This understanding was constructed in part through specific narratives about war babies carried by the global media, by nationalist players in Bosnia-Herzegovina during and after the war, by international lawyers, and by the transnational women's rights movement. These narratives interacted with an institutional culture within the child rights network that either precluded attention to children born of war altogether or posed obstacles to pursuing it for the political entrepreneurs who challenged the silence.

What this analysis teaches IR scholars more generally, particularly those optimistic about the role played by networks of normatively motivated policy practitioners in transnational civil society, is that the discourse of human rights is not a panacea for vulnerable populations. The case here confirms the findings of emerging scholarship in suggesting that the construction of specific categories of rights claims in international society does not follow a rational, linear process in which the most vulnerable populations receive attention on the basis of need and merit. Rather, attention to issues by human rights advocates is conditioned by myriad political, organizational, cultural, structural, coalitional, and economic factors; and some combination of these factors may draw attention away from certain individuals regardless of the merits of their case. At the turn of the twenty-first century, children born of wartime rape and exploitation constituted one such case. I conclude by suggesting that IR constructivists can learn much about human rights norms in world affairs by studying what does *not* get attention from human rights practitioners.

CHILDREN BORN OF WAR AND HUMAN RIGHTS

Children conceived as a result of violent or exploitive relations are living today in every corner of the globe. Born of conflicts and militarized sex relations, they face abuse, stigmatization, and discrimination. Although many are conceived in rape campaigns, others are born out of less overtly coercive exploitive relationships between soldiers and local women: prostitutes around military bases, aid recipients encouraged to trade sex for additional supplies, and young girls genuinely in love who believed they would be one day be wed to their foreign boyfriend, only to be abandoned when the soldier returned home, often to a wife and family there. When children result from such unions and are raised alone or abandoned by single women in postwar zones, they are often stigmatized as a result.

To date, no international organization concerned with children's human rights has published a systematic study estimating the number of such children worldwide. However, a group of Norwegian activists produced a report in 2001 synthesizing the anecdotal material available on the subject. This group, the

War and Children Identity Project (WCIP), was formed on the heels of a successful campaign by Norwegian *krigsbarn* (war children) whose mothers were impregnated by German men during the World War II occupation of Norway. These adult war children won a suit against the Norwegian government for compensation for failing to protect them from discrimination in the war's aftermath. Interested in situating Norway's *krigsbarn* in their broader context and perhaps exporting their model abroad, WCIP became the first organization to focus on war children as a global constituency. Its initial global report, authored by anthropologist Kai Grieg, estimated the total number of living war children at approximately 500,000.[9]

If these numbers are anywhere close to correct, children born as a result of wartime rape or sexual exploitation constitute a massive global underclass. Even looking solely at children brought to term as a result of deliberate impregnation as a tool of armed conflict, the list of potential cases is staggering, including those in Bosnia, Bangladesh, East Timor, Rwanda, Sierra Leone, and Darfur. Anecdotal evidence and press reports have demonstrated for almost fifteen years that such children born of war are at risk of infanticide, abandonment, abuse, neglect, discrimination, and social exclusion in conflict and postconflict settings specifically as a result of their biological origins.[10] Oral histories of adult war children from earlier conflicts corroborate such evidence.[11]

What is remarkable is that so little attention has been paid to this population by the network around children's human rights, particularly the organizations engaged in advocacy and programming for children in armed conflict. By "children's human rights network" I mean the transnational community of citizens, journalists, protection organizations, and statespersons who, believing that children possess certain fundamental rights as human beings, aim at the more widespread implementation of international child rights standards through persuasion or purposeful action. The network consists of the actors who promote the implementation of the principles, norms, and rules associated with the international regime for children's human rights.[12]

This network of organizations and understandings is embedded in the broader human rights regime about which much has been written.[13] A subset of organizations concerned broadly with human rights are those engaged particularly with children and armed conflict as a specific issue area. The principled belief at the core of this network's efforts is that children should be better protected from the effects of armed conflict. As the UN Web portal on this issue states, "International and local standards of conduct should be resurrected and respected, in order to prevent the abuse and brutalization of children."[14]

Given that such organizations claim to champion the human rights of all children and to be particularly concerned with "children in especially difficult circumstances," the "particularly vulnerable," or "children affected by armed conflict," one might expect the protection of children conceived through war to be a focus of concern for them. Yet despite consistent media and donor concern for this category of war-affected child, awareness of their particular vulnerabilities by gender-based violence specialists, and the presence of a few organizations such as WCIP lobbying specifically for their rights, major organizations in the growing advocacy network around children and armed conflict and the broader human rights regime have not openly defined children born to sexual violence survivors in conflict zones as a specific category of concern or sought to address the insecurities they face in postconflict zones. In 2004, while attention to other categories of war-affected child burgeoned in transnational civil society, a child protection official stated, "I can't think of any organization that has dealt with [children born of wartime rape] specifically." This continued to be true through early 2009, despite the widespread publicity regarding stigma and maltreatment of children born of rape in places such as Darfur and the increasing attention in transnational civil society to children and armed conflict generally.[15] Why?

This project uses a single case study, Bosnia-Herzegovina, as a lens through which to interrogate the broader silence on this issue from the global children's human rights regime and in turn to ask broader questions about the meaning and practice of human rights advocacy in world politics. Broadly speaking, human rights are a set of international standards said to govern relationships between sovereign governments and the citizens over which they have authority. What counts as a rights violation may be contested; these contests may be resolved in transnational space through the interaction between issue entrepreneurs, the nongovernment organization community, and UN agencies; the consensus may then be reiterated by actors who use naming and shaming strategies to hold states accountable to the standards they set through multilateral negotiations. But in the end, rights are implemented by states. Although in theory all human beings possess rights, they can enjoy them only insofar as authorities implement these standards through positive or negative action. Negative action means a state chooses *not* to torture or arbitrarily imprison people. Positive action means a state puts resources toward, for example, social safety nets to provide food and shelter for those who would otherwise go hungry.[16]

In theory, children possess human rights as individual humans, but they are governed by a very particular international regime because of their unique status and needs. Children have particular vulnerabilities, because of both their physical dependency on adults and their socially subordinate status. The Convention on the Rights of the Child addresses these vulnerabilities, calling on the state to provide for children's general social welfare and protect them from harm at the hands of adults. Although children are not endowed with the same rights and responsibilities as adults, the convention articulates the principle that decisions affecting children should be made with the child's best interests in mind. In short, the healthy social, physical, and emotional development of children becomes a matter of their rights.

What I am most interested in here is child rights talk. It turns out to be hard for international civil servants to think about children born of war using a rights framework, and this tells us something about both the concept of child rights and the broader institutional structures in which transnational human rights culture is created and maintained. By examining how different transnational actors report on conflicts, deliver humanitarian relief, codify war crimes in multilateral treaties, prosecute those crimes in international tribunals, and lobby states through UN channels to implement human rights norms, we can expose the obstacles to hearing rights claims from the many people shouting from the margins of world politics.

In short, examining what is *not* said by human rights practitioners or what falls beyond the bounds of human rights discourse provides insights about the human rights regime itself. By "centering the marginalized," theorists access otherwise hidden theoretical insights about broader phenomena.[17] My analysis demonstrates the way in which local and international understandings of human rights intersect, conflict with, and constitute the cultural framework in which war babies' existence becomes politicized. The "war babies problematique" provides a lens for reconsidering the very basis for human rights culture in world politics and the contradictions inherent in advocacy for children's human rights.[18] It allows us to see how human rights discourse and practice are constructed according to racist, sexist, and ageist assumptions. It forces us to consider whether such a framework is applicable to categories of human being that problematize these foundations. It allows us to analyze not only the efficacy of the children's human rights regime but also the way in which that sector in world politics itself helps structure the status and fate of these children.

A WORD ON THEORY AND METHOD

Insofar as I am exploring the social construction of categories and the relationship between international norms, local and global identities, and social outcomes, my analysis is grounded in constructivist theories of IR.[19] Constructivists argue that the constitution of social categories in world affairs is at least as important as the strategic pursuit of political outcomes, because it is through social norms and identities, articulated through language, that actors understand their interests in the first place.[20] IR scholars interested in how international understandings are constructed and change over time have aimed to theorize, for example, how altruistically motivated actors sculpt the global social fabric in the service of new moral ideals[21] and how such understandings, once constituted, both construct actors with certain properties[22] and affect actors' understandings of their interests.[23]

In the human rights domain, such scholarship has often emphasized the role of transnational networks of advocates in disseminating and promoting standards in international society and in specific local contexts.[24] At the international level, human rights networks have been credited with the emergence of treaties prohibiting the use of landmines,[25] criminalizing violence against women,[26] and ensuring the protection of civilians in armed conflict[27] and with creating the conditions under which international actors are persuaded to comply with such norms.[28] In order to promote the implementation of such standards, organizations often attempt to superimpose these internationally agreed-upon norms onto indigenous social systems by educating actors (often nonstate actors) in specific localities about their obligations and persuading them to comply.[29]

An implication of constructivism is that understanding the constitution of social categories in the first place is at least as important as understanding how they affect practice. Although early IR constructivist literature was often accused of failing to account adequately for the emergence or nonemergence of norms,[30] more recent work has taken up such questions.[31] Such an agenda directs attention, for example, to what human rights comes to mean, not just to states that are schooled by networks but to activists in those networks themselves. Why do they mobilize around certain international standards and not others? Why are some populations but not others recognized as categories of concern by international and nongovernment organizations? The constructivism here does not take the idea of human rights for granted but sees it as a contingent social institution that might easily have been—and might yet be imagined to be—quite different, and with different consequences for the life chances of different human beings.

Because the purpose of this research is as much to address silences and illuminate marginalized subjects as to contribute to an understanding of social reality, it falls into what Cox has called critical theory, as opposed to a more conventional, problem-solving constructivist approach that takes the existing order of things as a given and aims to explore social reality analytically without explicitly transforming it.[32] A conventional or "middle road" IR constructivist approach examines the constitutive effects of ideas without offering explicit normative arguments or reflecting on the role of theory in shaping social order. By contrast, critical theorists assume that the world might look different— *better*—than it does, not only in terms of solutions to specific sources of trouble but in terms of the very foundations of international order and justice. A critical theoretical analysis does not simply explain the world through a constructivist lens but is actively designed to provide an understanding of reality conducive to altering unjust social relations and views this emancipatory agenda as part of the function of research itself. Concerned with recovering and centering marginal subjects, critical theorists unmask and aim to transform the implicit power relations in conventional accounts of international relations.[33]

Even in such critical accounts of world affairs, children and the political construction of childhood have been neglected as sites for the reproduction of global norms.[34] As Watson notes, although there is a subject-specific literature in IR on child-related issues such as child labor and child soldiers and increasing attention is being paid to children as actors in world politics,[35] few IR theorists have drawn on the sociological literature analyzing childhood as a global political construct.[36] Following feminist IR theorists who highlighted gender as an ordering principle in world affairs, Helen Brocklehurst asks, "Where are the children?" in international relations theory. She analyzes intersections between constructs of childhood and security policy and explores how silences regarding children in the discipline of political science implicate and structure our understanding of the world.[37]

Here, I join these emerging voices in IR theory to argue not simply that children are present and must be accounted for on the world stage but that the ways in which the child as a social fact is constructed in different contexts fundamentally shapes international politics. Contingent understandings of children shape state, national, and ethnic identities, affect menus of options for foreign policy elites, enable specific war-fighting tactics, and structure the advocacy strategies of those who would bring moral pressure to bear on international actors. Because children born of rape live and sometimes die "on the margins of the already marginal,"[38] they constitute not just a normatively important subject in their own right but also a useful lens through which to obtain "otherwise inaccessible theoretical insights."[39]

Like Brocklehurst's, my investigation has also been informed by feminist readings of armed conflict and by feminist theories and methods. Conceptually, it is feminists in IR who have drawn attention to the identification and study of silences as a means of making visible social relations of power. Because it deals straightforwardly with exclusion, feminist IR offers a viewpoint and set of methods helpful and relevant to the study of marginalized groups. Substantively, IR feminists pioneered the study of wartime sexual violence as a site for the constitution of national and international norms and identities.[40]

Yet the substantive focus here differs from and extends IR feminist insights in new directions. Although much of the IR feminist canon defines a feminist approach as taking women's experience as a starting point, here child rights rather than women's rights remain the point of reference throughout.[41] The feminism here is thus less focused on women's experiences per se than on the broader project of overcoming gender hierarchies as they pertain to human security for all people, particularly for children conceived as a result of gender-based violence.[42] Rather than emphasize survivors' experiences per se, my goal is to explore the marginality of their children born of wartime rape and consider what this marginality means for children's human rights and for international relations.

Methods

I was warned at the outset that Bosnia would be a difficult case to generalize from and an unlikely place to gather reliable primary evidence on this population. For example, Raymonde Provencher, who traversed the globe to create the documentary *War Babies* with narratives from people in Rwanda, Bosnia, South Korea, Guatemala, and Bangladesh, told me that compared with Rwanda, where "there are so many babies and the subject is much more open," in Bosnia the issue was remarkably taboo.[43] "I wish you luck," she told me in a Montreal interview in 2003. Other respondents urged me not to treat Bosnia's war children as a paradigmatic case, given the particularities of the Bosnian experience.

It is entirely true that the experience of Bosnia's war babies is culturally specific, and the conclusions drawn in this case about the children themselves will not be generalizable to all other regions in which forced pregnancy campaigns have resulted in an influx of babies—to say nothing of contexts characterized by opportunistic rather than systematic rape, by sexual exploitation rather than violence, or by forced marriage. For example, there were fewer such children in Bosnia than elsewhere, given that women by and large had access to abortion during the early stages of pregnancy,[44] and contextual factors both complicated and mitigated the human rights abuses to which they were subject relative to other well-known cases.[45] It is also true (though not to the extent Provencher suggests) that Bosnian society is only gradually coming to terms with the prob-lematique of the *djeca silovane žene*, and this did indeed complicate the collec-tion of data when and where I went looking for verifiable information on the children themselves. Nonetheless, the process of trying to do so told me much about how the issue is conceptualized and situated relative to other concerns in postconflict Bosnian society and, in particular, among the international hu-manitarian and human rights organizations based in the region and beyond, in the transnational human rights network.

Indeed, because the focus of my project was not to empirically study the children as such but to gauge the local and international policy response to this population, Bosnia represented an ideal focal point for research. Although sexual violence is typical of many wars, the war in ex-Yugoslavia became inter-nationally famous for soldiers' maltreatment of women, and to this day many analysts assert that the crime of forced pregnancy was invented by the Bosnian Serb Army and its Yugoslav National Army supporters.[46] As a result, the war in Bosnia was a watershed in the development of international norms and institu-tions governing the conduct of organized warfare. It was a theater in which sites of power in the international humanitarian community were fundamentally revisited, which saw the emergence of myriad new organizations, and in which lessons from the field were learned and exported to other hotspots around the globe.[47] The mass rapes in particular were a catalyst to transnational feminist consciousness and to awareness in international institutions of the gendered nature of armed conflict and the necessity of addressing violence against women.[48] Though not new as a strategy of warfare, forced pregnancy was first articulated as a legal construct on the basis of the Bosnian mass rapes.

However, as Hansen describes, these emerging international understandings were also constituted by particular constructions of race and gender and, I ar-gue, of child rights.[49] They therefore had implications for the way in which the child rights agenda was understood and international children's policy under-taken during and after the war. My working assumption is that a detailed his-toriography of children's human rights in a specific country context, measured against the rhetoric of humanitarian and human rights organizations, govern-ments, and international standards on child protection, can tell us something useful about how the discourse and practice of children's human rights as a global construct is constituted and implemented.

The primary data gathered for this project consisted of 103 interviews with members of Bosnian and transnational civil society, collected during nine short field trips to Bosnia between 2004 and 2007 and a number of additional trips to human rights hubs including Geneva, New York, Montreal, the Hague, and Washington. I sought interviews with anyone who seemed to have something to say about Bosnia's children born of rape, children born of wartime rape in general, or rights-based programming for children and women in conflict zones more generally than that. As my project evolved, my dataset came to include interviews with journalists, novelists, film directors, and government officials. Another forty-two practitioners participated in a series of focus groups I organized in connection with the project. Finally, I have used my field notes from both trips to Bosnia and visits and participant–observation work at other sites in the children and armed conflict network as a source of data. Unless otherwise noted, quotations are taken from these interviews, focus groups, and field notes; to protect confidentiality and for consistency I have avoided associating specific quotes with individuals or their organizational affiliations where feasible. However, a complete appendix of the organizations whose staff were quoted as part of this study appears at the end of this book.

The method evolved and broadened over the course of the project. When I began to probe the humanitarian response, if any, to children born as a result of wartime rape, I was essentially attempting to measure a nonevent: the lack of attention to a specific subject by policy practitioners in the humanitarian sector.[50] I initiated the collection of primary data through in-depth interviews at headquarters and in Bosnia and, later, focus groups with humanitarian practitioners held in New York, Geneva, and Pittsburgh. These conversations allowed me to gather specific facts about war babies and other relevant political dynamics in Bosnia and beyond. They also served as a source of narrative testimonies from different perspectives. In other words, they were not only about the facts on the ground but also about the interpretation of these facts by the people I was interviewing.

I began by collecting documents and interviewing officials in the transnational humanitarian network, rather than with fieldwork in Bosnia, for ethical as well as methodological reasons.[51] Research on issues pertaining to mass rape in Bosnia is particularly fraught with difficulty because of the overexposure of that population to the Western gaze and the insensitivity with which journalists, aid workers, and Western researchers have historically treated the subject.[52] I adopted a layered approach to analyzing the issue that began by collecting relevant data at a distance, through secondary sources, with progressively more proximity to the children themselves. This enabled me to gain experience and knowledge by speaking to less vulnerable populations (e.g., international advocates) before approaching more vulnerable people (e.g., civil society groups in Bosnia, some of whose representatives are also torture victims). Beginning at a distance, I relied on a minimal network of contacts in the field, allowing these contacts to function as gatekeepers both to generate access and trust and to offset some of these ethical risks.[53]

My early field trips quickly led to more ambitious research goals. It was easier than I had expected to identify pockets of known children and stories about the issue. Moreover, interviews also led to heightened interest among Bosnian human rights advocates and international organizations in creating fact-finding or advocacy initiatives on behalf of these children. At times I involved myself in these activities as a participant–observer, thus both offering my expertise to the community as a means of giving back and monitoring the effectiveness of and obstacles to such advocacy.[54] For example, it was after my conversation with the regional child protection officer for the United Nations Children's Emergency Fund (UNICEF) that UNICEF of Bosnia and Herzegovina commissioned a pilot study on the issue over summer of 2004, in which I was asked to participate as a consultant. Involvement in this project afforded me a broader dataset on which to draw, because the UNICEF program officer in Sarajevo permitted me to use the resulting interview data and case history information as part of my book project. But more importantly, the experience allowed me to better understand how UNICEF's bureaucracy works, the agenda-setting process whereby an underrecognized issue is conceptualized and defined by a major international organization, and how "facts" are "found" (and sometimes lost) within the human rights community.

With only one exception, I did not pursue interviews with children in Bosnia (then between twelve and fourteen years old) as part of this study.[55] Information on specific children of war cited in this book was culled from media and human rights reports and from a small dataset of case histories on children and their families made available to me by UNICEF's Sarajevo field office in return for my assistance with the project. These case histories were compiled on the basis of interviews with social workers and civil society organizations whose clients included forced pregnancy survivors. The drawback of this method was that it used case workers' testimony as a proxy for actual data on the children. However, the advantages were that it engaged Bosnian civil society in helping to build the dataset, maintained an ethically appropriate distance between the international researcher and the vulnerable research subject, and went one step beyond the purely anecdotal data in press reports to actually begin systematizing reported cases of pregnancies carried to term and their outcome and to aggregate them in search of generalizable patterns.

In addition, although the key pattern that emerged from the human rights discourse was the lack of attention to this issue, part of my objective was to identify and interview people who had in some way participated in the project of constructing children of wartime rape as a category of moral discourse. These included journalists writing about "rape babies"; people involved in tentative, truncated suggestions in international documents that a study be conducted of these children; researchers who had investigated this issue in their work on children's rights or on mass rape; novelists, playwrights, and documentarians; and, in the case of Alen Muhić, one outspoken young person who views his identity and destiny as being at stake in the way in which postwar society views children such as him.

At the onset of the project I wrote field notes only during my trips to Bosnia, but I soon realized that in any conversational setting where I discussed my research topic I was also contributing to this process of social construction, and over the course of the project I began to keep detailed notes of these interactions and events as often as possible: at international conferences, at UN meetings where I was invited to present briefings on my research, in consultation with the humanitarian sector; in the classroom, over the phone with members of the press, and with my colleagues. The records of these interactions and lessons learned provided a supplementary source of data on how this topic does or does not fit into international rights discourse.

Outline

In the next two chapters I situate Bosnia's children born of war in the context of a much broader category of children born of rape and sexual exploitation in conflict zones worldwide, then document the glaring silence on this issue by the very network of organizations whose mandate it is to protect all children affected by war. Chapter 2 seeks to illuminate what is distinctive about their status and experiences as a result of their biological origins, situating these particular characteristics in a postwar context that has been very difficult on many children. Here I draw on and contribute to a small but growing body of literature tracking the fate of these people.[56]

Chapter 3 problematizes the lack of formal attention to these vulnerabilities by advocacy organizations. On the basis of interviews and focus group data, I argue that transnational advocacy agendas are based on internal and coalitional politics of transnational networks as much as on genuine humanitarian need. Advocates make strategic choices about where to place their resources and attention, constrained by the political context, their estimate of the probability of success, the feasibility of information gathering, and other concerns shaped in turn by the ways in which governments, the media, the academy, and local players construe an issue. When normative concerns come into play, they can mitigate against the construction of new rights claims as easily as they can facilitate them. This is particularly true when an issue poses a perceived threat to other issues in the advocacy pool, when a new cause places advocates in tension with partners on related issues, or when advocates guess that advocacy around a certain issue might actually lead to worse outcomes for the population of concern. Certain human rights problems may be avoided if they are deemed too sensitive.

The real question then is, What influences human rights advocates' understanding of their preferences? What makes an issue too sensitive? How do activists learn to think of a particular issue in such a way that it becomes obvious to them that it is not part of their mandate or concern? In this case, I argue that specific narratives about war babies' role during the war in former Yugoslavia made it difficult to think about their needs through a rights-based frame or to conceptualize them as children affected by war. Chapters 4 through 7 describe various constructions of children born to forced pregnancy survivors between the onset of the war and 2007, when I concluded data gathering for this project. During this period, attention to children of rape was far from absent in international law; in the news media; in nationalist and feminist depictions of wartime rape; in film, art, and literature; and in the discourse of various sectors of what David Rieff cryptically calls the "humanitarian international."[57]

However, rarely were children born as a result of rape imagined as subjects of human rights concern within these narratives. Instead, they functioned as symbols: Their identities and descriptions of their fate were manipulated and constructed so as to serve the interests of actors with very different agendas. Women's organizations focusing on helping rape survivors raise their children positioned the babies as a living component of the survivor's trauma, providing support to the mothers in lieu of effective protection to the children. International legal experts, intent on constructing "genocidal rape" as a new legal concept, overlooked the way in which existing international law essentialized children's ethnic identities and situated the children as tools of ethnic cleansing or biological warfare.[58] Nationalists in Bosnia and others seeking to construct Bosniaks as the prime victims in the war invoked the production of "little Chetniks" as evidence of Serb brutality, whitewashing rapes committed by Croat and Bosniak troops and mixed-ethnicity children born to ethnic Serb women.[59]

These various narratives, rather than the duty to protect vulnerable infants, underwrote policies—or, in too many cases, the lack of policies—to deal with these children in the aftermath of the war. Because interpretations of their needs were filtered through various organizational and ideological lenses, these constructions of the children's needs conflicted. Some were based primarily on securing the children's symbolic role as containers of group identity. Strategies to assist the children that relied on these ideas reproduced the exclusionist conceptions of identity that war babies' very existence belies, resulting in identity conflicts for some children and leaving others in a legal limbo. Other interpretations of the children's needs were based on promoting the needs and dignity of the rape survivors themselves, in an era when international attention to violence against women was emergent and on uncertain ground. These strategies resulted in inattention to children at risk from or abandoned by their birth mothers.

The empirical chapters examine how these contradictory narratives, and the strategy of avoidance adopted by humanitarian actors negotiating between them, contributed to and naturalized the advocacy silence in the broader child rights network. Chapter 4 traces the frames used by the Western print press to articulate the plight of "rape babies," which drew on and tied into discourses inimical to securing their rights after birth. These frames undermined or forestalled rights-based advocacy efforts on behalf of the babies by associating concern for their well-being with imperialist, nationalist, or feminist agendas.

Chapter 5 describes the various approaches (or lack thereof) to children of rape survivors by local and international Western and Muslim humanitarian organizations, many of which largely overlooked their needs—some due to institutional blinders, others out of a concern to survive in a turbulent political context. The inattention and lack of fact finding in the field during this and other wars contributed in turn to the taboos and lack of data about the more general subject of war babies later in the decade.

Chapter 6 examines international legal efforts to recognize and prosecute crimes that took place during and after this war in the former Yugoslavia. The structure of international criminal law and its evolving institutions also speaks in a very limited way of these children as subjects of human rights even as it broadens the space to articulate the wrongs against their mothers. In fact, the very way in which wrongs against women and national groups have been constructed has itself posed significant obstacles to addressing children of war as a vulnerable group.

Chapter 7 examines child rights policy in the former Yugoslavia since the end of the war, which has involved a mixture of postconflict nation building, stratification of religious communities, and the flowering of local civil society in relation to the international sector. Little space has emerged in this policy landscape for a discussion of how to protect war babies' rights; where the topic has been raised, it has been paralyzed by the appropriation of child rights for other ends or by substantial disagreements about how to translate international norms into local practice.

Chapter 8 revisits the impact of these different constructions on the calculations of human rights organizations about whether and how to formally address the rights of children born of war. Using UNICEF as an illustrative case, I demonstrate the institutional, political, and normative challenges to conceiving of this issue primarily through a child protection frame and the strategies UNICEF has used to gradually engage with the issue without compromising its existing organizational priorities.

This book concludes with some thoughts about the limits of transnational constructions of children's human rights. My analysis demonstrates that because of the importance social actors attach to children as signifiers of group identity, what masquerades as rights rhetoric is often about preserving social cohesion, policing conceptual and physical boundaries, and reproducing notions of self and other—all factors often inimical to the realization of rights in an individualistic sense. Activists genuinely aiming to promote a rights-based approach must maneuver between and be cognizant of such traps in order to achieve the normative changes they desire.

2.
"PARTICULARLY VULNERABLE"
Children Born of Sexual Violence in Conflict and Postconflict Zones

Children born of rape may be neglected, stigmatized, ostracized or abandoned. Infanticide may occur.
—World Health Organization, *Reproductive Health During Conflict and Displacement*, 114.

ACCORDING TO A REPORT from the War and Children Identity Project in Bergen, Norway, tens of thousands of infants have been born of wartime rape or sexual exploitation in the last fifteen years alone.[1] If one adds together the estimated numbers of war rape orphans, children born to women held captive as sexual slaves or "wives" of military troops, and children born to women exploited by foreign soldiers, peacekeepers, and even humanitarian workers, this emerges as a population of enormous global scope.

As this chapter details, in Bosnia such children sometimes face physical abuse or neglect, stigma, abandonment, and discrimination as a result of social perceptions about their origins, despite the best intentions of policymakers. But Bosnia is not an isolated or unique example. In Rwanda, sexual violence during the genocide produced an estimated 2,000 to 5,000 such babies.[2] In that context, there have been reports of infanticide and severe abuse and neglect; the children are often called "children of hate" or "children of bad memories."[3] Elsewhere in Africa, girls abducted into rebel armies and forced into sexual slavery often give birth to children of their captors, only to find themselves and their children stigmatized and marginalized upon their escape.[4] Many choose to remain with their abductors because they cannot return to their extended families for fear their children will be rejected or abused.[5] Anecdotal evidence suggests similar patterns in other post-conflict zones: Kuwait,[6] Liberia,[7] the Congo,[8] East Timor,[9] and Nicaragua,[10] to give a few recent examples.

The common experience these children face is the perception by the societies into which they are born that they are "of the other."[11] Because they are stigmatized as both illegitimate and "enemy" children, the human rights of children born of war may be compromised in a number of ways, from rejection, abuse, or neglect by immediate and extended family members, to stigma by the broader community, to lack of access to resources and denial of citizenship. As Rehn and Sirleaf wrote in a recent United Nations Development Fund for Women report, "[the children] . . . become the symbol of the trauma the nation as a whole went through, and society prefers not to acknowledge their needs."[12]

Children are protected as human beings under global human rights instruments, in particular the Universal Declaration of Human Rights. These various instruments guarantee children, like other human beings, the right to physical security, which in the case of children is related to the provision by others of food, medical assistance, shelter, protection, and a range of developmental needs.[13] At a bare minimum, this means that states are responsible for preventing infant neglect, abandonment, or death at the hands of family members or caretakers, something to which children born of war rape may be particularly, but not uniquely, vulnerable. The broader requirement that states ensure the necessary conditions for meeting children's other needs is reflected in global instruments that emphasize the "special care and assistance" to which mothers and young children are entitled[14] and "the provision for the reduction of the still-birth rate and of infant mortality and for the healthy development of the child."

The most important international legal instrument articulating children's rights is the 1989 Convention on the Rights of the Child (CRC), the most widely ratified human rights instrument in history. The CRC provides for all children's right to know their parents (Article 7), to an adequate standard of living, social security, and health care (Article 6), to a nationality (Article 7), and to protection against abuse, maltreatment, and neglect (Article 19).[15] The CRC also enumerates a long list of positive rights: Children are entitled to survival and to healthy physical and mental development (Article 6), to adequate health care (Article 24), to an adequate standard of living (Article 27), and to alternative care if deprived of a family environment (Article 19).[16]

As Leblanc notes in his exhaustive commentary, the CRC also enumerates a number of rights pertaining to the child's need to be integrated into a social community in order to exercise other rights and develop normally. Membership rights in the CRC include the right to be registered with the state at birth and to be given a name and nationality (Article 7) and the right to preserve one's identity, "including nationality, name and family relations" and to receive appropriate assistance in reestablishing that identity if in some way the child is deprived of it (Article 8). Article 7 also ensures the right to know and be cared for by one's parents to the extent possible, and Articles 9 and 10 govern separation from parents in extreme cases, stating that the "best interests principle" must be followed in such an event.

Finally, the CRC enumerates what might be called empowerment rights:[17] "rights that relate to a person being heard on matters that affect his or her life."[18] These include children's right to express views in matters concerning them (Article 12); to freedom of expression (Article 13); to freedom of thought, conscience, and religion (Article 14); to privacy (Article 16); to access information (Article 17); and to an education (Article 28).

In addition to laying out these various substantive rights, the CRC rearticulates the best interests principle as a guiding principle for the implementation of the CRC. Article 3(1) of the CRC states, "In all actions concerning children . . . the best interests of the child shall be a primary consideration." Although there has been a great deal of controversy in the literature on children's rights over how this concept is to be applied, at a minimum this suggests that policies regarding children should take into account these standards and should not be based primarily on the interests of other actors.

Additionally, children born of wartime rape are arguably protected by other international legal instruments relevant to the civilian population and to war-affected children in particular. The Fourth Geneva Convention and its Additional Protocols prescribe specific treatment for war-affected children. In addition to requiring states to provide for the basic needs and educational resources for children, it calls for preventing the forced recruitment of children, reuniting separated families, and laying down principles for rebuilding communities shattered by war.[19] Children's identity and family rights are also protected by Article 2(e) of the Genocide Convention, which considers the forcible transfer of children from one group to another as an act of genocide. Children are also protected by refugee law, in theory, to the same extent as adults.[20]

All these international standards incorporate, in principle, the assumption of impartiality: that children's human rights codified in law apply to all children, regardless of sex, nationality, religion, social origin, birth, or other status. As Cohen writes, "of all human rights principles, non-discrimination is . . . most consistently reiterated in human rights treaties": Both global human rights instruments and all three regional human rights treaties have made non-discrimination a central norm.[21]

Although there is no recognition in the international children's human rights regime that children born of wartime rape constitute a specific, protected category, several multilateral treaties do specifically outlaw discrimination on the basis of so-called illegitimacy.[22] By these standards, children born of sexual violence should not experience social stigma, discrimination, or a reduction in their physical and economic security on the basis of their nonmarital birth status, on the basis of their imputed ethnic origins, or because they were conceived as a result of violence.

In this chapter I describe the yawning gap between these lofty ideals and the fate of children born of rape into postconflict societies and problematize the inattention to this category by the international children's rights movement. I begin by discussing how the production of babies through sexual violence and exploitation functions as both a strategy of war and as an unintended side effect of militarized gender structures worldwide. Next, I discuss the situation facing babies conceived through such violence in wartime and postwar societies, positioning Bosnia's children of war rape in the context of this broader, global population.

RAPE, FORCED PREGNANCY, AND SEXUAL EXPLOITATION IN CONFLICT ZONES

During the war in the former Yugoslavia between 1991 and 1995, women on all sides gave birth to children conceived, often deliberately, by rape.[23] As in most other historical instances of well-publicized mass rape, the sexual violence in Bosnia was described at the time as "unprecedented."[24] Even those who understood that women have always suffered rape during war sometimes fell into the fallacy of thinking that the ethnic cleansing there breached some atrocity threshold beyond what had been seen in antiquity, during the Middle Ages or in the early twentieth century. For example, in her monograph *Rape Warfare* Beverly Allen wrote, "There may be nothing unprecedented about mass rape in war, but this [forced pregnancy] is something new."[25]

But mass rape and forced pregnancy were not inventions of the militias, primarily Bosnian Serb, who carried it out in the former Yugoslavia. Sexual violence has historically been, and continues to be, endemic in war-affected regions across the globe,[26] and although they are often not remarked on, babies are often produced as a result.[27] Babies were born to Kuwaiti women raped by Iraqi soldiers after the invasion of Kuwait,[28] to East Timorese women and Indonesian forces and paramilitaries in 1999,[29] and to female survivors of the genocide in Rwanda.[30] Evidence emerged in 2004 that Iraqi women may have been impregnated through rape in detention by U.S. forces.[31] Most recently, an increasing number of sources have documented this trend in the Sudan, where forced impregnation to make "lighter-skinned babies" has been used as a tool of ethnic cleansing.[32]

In general, wartime sexual violence takes many forms, with pregnancy and childbirth inevitably resulting from a proportion of cases.[33] Women may be raped opportunistically by soldiers who see access to enemy women as part of their reward for fighting.[34] Sometimes women and girls are raped publicly as a means of humiliating enemy communities[35] or terrorizing people into leaving a territory.[36] Rape may be used as a form of torture in detention to secure information about a woman's relatives or her own political activity.[37] In other contexts, women and girls are enslaved and used to service male soldiers during long periods in the field, as was the case with the "comfort women" of various Asian nationalities interned by the Japanese during World War II.[38] Although women of all ages are vulnerable to sexual violence, women and girls of childbearing age tend to be the prime targets.[39] It is therefore no surprise that in all the cases described here, pregnancy and childbirth often occur as a byproduct of rape.[40]

However, mass rape can also be and has often been used systematically for the express purpose of impregnating women on the other side of a conflict. In Bangladesh's war of secession from East Pakistan, for example, mass rape was used with the stated intent of altering bloodlines and resulted in a reported 25,000 pregnancies, many of which were carried to term.[41] In the ongoing crisis in Darfur, rape has been reportedly used as a means of creating "light-skinned babies" among Darfur's non-Arab populations.[42] In cases such as these, rape and forced pregnancy are used as a form of psychological warfare against not only the woman herself but her entire community and the nation of which she is a citizen.[43]

During the war in Bosnia-Herzegovina, sexual violence took place across the continuum described here,[44] and pregnancies resulted from opportunistic or single-incident rape as well as repeated rape in detention.[45] Reports of "rape camps" run by Bosnian Serbs, where Croat and Muslim women were held and raped with the deliberate intent to impregnate, drew particular condemnation by the international community.[46] A United Nations report issued in 1994 identified several patterns of rape, including the operation of such camps.[47] Testimonies gathered by the press, independent scholars, and various nongovernment organizations and UN fact-finding commissions as well as the Hague Tribunal have buttressed the claims that forced impregnation in these camps was systematic and deliberate.[48] There is evidence that soldiers were under orders to rape.[49] They often told their victims that they intended to make them pregnant and that they had been ordered to rape for this purpose.[50] That the creation of babies was an intended outcome of rape is further demonstrated by the fact that rape camps were staffed with gynecologists who frequently examined the detainees to determine whether they were pregnant.[51] Some pregnant women were given better treatment and food, and generally they were released only after it was too late to abort.

Although it is likely that the majority of rape-related pregnancies in Bosnia resulted in abortions,[52] some rape-related pregnancies were carried to term for various reasons. One well-cited reason was some women's lack of access to abortion. Despite the fact that before the war all abortions were legal in Bosnia-Herzegovina and allowable in Croatia after the first trimester in cases of rape, access to abortion for refugees remained limited. Women in flight or in refugee camps where reproductive care was not a priority had difficulty accessing such services.[53] Others were too ashamed of their condition to come forth early in pregnancy or denied their condition for psychological reasons.[54] In addition, a great number of women were intentionally detained in concentration camps until it was too late to undergo an abortion.[55] Women who sought abortions in late pregnancy were often turned away for legal or ethical reasons or because the procedure was deemed too risky.[56]

It is impossible to determine how many babies were conceived through this violence carried to term and born during or after the conflict, nor how many of the total number remain in Bosnia-Herzegovina today. Estimating the scope of the problem is complicated by a variety of factors. First, there are no reliable data on the total number of women who survived rape during the war.[57] Second, data on rape-related pregnancies tend to be anecdotal; systematic evidence on the percentage and sequelae of rape-related pregnancies exists only for isolated and nonrepresentative samples of victims.[58] Third, neither the government nor the humanitarian sector has kept official records or statistics documenting the birth of children of rape or tracked what has happened to them subsequently. This was partly because of the chaotic wartime environment[59] and the unpreparedness of the humanitarian sector to approach the problem of sexual violence in a careful and systematic way.[60] However, some actors intentionally hid evidence of these children's origins in an attempt to prevent stigma against them.[61]

A helpful estimate can be approximated by taking the most valid sample available and extrapolating the rape-related birthrate from that sample to the population of women estimated to have been raped during the conflict (although this number is also widely disputed). In 1993, the Mazowieki report confirmed a total of 119 rape-related pregnancies; of these pregnancies, 34 were carried to term, placing the birthrate from rape-related pregnancies in that sample at 28 percent.[62] If the European Community's estimate of 20,000 rape victims is to be believed, with a rape-related pregnancy rate of 9 percent, this could have resulted in as many as 1,800 pregnancies and 504 births nation-wide.[63] This number is consistent with conservative estimates of 400–600 given by doctors and aid workers in the field at the time and much lower than the wildly inflated estimates that prevailed during the war and the numbers available from other country contexts.[64]

What happens to the babies born as a result of such crimes? As detailed in this chapter, the available evidence suggests a bleak picture. In the next section of this chapter I provide an outline of the various harms to which these children may be subjected as a result of the manner in which they are conceived, drawing both on primary data from Bosnia and on available research and reports from other country contexts.

CHILDREN BORN OF WARTIME RAPE AND EXPLOITATION

Those concerned with child protection have often expressed a fundamental concern with mitigating the impact of armed conflict on the physical security of children. A second concern of the international movement to protect war-affected children is to assess and alleviate deprivation that results from war so that children can access the resources they need for short-term survival and long-term development. A third concern rose in the 1990s when the children's rights movement began addressing questions of the psychosocial health of children in various contexts. Birth as a result of wartime rape or exploitation has the potential to affect children physically, economically, and psychosocially, both as youngsters and later as adults, in ways that are relevant to the work of the international children's rights regime. I describe each of these general sets of concerns in the next section.

Physical Impacts

There is some evidence that certain health risks can accompany a pregnancy if the mother's reproductive health is compromised or if the mother experiences psychological and physical trauma while pregnant.[65] Where the pregnancy itself is construed as a trauma because of its origin, it can be hypothesized that this could affect the physical development of the fetus. A number of children in Bosnia who were born to rape victims are disabled, although it is uncertain whether factors relating to the rape itself were primarily responsible.[66] In general, there is reason to hypothesize that children brought to term as a result of such physical and psychological trauma, and in an environment where the mother continues to be under severe stress, may need particular medical care as neonates.[67]

For various reasons, women and girls who have been raped or are living in exploitative circumstances often try to abort such pregnancies.[68] If safe abortion is illegal or inaccessible, these efforts take place through the use of various informal means.[69] Such means are not always successful, and these pregnancies sometimes result in live births. We know little about the health effects of botched abortions on children brought to term.[70] Additionally, women and girls impregnated by rape often give birth without assistance, because they are in captivity or they wish to hide their pregnancy.[71] Such babies are at risk during childbirth, particularly if their mothers have experienced nutritional deprivation or lack of maternal care during pregnancy.[72] Moreover, the possibility of the mother's death or incapacity as a result of childbirth has important physical consequences for children born in isolation, without a support network nearby. For example, Hess has asked what happens to babies born in the bush to girl soldiers who die during childbirth. Are such infants automatically recruited into and raised by the armed forces, delivered to local communities, or simply killed or allowed to die?

Stories of infanticide pervade literary and social discourse on children born of war rape.[73] In a novel about forced pregnancy based on interviews with numerous rape survivors from the former Yugoslavia, Slavenka Drakulić describes two such incidents.[74] A recent Italian film about World War II portrays a group of pregnant rape survivors making a secret pact to kill their children; the award-winning *Turtles Can Fly* tells the same story, set in a Kurdish refugee camp.[75] Many real-life cases are rumored or reported by human rights and health workers who have known the victims. In Bangladesh, a social worker related stories of infants being put in dustbins by public officials after the genocide.[76] After the genocidal rapes in Rwanda, Human Rights Watch reported that "health professionals assume that a number of women gave birth in secret and later committed infanticide. They also believe that a number of women who gave birth in the hospital allowed their babies to die after returning home."[77]

Although many of these rumors are unverifiable and unsubstantiated by carefully kept statistics, there is direct evidence of a few such cases. In Kosovo, for example, a young woman raped by Yugoslav National Army forces snapped her newborn child's neck in front of World Health Organization nurses and then handed them the corpse.[78] In addition, several documents on gender-based violence in conflict situations, based on experiences in various field settings, warn that infanticide may be a sequela to rape-related pregnancies in conflict zones.[79] Although infant girls are at the greatest risk of infanticide worldwide because of the preference for sons, in the case of children conceived "of the enemy," anecdotal evidence suggests that male infants may be at a greater risk because they are viewed as potential fifth column combatants.[80] They may also be rejected more forcefully by their mothers, whose attitudes toward males in general may be adversely affected by the experience of sexual violence.[81]

As early as 1993, reports of infanticide began surfacing from the former Yugoslavia, and some of these were later confirmed. The director of the Documentation Center for Genocide and War Crimes in Zagreb stated that women raped in Bosnia who could not get abortions abandoned their infants "or they kill the babies . . . although we've never been able to prove it."[82] A women's advocate from Croatia recalls one survivor who threw her newborn child into the Sava River.[83] Medica Zenica, a women's organization that worked with many rape survivors during and after the war, kept careful statistics on the sequelae of rape-related pregnancy during the conflict. Out of a sample of fifteen rape-related pregnancies, thirteen of which were carried to term and three of whose mothers chose to raise the child with psychosocial support from Medica, one child was eventually killed.[84] Distraught mothers did not pose the only such risk to the children. Some survivors have testified that children born to detained women in the former Yugoslavia were killed by their captors after birth.[85]

Failure to keep records of which children had been born as a result of rape and were therefore at particular risk of infanticide has impeded monitoring of their situation. It also makes it impossible to ascertain the total number of infant deaths by abuse or neglect during and after the war that were related to the child's biological origins or the total percentage of children born of rape who were killed by their mothers or extended families. Information on general infanticide rates in Bosnia is unavailable, but a study in Croatia of infanticide rates from 1989 to 2002 found that the general neonaticide rate was approximately 8 in 100,000, or 0.008 percent. In comparison, the percentage of neonaticide among reported case histories for children born of rape in Bosnia is quite high, with 8 percent of cases (two out of twenty-three) resulting in an infanticide attempt and 22 percent of cases (five out of twenty-three) involving consideration of infanticide.[86] The rate of infanticide in this case history dataset is eight times higher than the entire infant mortality rate in Bosnia for 2003 (15 in 1,000, or 1.5 percent).[87]

Infanticide is not only directed at some children born of war rape but also seems to be constructed by some actors as a legitimate response to bearing a child of rape. A women's advocate working with Kosovar rape survivors, referring to a particular infanticide, was quoted as saying, "The attitude that she is a cold-blooded murderer is wrong. Who knows what this poor girl has been through?"[88] Beverly Allen, whose path-breaking 1996 book *Rape War-fare* defined forced pregnancy as genocide and as a form of biological war-fare, suggested that infanticide should be considered a psychologically healthy reaction for a mother impregnated by rape.[89] Even testimonies from women who aborted or chose to raise their children suggest that they considered in-fanticide a socially acceptable option: "Thank God for the abortion," a survivor was quoted as saying in a recent documentary; "If I had given birth, I would have killed it."[90] A Rwandan forced pregnancy survivor relates, "I was angry about the pregnancy and even thought about getting an abortion, but I had no money. . . . I gave birth to twins in January 1995. At the time, I accepted them. I could not think about killing them."[91] Evidence that this response is normal-ized in some contexts as a means of dealing with an influx of children born of war strongly suggests that infanticide is a serious physical risk to the security of infants born of rape and exploitation.

Children of war rape who are allowed to live may be abused or neglected.[92] Indeed, family abuse and neglect of children in general are likely to increase under conditions of armed conflict and societal stress and, like domestic vio-lence against women, are among the most understudied and under-discussed dimensions of children's suffering during war. But children conceived in rape may be at a greater risk of such abuse, either by their mothers, who may be physically or psychologically unable to care for them, or, if the mother accepts the baby, by the extended family.

A number of reports document the correlation between psychological se-quelae of rape and the risk of abuse or neglect of children born as a result.[93] In cases of wartime rape, neglect of infants carried to term is understood as a key symptom of sexual trauma.[94] Abuse is often reported by women who have raised their child conceived of rape, either willingly or because they had no acceptable alternatives. Describing a reluctant Rwandan mother, one journalist reports,

> Sometimes she awakes resentful. It is during those days that she finds her tem-per short and she hits her child. A few times she has tried to give him away. Out of anger she tells him lies: "You are not even mine. I picked you from the trash." Sometimes she cries for hours, unable to function. "I really beat him for such petty things, and I feel I can't love anyone," she whispered.[95]

In Bosnia, war rape survivors have described their child as a reminder of what happened, particularly when they see the perpetrator's features in the child's face: "Even now, when my daughter gets angry there is something in the expression on her face that reminds me of the one who did this to me. I feel like hitting her in those moments. I have to walk away to calm myself."[96]

These outcomes are not deterministic. Women who consciously choose to raise their children, who might otherwise have given up their babies, in some cases are able to overcome their trauma and experience mothering as a method of healing: "It was my daughter who helped me back to some sort of normality. Perhaps that is why I love her so much," one survivor said.[97] Rape survivors' abilities to nurture their children are shaped by the resources and support available to them: financially, logistically, and, most importantly, emotionally.

Yet this support is often not available, either from families, communities, or the state. Children whose mothers do summon the courage to care for them often face rejection and abuse from extended family members or communities. A forced pregnancy survivor in Rwanda testified, "Almost all my family members have refused to accept the baby—it is a child of an Interahamwe. They have told me that they do not want a child of wicked people. They always tell me that when my baby grows up that they will not give him a parcel of land. I don't know what is going to happen to him."[98]

In 2004, the United Nations Children's Emergency Fund (UNICEF) field office in Bosnia-Herzegovina collected confidential case histories on specific children born of rape from civil society organizations who knew of such families. Thirty-nine percent of the case data included references to an initial rejection of the rape survivor or her baby by one or more family members.[99] According to one case study, the survivor's "whole family and even her mother kept telling her that 'she gave birth to a Chetnik child.'" One family referred to in a document from Medica Zenica, a women's organization working with trauma survivors, had reportedly taught their daughter's child to explicitly identify his existence as a mistake, forcing him to introduce himself to household guests as "I am the product of my mother's shame."

In other cases, whereas the child's extended family might treat the child with love, stigma might be expressed by neighbors, peers, or other community members. During the war in Bosnia, the media and various fact-finding missions on rape mentioned the concern of local actors that children born of rape in Bosnia would be stigmatized along with their mothers after the war.[100] A rape survivor was quoted as saying, at the time, "Where I come from, everyone would think of the kid as filth."[101] In Uganda there is a pattern of physical abuse of small children conceived in the bush by abducted girls. Such children are often viewed with suspicion by the mother's community when she returns home, and some are even blamed or beaten in cases in which, for example, their playmates get hurt.[102]

Economic Impacts

Children of rape or exploitation who are raised by their mothers are likely to suffer extreme economic marginalization. This is related to the status of women in war-affected societies in general, and exacerbated by the specific stigma of rape, which may actually be heightened by a woman's "scandalous" choice to raise her child.[103] First, the child constitutes evidence of the assault, which could otherwise be denied or repressed. To the extent that silence about one's victimization is a protection mechanism, this option may be unavailable to women who bear their children conceived in rape. Second, the child may represent an insult and a continual reminder of collective violence to the surrounding community: "The perception of public ownership of women's sexuality . . . makes it possible to translate an attack against one woman into an attack against an entire community; the impact is multiplied when the woman becomes pregnant."[104] Third, the enmity toward the child may be projected onto the mother, who in addition to being seen as dirty or unmarriageable as a result of the rape may also be viewed as complicit or traitorous for not rejecting her child. All these factors generate tremendous social difficulties for women who choose to raise children conceived of rape.

Above all else, a single woman raising a child needs a source of income. If she lacks a reliable family network for assistance, the child's presence may prevent her from working or receiving job training if alternative childcare arrangements cannot be made. In Sierra Leone, for example, demobilized girls impregnated by rebel captors in the bush considered job training the most important form of support they could receive. Unfortunately, the lack of childcare assistance from their families or the rehabilitation programs themselves made it difficult for these mothers to attend job skill training.[105] Because of this lack of support, many girl mothers became prostitutes, exposing their children to a range of psychosocial, economic, and physical risks. Mothers who resort to such means of survival increase their risk of contracting HIV and thereby increase their baby's risk of contacting this virus through breastmilk.[106]

Financial hardship was one of the most common concerns cited in the Sierra Leone interview dataset. These concerns were also highlighted in UNICEF's case histories as being a particular problem for Bosnian families. In one case, "the mother is without employment, the girl goes to school, they are living in difficult financial circumstances, below the minimum required for sustenance; they even do not have the bed for sleeping and the girl dreams of having a TV set." In several case histories collected by the research team, it was reported that desperate mothers were eventually forced to institutionalize their children because of a lack of financial resources and support from their extended families or welfare agencies.

Because of social and economic pressures such as these, children born of rape and exploitation appear likely to be abandoned, although this likelihood seems to vary by context. In Bosnia, it is guessed that most babies carried to term by rape victims were abandoned at birth by their mothers.[107] According to one respondent who reported the cases of twenty-seven women seen by her organization who gave birth as a result of forced pregnancy, only four kept their children, and all of these women emigrated from Bosnia. This differs from the situation in Rwanda, where many of these children are being raised by their mothers. Some claim that a lack of alternatives, as opposed to maternal acceptance, may be responsible for this trend. According to one news article, a survivor said that "she would gladly give up her 19-month-old boy to anyone who was willing to raise him. No one has offered."[108] By contrast, some aid workers report a surprising level of acceptance of the babies among East Timorese rape survivors.[109] However, such reports conflict with evidence that many children born of rape in East Timor are now in institutions.[110]

It must be emphasized that even in very conservative societies, women do not always want to surrender their children conceived of rape. Portrayals that this is a uniform response may result partly from a social expectation that this reaction is normal. To the contrary, there is evidence of governments forcing abortions or adoptions on women who preferred to keep their babies.[111] Some women have testified that the choice to raise their child was a means of overcoming the horror of rape.[112]

However, anecdotal evidence suggests that abandonment of these children is common due to a combination of factors. The initial choice to raise a baby is no guarantee that a woman will be able to follow through on this decision. In several cases, Bosnian women who attempted to raise their children were later forced to place them in institutions by economic hardship or psychosocial difficulties. A social worker associated with the women's organization Medica Zenica in Bosnia-Herzegovina told me,

A sad story: Mother was raped somewhere in eastern Bosnia; she escaped to Serbia because it was the nearest place without the war to avoid further abuse. She presented herself as a Serb because she didn't have any documents. . . . She gave birth to the baby and she was raising the kid for a year alone. And suffering and torturing herself. When the baby turned one year old she gave it to the orphanage. After a year the baby was two years old; they gave her child back from the orphanage because they said the baby couldn't stay there because it was not Serb. So she managed somehow to reach her parents in Bosnia; the war was ending. She came to Sarajevo with the child to her parents. So the parents told her, "We accept you, but we don't accept this Chetnik." That's how she found out about Medica. Then she came to Medica to seek assistance to solve her personal dilemma of whether to keep the baby or give it to the orphanage. Because she couldn't give the baby up so easily after that time. Then she was working with the baby, it was so obvious that the baby was really tortured by this separation from the mother all the time, it was obvious because the baby was afraid to let the mother walk away from it even for a little bit. It turned out they had been working on reintegrating the two of them. That's when she decided to keep the baby. For a couple of months Medica lost contact with her. A couple of months later we received a letter from the Center for Social Work asking for our estimation on whether the child should be given to the orphanage. This is when I realized the community didn't do anything to assist the woman when she had decided to keep the child. . . . Last I heard the child was given to the orphanage. I assume that it was in Sarajevo.

In general, it is unknown how many such children are abandoned after a period in their mother's or birth family's care or what happens to them after abandonment. In general, the extent to which abandonment affects young children's economic well-being depends on the social mechanisms that are in place for providing alternative care.

It is typically assumed that the best outcome for a neonate is achieved when he or she is placed as quickly as possible with an adoptive family. The availability of such families and a means to connect them to babies depends on the context and on whether social services exist. Even where such mechanisms are in place, there is conflicting evidence about the likelihood of children born of war rape being adopted rather than institutionalized.

A baby's prospect of being adopted may be indirectly affected by physical or mental disabilities.[113] A number of children born of rape in Bosnia were disabled, and although it is uncertain whether factors relating to the rape itself were primarily responsible, there is evidence that such children are less likely to be adopted.[114] A Croatian doctor interviewed by a journalist in 2003 recalled that he had considered adopting a child born of rape who had been admitted to his center, but his "wife wouldn't even consider adoption."[115] Families that have done so have often had to deal with the ostracism engendered by raising a child "of the enemy."[116] In the case of the Muhić family, this included death threats and at least one attempt on Alen's adopted mother's life.

On the other hand, being born of war rape appears to be an advantage rather than an obstacle on the international adoption market. In the case of Bosnia, waiting lists existed in Western countries of couples specifically asking to adopt "rape babies,"[117] and after the 1971 war in Bangladesh, many children born of rape were exported to the West.[118] In many cases, such a child's opportunity for placement depends on political rather than market factors. Some postwar governments actively seek to remove the children from the national population, whereas others will not allow such children to be adopted abroad. The new government of Bangladesh constructed a "marry-off" campaign for women raped during the war. Only women who were willing to relinquish their babies conceived in rape to adoptive parents overseas would be eligible for marriage.[119] By contrast, governments in the Balkans opposed the export of such children for symbolic reasons. By some accounts, the government was worried about being accused of selling the children, as had happened in Romania.[120]

Policymakers were also under pressure from religious authorities who, depending on their understanding of the child's identity, sought to limit which couples could adopt, either domestically or abroad. For example, the transnational Islamic community argued that children born to Bosnian Muslim rape victims must be raised by Muslims.[121] In other cases, governments are reluctant to surrender "their" citizens to foreign countries because of concerns about postwar demographics.[122] "We have hundreds of thousands of orphans," said a Rwandan minister. "Adopting them to the outside means you are looting an entire population."[123]

The refugee policies of host countries also affect war babies' economic status and their prospects for adoption if they are abandoned by their mothers at birth. For example, it is notable that although the United Kingdom actively sought to streamline its international adoption procedures to import "rape babies" from the Balkans, it maintained restrictive asylum laws that prevented pregnant rape victims from immigrating.[124] Similarly, the desire for Bengali babies demonstrated in countries such as Canada did not extend to providing asylum for their mothers.[125] The life histories, economic prospects, and eventual national identities of children born to pregnant women seeking refuge in neighboring countries will be affected by whether their mothers obtain asylum. In addition,

the psychosocial and economic assistance that is available to mothers in host
countries and the extent to which social safety nets are available for women
who choose to give up their newborns will affect a child's future.

If an abandoned child is left in the care of authorities in a war zone, rather
than being killed or left to die at birth, and if immediate adoption is not a possibility, he or she is likely to end up institutionalized. In East Timor, for example, "the orphanages are filled with these children of the enemy."[126] In such
cases, ambiguity regarding a child's biological origins can impede placement
and perpetuate the experience of institutionalization. One girl in Bosnia was
reported in 2003 to have been in a legal limbo for twelve years because her
mother abandoned her without instructions as to adoption. Unfortunately, the
municipality in eastern Bosnia from which the mother originated now lies in
the Republika Srpska, which requires the authorities to admit responsibility for
the child's origins or her well-being in order to proceed with adoption hear-
ings. Toomey states,

> In the absence of any record of what her mother wished to happen to her
> child, authorization for her to be adopted would have been needed from the
> social-services department in the municipality where her mother lived be-
> fore the war. But that now lies in the Republika Srpska. In order for the Serb
> authorities to give permission for Samira to be adopted, they would have
> to accept financial responsibility for the special care she needs; they would
> also, indirectly have to acknowledge the circumstances under which she
> was born.[127]

Some children born of rape or exploitation become stateless if they are denied citizenship by the countries in which they are born, either as a deliberate
form of discrimination or as a result of indirect factors, such as jus sanguinis
citizenship laws. Lack of formal citizenship can have an economic impact if
children are denied access to medical care, education, or other social benefits.
Statelessness also affects a person's freedom of movement, ability to receive asylum, chances of being formally adopted, and vulnerability to trafficking.

According to Grieg, children fathered by American soldiers in Vietnam
were denied medical care, welfare, and education because it was "customary
for fathers to claim legal paternity and to register births. . . . The implications
of this are tremendous. Without citizenship the children are doomed to be a
pariah in their birth country."[128] Children conceived as a result of Iraqi rapes
during the occupation of Kuwait were reported to have been protected financially but denied citizenship.[129]

In Croatia, children born to female refugees who had crossed the border from Bosnia were sometimes denied both Croatian and Bosnian citizenship.[130] According to a legal analysis undertaken by the Center for Reproductive Law and Policy in 1994, only children with one Croatian parent could be considered Croatian, although an additional provision guaranteed citizenship to children "found abandoned." "Babies born of rape, however, are unlikely to be covered by this provision as their mother is usually known."[131] In 1996, it was reported that babies born in Croatia to rape survivors fleeing Bosnia were being denied the right to go to school in Croatia.[132]

Psychosocial Impacts

Little is understood about the psychosocial impact on children born of wartime rape, and children in different circumstances probably will experience different effects. Based on available evidence, however, it seems clear that children's development, sense of identity, and psychological health may be affected in a variety of ways over the course of their young lives as a result of the details surrounding their conception.

In infancy, the main psychosocial impact on children born of rape stems from the possibility of neglect and the lack of long-term, supportive family relationships. Although these difficulties are not limited to these children, they may be particularly vulnerable to their effects.[133] If a child is kept by her mother, she may experience difficulty bonding;[134] some rape survivors who have had no choice but to raise their child have reported extreme ambivalence toward them.[135] But some rape survivors have expressed deep love for their child, constructing their baby not as a burden but as a gift from God after all else was taken from them.[136] More research is needed on the factors that lead to positive relationships between a rape survivor and her child.

Although there is a lack of evidence about these positive relationships, the psychosocial effects of maternal ambivalence and distress on young children are profound. According to psychologists who have worked with such families, many children exhibit attachment difficulties both with their mothers and with others. Additionally, some children become depressed, excessively clingy, or fearful of losing their mothers. One Bosnian child, whose mother had attempted to institutionalize him for lack of financial means and who had been rejected by the mother's family, had "developed a constant fear that his mother would abandon him" by the time the woman and child reached Medica Zenica.[137] A study on children of rape born to Medica Zenica's clients detailed a variety of attachment disorders and insecurities among the children resulting from precisely this type of ambivalent response by the mother. Several of the children in the study expressed a belief that their mother did not love them and greatly feared abandonment.

Even children whose mothers attempted to maintain a positive relationship were said to be indirectly affected by their mothers' psychological trauma. Thirty-seven percent of the women raising children in the dataset gathered by UNICEF in 2004 were reported to have been suicidal since the child was born. One organization reported that a mother told therapists that she planned to kill herself when her child turned eighteen. Some children developed a reverse parental relationship in which they felt the responsibility to protect and care for their mothers and blamed themselves for her distress or depression.[138] The aforementioned child was described as "constantly concerned for her mother who has isolated herself from the society and keeps quiet most of the time. . . . She fears that the mother will die, because she constantly takes medicines."

The Graça Machel Review states that "with supportive caregivers and secure communities, most children will achieve a sense of healing," but in social environments where a child is stigmatized or unwanted, such a child may lack precisely these relationships.[139] As a child grows older and develops a sense of self and a need for social acceptance and belonging, he or she becomes sensitive to stigmatization or emotional abuse from close relatives, peers, and members of the broader community.

In the early childhood years, children born of war may be scorned, teased, or stigmatized on the basis of their social origins, particularly if they are living with their mothers in close-knit communities or if their physical features identify them with their father's lineage. Amerasian children growing up in Vietnam after the war were labeled "dust of life" by their neighbors and classmates.[140] "Many children tried to hide their true identity and escape discrimination by quitting school."[141]

Anecdotal evidence gathered by the media provides support for the hypothesis that such stigma exists in Bosnia as well. At age three, Alen Muhić told journalists of hating being called "Pero," a derogatory Serb name, by members of his community, although at the time he did not understand the meaning of the term.[142] "People have something against these children, even though they are not to blame for any of this," a doctor told a reporter after the war.[143] Even some rape survivors have internalized the idea that the children are somehow tainted by the perpetrator's blood. One woman quoted in a recent documentary, who aborted her rape-related pregnancy, referred to other children born of rape this way: "I know some of these women had these children, because they were detained and they had no choice. I think those children will grow up to be just like their fathers."[144]

Social workers interviewed by UNICEF in 2004 reported that rape survivors and their children were sometimes stigmatized in this way: "She has four other kids, her husband had been killed earlier so everybody asked her 'where did the fifth one come from?'" A news article from 2003 described the way in which a Bosnian community ridiculed one survivor:

> For years [Jasmina] suffered taunts from those who knew, or suspected, what had happened to her during the war, and who would openly deride her daughter as "that bastard child." Sometimes, when she took her daughter out for a walk, they would shout after her: "There goes that whore, and look, she's given birth to another whore."[145]

Many people I have interviewed in Bosnia assumed that young children don't understand enough to be harmed by name-calling, even though this kind of rejection has been shown in other contexts to have dramatic effects. Older Amerasian children have reportedly mutilated themselves in attempts to look more white or more Asian.[146] Children who are never told of their origins while they are young may intuitively internalize this societal stigma: An adult war child fathered by a German soldier who was raised in postwar Norway told me, "No one ever told me why I was different, but I always knew there was something wrong with me." Similarly, institutionalization may also generate a sense of isolation from mainstream society, particularly where it constitutes the sole and official response to such children's upbringing, as in Kuwait after the first Gulf War. "When they enter school they're always asked the same question: why do you come with a government bus, where are your parents?" a social worker at Dar Tufalah Orphanage said. "They come back and cry and I have to comfort them."[147]

Given the various impacts described in the preceding sections, it is unsurprising that conventional wisdom in early psychosocial development concludes that it is best for such children to be adopted at birth into a social environment where their biological origins are unknown.[148] Yet as children enter adolescence and young adulthood, they begin to reinvent themselves, create a meaningful mosaic of their identities, and ask questions about their roots and origins. Children who have been adopted begin to demand information on their biological parents; children with one absent parent may begin to demonstrate an interest in making contact. For children born as a result of war, there may be a particular need (as well as a difficulty) in establishing contact with their parent in order to ascertain "who they are." Numerous such cases of World War II–era European children in search of their North American fathers are documented in the recently published *Voices of the Left Behind*.[149] These issues can arise even for children adopted under the most auspicious circumstances. As Ryan Badol, a Bengali-Canadian war baby, related in the 2001 documentary *War Babies*, "My interest in my birth mother changed. . . . I [developed] a wish to know more and more [not just about her but] about all the birth mothers."[150] Adoption reunions can be immensely complicated both for children and birth mothers even in the best circumstances; in cases such as these, numerous legal and psychosocial elements will come into play that have been given little consideration by actors concerned with the human rights of children in armed conflict.[151]

Similarly, for many children left behind by soldiers in Asia, Africa, or Europe, the desire to trace and make contact with their birth father becomes imperative during adolescence. Numerous advocacy organizations, such as Traces, Project Roots, and the War and Children Identity Project, are now involved in connecting such children with their biological fathers. For older children born of war, the inability to trace one's roots can become a source of psychosocial strain. States often place barriers on such people's ability to trace their parents. For example, Canada's Privacy Act protects World War II veterans who impregnated Dutch and British women after the war from unwanted contact by the women or their adult children.[152]

Adults in Bosnia tend to believe that these barriers are the best way to protect children from stigma and trauma. A common coping mechanism in Bosnia, apparent in both interviews and case histories, is for families to avoid telling the children how they were conceived. Only one child in the UNICEF dataset was made aware of her origins from the start. Mothers who kept their children tended to make up stories about dead fathers. Christine Toomey interviewed an activist who ran a safe house for pregnant rape survivors on the Croatian coast during the war. According to this activist, all thirty clients insisted they would never tell their children the true story, and they made up imaginary fathers to describe when asked.[153] Although many adults I surveyed believed shielding young children from the truth is an appropriate practice, others emphasized the psychosocial trauma that this can generate if children discover the truth:

> Of course they are traumatized. Maybe when they are smaller they don't know what happened, but one day. . . .

Child must know who he is. Why he is left in orphanage, why adopt him, who is his parents. He must know and that is fair really. But I don't know how he feels if you say that his mom was raped in war and all that. Maybe that would help him to understand why she left him, maybe he can forgive her. But you must find the best moment. You must be really clever with that and careful.

For those who know their origins and are attempting to create a functional social identity, lack of official discourse and information can be an impediment. Many Amerasian war children considered it a moral victory when the U.S. government recognized and took responsibility for their existence by awarding them immigration rights under the Homecoming Act of 1987.[154] By contrast, as the film *War Babies* documents, Ryan Badol's efforts to gather information on his background were frustrated by the Bengali bureaucracy and ongoing discourses of denial. In the end his greatest desire remains simply to raise awareness of the issue "so that it can be talked about."[155] Other adult war children continue to lobby for recognition and rights under international law.

VULNERABLE YET OVERLOOKED: THE PUZZLE

International standards demand that all children are entitled to survival, a family, a nationality, and equal treatment and to have their basic social, physical, and developmental needs fulfilled. Yet as this chapter details, children born of wartime rape into postconflict situations are often denied these rights. To anyone familiar with governments' records of human rights compliance more generally, this is no surprise. What is more puzzling is the lack of advocacy attention to the population by transnational civil society actors whose mandate is to promote such compliance.

Today, there is little mention of this category of child in the international discourse on war-affected children.[156] When I began interviewing representatives of leading child protection organizations in 2003, it was difficult to find anyone who had spent time thinking about what had happened to the babies born as a result of rape in Bosnia, East Timor, or Rwanda.[157] Despite media and donor concern for this category of war-affected child, awareness of their particular vulnerabilities by gender-based violence specialists, and the presence of a few small organizations lobbying specifically for their rights, major organizations in the growing advocacy network around children and armed conflict have not defined children born to sexual violence survivors in conflict zones as a category of concern. As recently as 2004, while attention to other categories of war-affected child increased, a UNICEF child protection officer stated, "I can't think of any organization that has dealt with [children born of wartime rape] specifically."[158] This continued to be true through early 2006, despite the widespread publicity regarding stigma and maltreatment of so-called Janjaweed babies in Darfur[159] and the increasing attention in transnational civil society to children and armed conflict generally.

At first glance, it seems obvious why the international community overlooked this category of child: Their needs and vulnerabilities are so complex and overwhelming, the human rights community may not have known what to advocate for. But this alone cannot explain the silence from human rights organizations and activists, because other equally complex issues were tackled in the 1990s and early 2000s. For example, rape itself and the complex psychosocial, physical, and economic impacts on male and female survivors defy easy attention and concrete responses. Yet the human rights community made it a priority in the 1990s to grapple with that ambiguity and to speak out on behalf of survivors. Other complex social problems relating to stigma, marginalization, and the body, such as HIV and AIDS, caste discrimination, and honor killings have all been the subject of specific agenda-setting and programmatic efforts by human rights actors since the end of the Cold War. Many are at least as complex, structural, and seemingly insoluble as the difficulties faced by children born of war.

As the rest of this book demonstrates, the explanation must be more complex. In the next chapter, I begin by thinking about how the world of transnational advocacy is structured and functions, situating children born of war as one of many issues considered too political, too sensitive, or too risky for global attention at particular historical moments. The chapters that follow dig deeper to discover how that consensus emerged in the human rights community, fueled by multiple narratives that cast the babies as symbols of atrocity rather than subjects of human rights law. Only in the early twenty-first century did currents of change begin to emerge, and these have been stilted, slow-moving, and full of pitfalls. For now, the war babies of Bosnia-Herzegovina, like those in conflict-affected societies elsewhere, remain underacknowledged and underserved.

3.

"DIFFERENT THINGS BECOME SEXY ISSUES"

The Politics of Issue Construction in Transnational Space

We tend to think of children affected by war primarily as child soldiers. There are several categories of children affected by war; and a dire lack of information for this particular category.

—Focus group participant, University of Geneva, 2005

SINCE THE EARLY 1990S, the protection of children in armed conflict has occupied unprecedented international attention.[1] In the transnational spaces beyond Bosnia-Herzegovina, a broad network of tireless people is dedicated to promoting child rights in conflict zones. They advocate for a child rights perspective in international institutions, in national legislation, and in communities, households, and refugee camps. They oppose the recruitment of children as soldiers, they talk about "zones of peace" for immunization, they champion the right to play and learn. The principled belief at the core of this issue network's efforts is that all children should be protected from the effects of armed conflict. The UN Web portal on this issue states, "International and local standards of conduct should be resurrected and respected, in order to prevent the abuse and brutalization of children."[2]

In many respects, the activities of this network have had a fair amount of success. They have transformed the international security agenda. In 1994, following a recommendation from the General Assembly, the UN secretary-general commissioned a global study on the effects of armed conflict on children, and the resulting document, the 1996 Graça Machel report, galvanized the human rights network, the UN, and governments worldwide.[3] As UN secretary-general, Kofi Annan established the Office of the Special Representative of the Secretary-General for Children and Armed Conflict, appointing Olara Ottunu as the first special representative in 1997. Simultaneously, the newly christened Office for the Coordination of Humanitarian Affairs was developing its "protection of civilians" mandate, with an emphasis on children and war incorporated as a component. Even the UN Security Council, once concerned only with issues of "high politics," undertook a series of thematic debates and resolutions on children and armed conflict in 1999; the most recent of several high-level reports was released in 2008.[4] The first indictment of the new International Criminal Court centered on crimes against children.[5] Defense think tanks in capital cities now include research on children and armed conflict, as do most human rights organizations.[6]

These shifts in the global agenda are not merely cosmetic; they have translated into concrete support for many children. For example, after Sierra Leone's ten-year civil war ended, the United Nations Children's Emergency Fund (UNICEF) and other agencies helped rehabilitate nearly 10,000 combatants under the age of eighteen; 20,000 were reintegrated into society in the Sudan.[7] In 2007, former child fighter Ishmael Beah went on a speaking tour in the United States to promote his memoir of life as a soldier for the government of Sierra Leone, speaking in particular of the UNICEF aid workers who rescued and rehabilitated him.[8] In short, the activities of this transnational network carry real significance not only for the development of international ethical norms but also for the life chances, physical security, and dignity of people in conflict zones. By extension, when the network overlooks specific problems, it exercises omissive power with concrete impacts on human security. For example, until 2003 very few organizations that dealt with child soldiers acknowledged that girls, as well as boys, were recruited.[9] Only after they began to do so did practices such as allowing an abducted "wife" to demobilize as her "husband's" dependent change.[10]

Although child recruitment is the most salient issue on the "children and armed conflict" agenda, it is one of many issues on which this community of practice focuses. The child rights network is also concerned with displaced children, refugee children, children exploited for their labor or for sexual services in camps for internally displaced persons, trafficked children, or those experiencing psychosocial trauma. Often, the agenda of the "children and armed conflict" network has included attention to issues of stigma and abuse of children by their own communities. The child protection network now deals with minority children such as the Roma and with stigma against AIDS orphans and former combatants.

Yet throughout the period of my research and at the time of this writing, the situation of children born of war, in Bosnia and elsewhere, remained largely a nonissue for this network of conscience. This silence is evident in the "Issues" links on Web sites of major humanitarian organizations engaged in child protection.[11] On the agendas of such Internet portals to the children's rights community one can find issues as varied as landmines, small arms, child soldiering, trafficking, unaccompanied children, and, increasingly, the girl child. But the stigma faced by children born of war and ways in which human rights actors might address this stigma so as to ensure their protection have attracted remarkably little attention from a children's rights perspective. Until very recently, it did not occupy agenda space in its own right, nor was it mentioned explicitly under themes such as "discrimination" or "unaccompanied children." For example, a content analysis of the online advocacy discourse for thirty-three major advocacy organizations' Web sites in 2005 found no references to stigma against children born of wartime rape.[12] Nor did it draw attention as a research priority or knowledge gap at conferences on data gathering with respect to war-affected children during this period.[13]

That these children as a category have been generally absent from the formal network agenda is confirmed by in-depth interviews I conducted with humanitarian practitioners and by the findings of focus group research conducted at the University of Pittsburgh between December 2004 and March 2005.[14] When asked to describe the key protection issues for children in conflict zones, no participants referred to children born of wartime rape as a category particularly affected by armed conflict. One stated, "You ask what is known about these children? You might begin by asking what is not known." An interview respondent told me, "I can't think of a single organization that has addressed these children directly."

These impressions by practitioners do not mean that nobody was thinking about the babies as such in the 1990s and early 2000s; organizations and individuals existed that cared about the issue. These groups included the War and Children Identity Project (WCIP) in Norway, established in 2001 to raise awareness of the human rights of war children as a global constituency. Human rights intellectuals were working to define this population as a category of concern in workshops, written articles, and international forums.[15] Other agenda-setting efforts from within the human rights advocacy sphere include five separate international documents that have called for greater advocacy and programmatic attention to children born of wartime sexual violence by organizations engaged in child protection in conflict zones, language that was pushed by concerned insiders in the human rights and humanitarian network.[16]

But when such "issue entrepreneurs" attempted to engage the agenda-setting machinery in the UN system in the 1990s and early 2000s, they faced resistance, and their lack of success in promoting a child rights view of this problem prevented the dissemination of awareness throughout the child protection network. Moreover, where this resistance was overcome, it was primarily through connection of the issue not to child rights discourse but to concerns over sexual violence prevention and response.

For example, the few instances of advocacy language about children born of war appear primarily in documents on gender-based violence, including the International Committee of the Red Cross's *Women and War* study, the secretary general's *Report on Women, Peace and Security*, and the United Nations Development Fund for Women's independent experts' assessment titled *Women, War and Peace*. UNICEF concluded at a 2005 meeting that any efforts to meet such children's needs should be addressed in the context of programming for their mothers. Similarly, when the Office of the Special Representative of the Secretary-General for Children and Armed Conflict mentioned babies born to girl soldiers for the first time on its Web site in 2007, this concern was raised as a subset of issues affecting girls in war. In short, rape survivors—including older girls who suffer sexual violence and pregnancy—remain the advocacy focal point for the few in the child rights network who have taken notice of the issue at all; the child rights movement more generally remains largely silent on the broader issues affecting children of war.

The history of this floundering issue raises a number of interesting questions. First, why did the vulnerabilities of these children come so late to the radar screen of organizations concerned with child protection in conflict zones? The very hesitant and limited steps taken with respect to this population are in stark contrast to the attention paid since the early 1990s to not only child soldiers but also girls in armed conflict, displaced children, AIDS orphans, trafficked children, exploited children, and a laundry list of other categories of concern within the network around children and armed conflict.[17]

Second, why have issue entrepreneurs concerned with this problem been so unsuccessful at pitching an explicit, comprehensive advocacy approach to major governments, international organizations, and nongovernment organizations (NGOs)—the same entities who have led the norm creation process in other areas such as landmines, the creation of the International Criminal Court, and the protection of child soldiers? Third, why has concern for these children, where it is now being formulated, been situated under the umbrella issue of sexual violence rather than the umbrella issue of child protection?

BYSTANDING, ISSUE ENTREPRENEURSHIP, GLOBAL GATEKEEPING, AND RIGHTS ADVOCACY

Asking why an issue such as child soldiers gets catapulted to global prominence and yet another, such as children born of war, gets framed largely off the international agenda begs broader questions about the politics of human rights agenda setting. Why do some issues get noticed by issue advocates and others do not? Why are some issues, when noticed, not perceived as lending themselves to advocacy attention? In short, why do human rights activists sometimes play bystander? And how do issues spread through a network once they get noticed by political entrepreneurs, and why do some issues fail to do so?

Early literature on advocacy networks emphasizes that "not all principled ideas lead to network formation, and some issues can be framed more easily than others so as to resonate with policymakers and publics."[18] By the same token, some issues resonate more easily with potential political entrepreneurs within advocacy organizations. According to Jenson, existing political discourses set boundaries around acceptable political action, "limiting the range of issues considered to be included in the realms of meaningful political debate, the policy alternatives feasible for implementation, and the alliance strategies available for change."[19] What draws attention as a genuine issue at a particular time is structured in part by the existing issue pool, existing institutional discourses aggregated across a network, the rules and norms of the political community in question, and the external political context.[20]

Such pressures can create a cognitive dissonance that draws practitioners' attention quite unwittingly away from issues that do not fit.[21] According to Erica Bouris, one factor that increases the likelihood of such dissonance is the extent to which a problem invites a simple and coherent frame of moral victimhood or requires a complex understanding of political victimization and vulnerability.[22] If an issue is complex enough, practitioners may not even arrive at the moment when they think carefully about whether it is too complex; they may simply keep their attention on more readily formulated problems. Particularly toward the beginning of my study, my informants often spoke with surprise at how they had simply never thought about the issue before:

> It seems when you think about it that this is an obvious category of child to be concerned about after the conflict, but I can't think of any organization that has focused on them specifically. . . . Of course, there is a broad range of issues competing for attention and many contributing factors that determine which issues get on the agenda.

I don't know, there is something about this issue that doesn't spring to mind—
we always think about rape as something that happens to a woman, but we
don't think about the children who are born as a result.

Such an effect is not deterministic: Individuals located within a network
may nonetheless take note of and aim to create a space for articulating a new
issue, no matter how complex or counterintuitive. Where an issue seems ill
suited to an advocacy domain or is considered highly sensitive, however, those
efforts may be constrained or resisted. For example, the influential 1996 report
by Graça Machel titled *Impact of Armed Conflict on Children* did not address
children born of sexual violence or exploitation. But in 2000, when the Canadian government organized a review conference to assess progress made with
respect to protecting war-affected children, several staffers involved in assisting
Machel with drafting a follow-up document saw the report as an opportunity
to bring some attention to children of war. One described to me the challenges
of doing so:

What we had seen in the field was really alarming. It seemed to be a real gap
and something that we just heard horrifying anecdotal stories about but were
unable to document or quantify and therefore slipped through everybody's
agendas. You couldn't focus on it directly.

The person who anonymously told me this story, along with several colleagues on the Machel review team, worked to ensure that language regarding
children born of rape ended up in the report that framed the agenda for the
2000 International Conference on War-Affected Children in Winnipeg.[23] The
document, given to conference attendees, included a recommendation that a
global study be done titled *Where Are the Babies?* to follow up on the situation
of children of rape and their mothers.

But at Winnipeg, whereas other issues raised in the review document were
addressed in specific sessions at the conference and discussed in the NGO draft
outcome document, no references to children born of rape made it onto the
agenda at the conference or the materials that resulted. The only reference to
forced pregnancy as a child rights issue in the document concerns underage
victims of rape who become pregnant.[24]

This story suggests the challenges of conceptualizing certain kinds of issues
within an advocacy discourse, incentivizing a bystander role for busy advocates
dealing with many pressing issues. It also suggests a politics of agenda setting
that constrains the spread of new issues through an advocacy network. Early

literature on advocacy networks envisioned the human rights community as a friendly web of like-minded activists, characterized by "voluntary, reciprocal and horizontal patterns of communication and exchange" and linked by their common principled commitment to human rights.[25] But in practice, the human rights network is a hierarchy in which many issue entrepreneurs agitate for their causes to be heard, and a few leading organizations in any issue area determine, through their internal agenda-setting process, which causes belong on the global agenda.[26]

"Political entrepreneurs" interested in getting a new issue or problem on the international agenda rarely have the resources or influence to do it themselves, so they pitch their ideas to organizations that do.[27] In the human rights area, for example, Human Rights Watch (HRW) and Amnesty International often must choose causes to adopt from the many claims they hear articulated by aggrieved groups worldwide.[28]

Although many people in large NGOs or UN agencies do not see themselves as powerful because their reference point is generally their relationship to governments, choosing which claims to legitimize is an important form of power vis-à-vis less central organizations in global civil society.[29] One informant told me,

> Different things become sexy issues, and we've had a role to play in highlighting one issue or another, or knowing something needs attention, a whole lot of organizations will throw themselves at family tracing, child soldiers, sexual violence, then everything else falls through the cracks.

In short, some issues are adopted onto the agendas of major international organizations and NGOs, and of these a few, such as child soldiers, result in major transnational campaigns and new treaties, norms, or state policies. Others fail to capture advocacy attention because it is not obvious what can be done. And some, such as war children, are pitched by political entrepreneurs but given little attention by these state, NGO, and UN authorities in global civil society, often for both strategic and principled reasons.

Consider the moment when activists from the Norway-based WCIP approached the Norwegian government to fund a conference and lead a treaty-making process on the specific issue of war children. WCIP's goal was an optional protocol to the Convention on the Rights of the Child that would comprehensively address the situation of children born of war and would call on states to undertake specific initiatives to ensure that such children were protected from stigma and discrimination, that they could access information about their parentage, and that their life experiences would become part of the public agenda.[30]

In 2003, activists from WCIP believed the that time was ripe for international attention and that their government was in an ideal position to become a norm leader on the issue. Norway was well known as a good international citizen, having worked closely with Canada to champion the anti-landmine campaign and the campaign to ban child soldier recruitment. The issue also resonated with Norway's domestic experience after World War II: In 2001, under pressure from domestic lobbyists, the government issued an apology and provided compensation to Norwegian children of Nazi fathers who were stigmatized as *krigsbarn* after the war.

But the WCIP activists I interviewed were surprised to discover that their government, renowned for its international moral leadership in the human security area, considered war children too complicated an issue. The request for funding was denied, the conference failed to materialize, and without a government's strong backing and the institutional access to the global policy arena it entailed, the idea of a new treaty was stillborn.

A similar episode of advocacy gatekeeping occurred in 2006. In December 2006, activists from several countries met in Cologne, Germany, to discuss strategies for addressing the social problems faced by children fathered by foreign soldiers. This meeting had been organized collaboratively by WCIP and social scientists at University of Cologne Central Archive for Empirical Research. The event drew together researchers from Eastern Europe, the United States, and Africa to consolidate the evidence base on children born of war. Activists and researchers at the meeting drew on historical case data from the post–World War II era in Scandinavia and evidence from more recent conflicts in Bosnia, Uganda, and Rwanda to make the case that children born of war faced specific vulnerabilities and had specific needs in conflict and postconflict zones. Their ideas and proposals ranged from fact finding in places such as Darfur, to implementing a sensibility about the issue into training for humanitarian practitioners, to an international conference whereby states would be asked to take seriously their responsibilities to children born of war after conflicts.

A UN representative had also been invited: a UNICEF officer with some involvement in that organization's considerations about how it might address babies fathered by peacekeepers and UN personnel. The political entrepreneurs at this meeting imagined that the support and legitimation of a powerful authority such as UNICEF would lend credence to their concerns, assist in the process of awareness raising throughout the child rights network, and provide valuable contacts throughout global civil society.[31]

But over the course of two days, the UNICEF representative consistently argued against the idea, stressing a variety of organizational, conceptual, and logistical issues. Although he was deeply sympathetic toward the subject, his position was that the issue was too multifaceted to encompass under one rubric, that it was not obvious that such children's needs were unmet by existing human rights programming, and that any additional threats to their rights (such as stigma) did not fall properly under UNICEF's mandate. Toward the end of the conference, despite case data, statistical evidence, and eloquent rights-based arguments made by several of the activists, he stated firmly, "I remain to be convinced of the merit of UNICEF treating these children as a specific group."[32]

These stories suggest that human rights agenda setting requires much more than dedicated moral entrepreneurs identifying and naming a problem. There must also be a space within a network's discourse for acknowledging such an issue, and it must resonate with established players in a transnational network whose attention and resources ensure visibility and dissemination. For some problems this happens easily; for others it happens slowly or not at all. In the end, it was up to other players within UNICEF to repackage the issue in such a way as to better fit the mandate of the organization; only very recently has UNICEF begun to develop that consensus. In so doing it is making possible a more open advocacy on the issue but also narrowing the issue from what the original advocates were proposing.

If it is the most central organizations in an advocacy network that have the power to legitimize or to block new issues from global agenda space or to reframe issues entirely, then a large part of the answer to the question asked in this book must center on the way in which such central players in an advocacy network understand their preferences. What persuades powerful players in transnational advocacy networks, such as UNICEF, the Norwegian and Canadian governments, the UN secretary-general, to pay attention to an issue they hadn't thought of before? What makes people with access to such network hubs likely to notice certain issues more than others? Once they do so, what drives the decisions of such organizations over whether and how to adopt a new issue within their organizational agenda space? Although these general questions cannot be definitively answered by examining one case, the aim here is to develop general hypotheses by answering this question in specific. Why did issues such as HIV and AIDS and child soldiers become prominent on child protection organizations' agendas in recent years, while the problem of stigma against children born of war was met with resistance?

SOME UNCONVINCING ANSWERS

A close examination of the case in this book calls into question a number of standard factors sometimes assumed to drive the decisions of human rights organizations. One is the idea that the nature of an issue itself ensures its suitability, or lack thereof, for global attention. According to Keck and Sikkink's landmark study on advocacy networks, the issue attributes most helpful in terms of framing issues are "causes [that] can be assigned to the deliberate actions of identifiable individuals"; "issues involving bodily harm to vulnerable individuals, especially when there is a short and clear causal chain assigning responsibility; and issues involving legal equality of opportunity."[33]

But this suggests that children born of war should be more likely to be on the agenda than child soldiers, for example, because as infants they should be perceived as highly vulnerable and innocent and because the rights violations they experience include bodily harm and discrimination. By contrast, child soldiers, many of whom maim, kill, rape, and gain social benefits and security from participation in armed groups, are a particularly problematic category to cast as uniformly innocent and vulnerable. In many cases child soldiers themselves perpetrate atrocities; they are as likely to have joined voluntarily as to have been forcibly abducted, and as one humanitarian official told me, "Compared to some other children experiencing the effects of armed conflict, child soldiers are extraordinarily well off."[34] Yet advocacy on their behalf has been enormously successful, whereas newborn babies resulting from sexual violence, who are more arguably both innocent and defenseless, have not been articulated as a priority for the child protection community.

One insight from Keck and Sikkink's issue attributes thesis does find some support in my data. They observe that "problems whose causes can be assigned to the deliberate (intentional) actions of identifiable individuals are amenable to advocacy network strategies in ways that problems whose causes are irredeemably structural are not."[35] For example, HRW gravitates toward issues in which a perpetrator can easily be named and shamed: As a representative of HRW's child protection unit told me in 2000, "We like to know who we can point the finger at." Clifford Bob's analysis suggests this is true of many human rights NGOs.[36] However, although this concern has certainly played a role in dampening advocacy around children born of war, there are limits to this argument as a general explanation of nonevents in human rights advocacy, because groups such as HRW have been known to diverge from this formula in other areas. For example, honor killings, committed not by the state but by families and enabled by complex and hard-to-change social norms, are now nonetheless on the human rights agenda.

Richard Price suggests that the promotion of new issues in international society is most likely to succeed if the issue can be grafted onto preexisting norms and categories of concern.[37] It is much easier to add a new issue to a preexisting campaign than it is to create issues out of the blue, he argues. But the absence of these factors can't explain inattention to children born of war. As chapter 2 already described, numerous international legal standards should be easily applicable to the kinds of rights abuses these children face, and as noted earlier, there is a well-organized network of organizations mandated to protect all children in armed conflict.

The global media are sometimes described as a possible source of advocacy momentum around specific issues.[38] The contagion effect of targeted media coverage is often cited as a driving force behind disproportionate attention to certain regions[39] or categories of victim.[40] If such coverage is lacking, this line of thinking tells us, this could explain the absence of advocacy as well. But as chapter 4 demonstrates, media attention to this issue has been plentiful: Numerous reports of "rape babies" in war zones from Bosnia to Rwanda to East Timor to Sudan have appeared in the press.

James Ron and Alexander Cooley tell us that we ought to think about human rights advocacy as a marketplace of ideas or of short-term contracts in which public attention toward a problem generates pressure to appear to be addressing it.[41] Similarly, Clifford Bob suggests that savvy advocates gravitate toward "hot" issues likely to draw donor funding and public support for their organizations. The logic of these arguments is that greater public awareness of a social problem contributes to market incentives for transnational advocates to adopt it as a cause: "Today's dominant issue areas and their thriving niches reflect broad agreement among powerful publics in the developed world about today's most important social problems."[42]

However, a number of celebrities[43] and states (particularly Britain) expressed interest in war babies at various pivotal moments during the Bosnian conflict,[44] but despite the predictions of realism or resource mobilization theory that transnational advocacy is driven by the concerns of powerful governments and donors, issue space failed to emerge in the 1990s that might have harnessed publicity (and financial contributions) on behalf of these children.[45] When attempts were made to create such space, they did not result in concerted action.

It seems that celebrity, activist, journalist, and state norm leaders' interest in specific issues can be no more than an exacerbating factor in issue adoption, given other permissive conditions within and between transnational advocacy networks themselves.

Moreover, in interviews and focus groups with human rights advocates I saw little evidence of the perception that media, donor, or public attention is a helpful catalyst for advocacy. Although they do experience such pressures, child protection organizations sometimes find themselves playing defense against a donor establishment and media perceived as sensationalizing issues best kept under the rug rather than playing a more helpful role in setting the agenda. Focus group participants told me skeptically,

> This sort of thing grabs a lot of people, the media grabs international attention, the politicians, . . . and I'm a little worried that we're going to create this sort of situation if we start focusing on this in this way, as a humanitarian epidemic.

> I think there's something kind of instinctive that says, oh, we need some sort of category like this that would give additional vulnerabilities, this will somehow grab the attention of donors or the international community or whoever. But my concern is that in examples where this has been done before there has either been a horrible backlash or it just doesn't make any logical sense.

What else might explain the lack of attention to children born of war? The idea that a specific organizational culture drives issue adoption decisions carries some weight. As I document in chapter 8, for example, UNICEF's particular organizational culture and mandate account partly for both the timing and nature of its approach to this issue. But factors unique to any one organization cannot explain the broad trends toward obfuscating this problem through the human rights network. A series of four focus groups with human rights practitioners drawn from a variety of organizations all showed the same thing: When asked to describe the vulnerabilities of children and women in armed conflict, participants never mentioned stigma and abuse against children born of war unprompted. When asked to think specifically about children born of rape or exploitation in conflict zones, respondents were quick to suggest that this was an important dimension of the humanitarian context in conflict setting. Yet participants based their comments primarily on inference rather than experience and pointed generally to the lack of data or programmatic attention to these children by the human rights network.

There is very little data. . . . We have good data now on the consequences of sexual violence for women, but looking specifically at what happens to the children, I've not seen it in the literature.

Places such as Pakistan where there have been instances, it has been an issue, but no one's ever followed it up. It's been an issue that women have been raped, but then what happened to their children, they just disappeared into history.

Many of my interview and focus group respondents who do child protection work raised an alternative explanation for the lack of specific attention to these children: that many practitioners genuinely believe that the best interests of the child are not served by articulating their problems through a rights-based lens. In fact, several of my informants argued that advocacy on behalf of a population could actually jeopardize their human rights:

Advocacy is important at a global level, but on the ground how do you tabulate without identifying the kids, how do you identify without stigmatizing, how do you gather data without naming?

Categorization may be helpful in leveraging funds and in advocacy, but categorization can also be risky as it can lead to stigmatization or other negative impacts.

There can be unintended consequences from our good intentions.

Such concerns are genuine, well founded, and prevalent in my dataset. But as an explanation for the avoidance of this issue, they do not provide a convincing account. For one thing, there is no consensus on this point in the child rights network. Although voices arguing against advocacy have predominated so far, there are also insiders who argue for a more comprehensive approach to children of wartime rape. Some said forcefully in focus group settings, "If you don't classify, if you don't identify, if you don't know, then how do you plan the policy and the programs, and how do you do the advocacy?" and "There's no public policy without some sort of information that says, you know, here is a problem."

More importantly, the same argument would be relevant for a variety of issues that are nonetheless very salient in global civil society: stigma against HIV and AIDS victims, child soldiers returning to their communities, disabled peo-

ple, and ethnic minorities. Indeed, the same argument was once used to justify inattention to the needs and vulnerabilities of sexual violence victims. This
has changed, and, most activists would argue, rightly so. So although rights-
based concerns are genuine, have merit, and are an important part of the story,
they are insufficient in themselves to explain the lack of attention to this issue.
Something about this issue convinced activists at many locations in the child
rights network that the political and normative risks of advocacy outweighed
the possible benefits, causing many to ignore the issue and others to oppose
open advocacy for children of war altogether. What impeded attention to this
very vulnerable category of child in the broader child rights network, during a
period when so many other causes proliferated within that network?

BLAMING AND FRAMING: HOW WRONGS MATTER IN
RIGHTS ADVOCACY

In the rest of this book, I argue that the reluctance to openly advocate for these
babies is rooted in the way children born of war have been constructed not as
subjects of human rights concern but as symbols of human wrongs inflicted on
other populations. The next four chapters demonstrate how representations of
the children functioned not to promote their human rights as war-affected people but instead to frame sexual atrocities in Bosnia as crimes against women,
as genocide against ethnic groups, and as a deviation from a civilized, global
"imagined community." These narratives made it easy to overlook children of
war and created a context in which human rights advocates came to view a
child rights approach to the issue to be particularly sensitive and risky.

   In short, what distinguishes successful from unsuccessful international issues is not the actual nature of an issue but rather advocates' perceptions of the
political and normative costs of advocacy. This in turn is a function of the way
in which an issue is perceived to fit within an existing set of narratives about
human rights. Other factors matter, but they constitute permissive conditions
only. If a potential set of rights claims is perceived to clash with existing understandings of atrocity—with preconstructed wrongs—this can inhibit organizations with prior commitments to validating earlier claims. Indeed, the way
in which those earlier wrongs are constructed can determine how such a new
rights claim will be conceptualized when it is raised.

   In the case detailed here, the failure to construct children born of war as
an international cause resulted largely from the way in which atrocity narratives were constructed in the 1990s around adjacent issues, particularly ethnic

violence and sexual violence. Children born of war came to be viewed through the lens of children born of rape as it was practiced during a conflict perceived to be genocidal. As signifiers of group identity and physical trauma to mothers, they were imagined to be carriers of atrocity rather than human beings in their own right. This frame complicated protection efforts for the children in Bosnia, as described in chapters 5 and 7. It also limited the advocacy space for thinking broadly about the vulnerabilities of such children as a global population of concern. First, the "children as consequences of atrocity" frame created the perception of conflicts of rights, between the children and their mothers and between the children and the ethnic communities into which they were born. Second, the atrocity frames created ambiguity about which types of advocacy organization owned the issue, setting the stage for these children to fall through the cracks in global and local advocacy discourse and in rights-based programming. Third, these narratives shaped strategic choices about whether to connect the issue to existing work on social exclusion and child protection or to sexual violence response, a choice that has important implications for advocacy and programming.

In the next few chapters, I trace the emergence of these narratives about children born of rape during the war in the former Yugoslavia in a number of sites where understandings of postconflict human rights get constructed: the media, the humanitarian sector, international criminal tribunals, and postconflict political discourse. In each chapter, I situate these narratives in their political and institutional contexts and then show how they occluded attention to these children's rights. Representations of the children functioned not to promote their human rights as war-affected children but rather to frame sexual atrocities in Bosnia as crimes against women, as genocide against national groups, and as a deviation from a civilized, global society. As a result, policies to address these children's needs were often defined in terms of state sovereignty, national reconciliation, or related, evolving issue agendas rather than out of a concern primarily for the best interests of the children.

I return to the question of agenda setting (or agenda denial) in transnational advocacy networks in chapter 8. There, I demonstrate how these specific, earlier constructions—and the political context they generated and sustained—structured the decision making of major child rights organizations as they struggled with whether and how to frame stigma against children born of war as a human rights problem in its own right and whom to blame for it. This story, though still unfolding, is one of reluctant norm leadership by a few savvy, courageous individuals in organizations generally indisposed to tackling such politically sensitive subjects.[46] Whether this changes in the future will depend a great deal on whether they can successfully repackage these children's vulnerabilities through a children's rights frame and sell this new frame to the transnational advocacy community. What is certain is that nothing like this type of issue creation occurred between 1991, when reports of babies born of rape in Bosnia began to hit the Western headlines, and 2007, when I stopped gathering interview data for this study. The next few chapters begin to explain why.

4.

"A FRESH CROP OF HUMAN MISERY"

Representations of War Babies in and Around Bosnia-Herzegovina, 1991–2005

No one knew her name when she arrived. The staff at the hospital where she was abandoned at birth christened her "Emina." A temporary name, for an anonymous, unloved baby whose future is uncertain. . . . To the nurses, she is just another tragic victim of the unspeakable Bosnian rape camps. . . . Her mother could not bear the shame of that birth. . . . She is 16, a Muslim schoolgirl from eastern Bosnia, made pregnant after being raped repeatedly by Serbian soldiers. . . . When her daughter was born she told doctors to take it away. . . . Meanwhile, in the same maternity ward where Emina lies this morning, happy fathers are arriving with flowers for their wives and newly born children. These are children born of love—while in the next cot is Emina, a child born of inhumanity.
—Willsher, "The Baby Born of Inhumanity."

I FIRST HEARD OF what was happening to Bosnia's war babies as a college student reading the news article excerpted here on the brand new World Wide Web. At the time I was an undergraduate government major in New Mexico, far from Bosnia, with little certainty about career directions, and three messages jumped out at me from that piece: Children are being horribly affected by war and by war rape, all this is happening in Bosnia for reasons and at a scale that is unprecedented, and something should be done. This is the moment I hark back to when people ask me today how I became interested in this subject, and so it is a moment I have theorized about in considering the role of the global media in provoking attention to children born of rape.

It was not until the winter of 2006, when I was finishing the archival research for this book, that I was able to track down a copy of this article that had so influenced my emerging political consciousness about children's rights and gender-based violence. Approaching the same text for the second time, with ten calendar years, seven years of graduate education, and four years of fieldwork under the belt, I saw it in quite a different light. Filtered through these lenses, several distinct patterns become apparent.

First, that article, like many other images of the conflict, describes the rapes in Bosnia in ethnic terms, essentializing the identities of the perpetrators, the victims, and their babies. One reads how "Muslim schoolgirls" were raped by

"Serbian soldiers" to produce "Serbian" children. Second, the emphasis is on women as victims of childbirth. "Rape has become a weapon of this war," the article states. The victims "cannot bear the shame" of giving birth to babies they cannot possibly love. Third, the babies themselves are described in the most hopeless terms, highlighting the barbarity of a country that could produce and then abandon such "tragic victims." This discourse led to calls for humanitarian intervention but also validated essentialist stereotypes of Bosnia as an uncivilized, patriarchal place, incomprehensible to and apart from Western Europe.[1] In other words, the piece situates these babies as the byproduct of women's victimization at the hands of age-old ethnic enemies who could be stopped only by the intervention of good-hearted outsiders.

This chapter explores the role of the global media in calling attention to children born of wartime rape in Bosnia and examines media frames to understand why the agenda-setting function attempted by a number of journalists has not resulted in the emergence of children born of war as a category of concern on the international agenda.

On the surface this is a puzzle. Domestic agenda-setting theory, often imported into studies of international human rights politics, posits an important relationship between media coverage, public awareness, and the policy agenda.[2] Although in theory journalists do not tell the public what to think, they do tell people what to think *about*.[3] The CNN effect is often cited as a causal factor in drawing international attention to human rights abuses in certain countries, and press coverage is understood to be vital to the emergence of specific issues on the global agenda, leading former UN secretary-general Boutrous-Ghali to allegedly remark, "CNN is the sixteenth member of the Security Council."[4] This argument has more recently been extended to the entertainment industry as well: Documentaries such as *Sicko* and even blockbuster films highlighting social issues such as *The Day After Tomorrow* and *Blood Diamond* are increasingly said to mobilize public opinion in favor of specific transnational campaigns (in these cases, health care, climate change, and conflict diamonds).[5]

If all this is true, lack of attention to war babies on the international agenda is a puzzle, because there has been no shortage of attention to the issue in the print news and the film industry. Numerous reports of rape babies in war zones from Rwanda to East Timor to Sudan have appeared in the press over the past ten years and continue to be a regular feature of atrocity reporting from hotspots around the world. In Bosnia in particular, there were many stories in the global press about the mass rapes, the resulting pregnancies, and the newborn babies who were abandoned in orphanages. As Linda Grant wrote in early 1993,

"The media was desperate for rape babies. . . . Rape in Bosnia was the hottest story of the year."[6]

In addition, films about children born of war have been produced to wide acclaim in the last decade. Some, such as *Turtles Can Fly*, portray the vulnerability of younger infants who are in the care of their traumatized mothers. Others, such as *The Beautiful Country, Mirka*, and *Grbavica*, detail the search of older war children for their birth mothers or their struggles over sociopolitical identity in postwar contexts. Documentaries such as *Boy from a War Movie* and Macumba Productions' *War Babies* chronicle case studies of actual war children and their relationship to their families and nations. More recently, political blogs have started to take up this issue as well.[7] A common theme throughout these media sources is the argument that states are failing these people.

Yet this public visibility in the broadsheet press, electronic media, and film industry has not translated into specific support for these children. With all the attention on this issue, why did so many people read the stories, watch the films, and then move on to other matters? I argue that these events are puzzling only if we assume that the goal of the media was to put rape babies' human rights on the global agenda. This does not appear to be the case.

Instead, narratives throughout the press coverage of this conflict and in the resulting films constructed war rape through lenses of nationalism, feminism, and humanitarianism rather than through a children's rights frame. These three dominant constructions played into the Western public's concern for the conflict itself rather than with the specific intergenerational trauma suggested by the babies' existence. In part, this explains why attention to these babies dropped off the international agenda as the war ended and resurfaced only around the around the ten-year anniversary of the conflict.

In this chapter I first describe the salience of war babies in media coverage of the wartime rape in Bosnia-Herzegovina. I then analyze three specific frames used to describe children born of war rape in Bosnia and demonstrate how they fed into the three dominant constructions of human rights in the war. In all three cases, these frames obscured attention to the specific needs of the babies themselves. And they combined in powerful ways to preclude important policy questions about the children as subjects of human rights, by structuring the normative context in which humanitarian organizations could press claims, by feeding a nationalist discourse useful to postwar propagandists, and by associating the babies with the harms inflicted on women during war. Each of these arguments is taken up in a subsequent chapter.

THE WESTERN MEDIA AND BOSNIAN RAPE BABIES

The crusade to focus attention on mass rapes in Bosnia is often said to have started with journalist Roy Gutman's story "Mass Rape: Muslims Recall Serb Attacks," which appeared in *Newsday* on August 23, 1992,[8] but earlier articles situating forced pregnancy and rape as deliberate strategies of the war appeared in the Western press as early as August 8.[9] Later that fall, the Bosnian government issued a statistic indicating that 50,000 Muslim women had been raped; the European Community followed this up in December with an estimate of 20,000. These numbers, coupled with the graphic stories of many victims, were enough to mobilize attention toward the situation of Bosnian and Croatian women, and by early 1993 a spate of rape stories had exploded across the Western media. A Lexis–Nexis search using keywords "rape" and "bosnia" and ("babies" or "pregnancy" or "children") identified fifty-four articles appearing in the press between August 1992 and August 2005.[10] References to babies of rape appeared in general articles and specific op-eds about mass rape in Bosnia, and entire pieces were dedicated to the babies themselves. War babies were also highlighted on the TV news, in books such as the novel *S.*, and in plays such as the *Vagina Monologues*.

On one hand, it is possible to view the media as playing a helpful agenda-setting function by spotlighting gender-based violence during the war. Rape reporting served as a catalyst to reframe women's rights as human rights and helped spark a successful transnational campaign against gender-based violence.[11] In telling the Western public to think about gender-based violence, the media helped set the stage for the articulation of mass rape as a threat to international peace and security by the UN and gave legal activists leverage to address sexual violence in the subsequent international tribunals.

At the same time, the Western media were severely criticized for their role in human rights reporting during and after the war, particularly around the sensitive issue of sexual violence.[12] One set of critiques centered around the questionable sources some journalists used in publicizing reports of rape. According to Rose Lindsey, stories of rape were derived in large part from "spin doctors from the predominantly Muslim Bosnia-Herzegovinian government who were 'selling' the rape stories to western media organizations."[13] Others have accused Western news accounts of being brazenly sexualized, even pornographic.[14] Reporters were also criticized for the way they interacted with survivors in the field.[15] Journalists seldom offered psychosocial assistance, such as referrals to available counseling, or undertook sensitivity training before conducting interviews with trauma victims. Sometimes, women were interviewed in front of family members or were asked leading questions. There were cases in which a reporter promised confidentiality but ended up publishing a survivor's narrative using her actual name, or changed the name but included a picture of the street she lived on. It is not surprising that several cases of suicide followed the publication of articles about specific rape survivors.[16]

Rape-related pregnancies were a staple trope in media accounts of the war. I was told in interviews with women's organizations in Bosnia-Herzegovina that the ideal rape survivor sought by journalists during the war was "preferably someone who had had a baby born of rape" during this period. Duska Andrić-Ružičić writes of reporters' requests for information from Medica Zenica, "I cannot recall a single contact with any journalists in the last seven years that did not contain a request along the lines of 'Could you get me an interview with a woman who was a victim of war rape, who was impregnated and had the child?'"[17] Journalists frequented the maternity wards of hospitals in Sarajevo and Zagreb, eager to be the first to interview new mothers who had a war story to sell. An op-ed written by Linda Grant in 1993 describes how "in a maternity hospital in Zagreb, a British journalist and a French camera crew degenerated into an undignified tussle over the bed of a teenage girl who was pregnant after being raped by a Serbian."[18]

Children themselves were rarely old enough to be interviewed, although in 1996 *Newsweek* reporter Stacy Sullivan managed to quote three-year-old Alen Muhić regarding some teasing he experienced on the block, when children called him Serb names.[19] More typically, the testimony about the babies came from their mothers, nurses, or psychiatrists and sometimes from sympathetic people in the community.

Muharem Muhić, Alen's adopted father, reported that the Western media had been a constant presence in the family's lives. Although he said it made him proud to see his family in the paper, it troubled him that reporters rarely sent copies of what they had written, sometimes got the facts wrong, and seldom followed up. There is also a strong sense in this family that remuneration is appropriate when informants spend the time and emotional energy to provide stories to the media. This stands in contrast to Roy Gutman's method for identifying reliable sources among a conflict-affected population, which includes never paying.[20]

In an analysis of the coverage of rape babies in the broadsheet press, Penny Stanley critiques representations of mass rape in newspapers but argues that the media played "a decisive role in making the subject of rape visible."[21] She suggests that the storyline about rape babies in particular appealed to many readers and publishers, especially when linked to the possibility of domestic gains for Western adoptive couples, because it constituted a "positive outcome" of the war: Babies of rape were "one war issue that might have immediate practical consequences [for British or U.S. parents], and would possibly not be halted by complex political bureaucracy."[22]

Yet if babies born of rape were so salient in war reporting from Bosnia, both in their own right and in the context of rape, and if coverage of rape as a whole catalyzed the human rights community to address sexual violence as a crime, how can the relative inattention to the babies by the community of organizations engaged in child protection during the war be explained? I argue that the frames used by the media not only failed to provoke a rights-based approach to the children but perhaps even inhibited such a response. Rather than evoking concern over the rights of the child, these war stories constructed the babies as signifiers of atrocity against women, against cultural groups, and against the "civilized" international order. I will deal with each of these in reverse order and discuss how each frame created a permissive context for overlooking these children, a claim that is fleshed out in later chapters.

"This Latest Bosnian Atrocity": Imperial Humanitarianism and the Balkan "Other"

A fresh crop of human misery is sprouting from the bloody battlefields of the former Yugoslavia: babies conceived by rape and abandoned by ashamed mothers. The latest born was No. 508, a 7 1/2-pound boy with thick black hair transferred Tuesday from Zagreb's Sveti Duk maternity clinic to an orphanage after his mother refused to see him or even give him a name.[23]

According to several media framing studies of war coverage, a dominant misconception created and reflected by the media was the idea that the people of the Balkans had been at each other's throat since time immemorial.[24] This view was popularized by journalist Robert Kaplan's monograph *Balkan Ghosts*, said to be read closely by President Clinton, and was reflected in elite Western discourse and written accounts of the war. In 1993, the *New York Times* described Bosnia-Herzegovina as "a vast and perilous ethnic morass that innocent outsiders enter at their peril."[25] Even earlier, Warren Christopher, then U.S. secretary of state, was quoted in *Newsweek* as referring to Bosnia as "like one of those great beasts down there . . . one of those great messes."[26]

Constructions of both forced pregnancy itself and the reaction of victimized communities to an influx of rape babies played a role in creating the impression that Bosnia-Herzegovina was a land beyond the pale, a nation apart from civilized Europe. As Hansen writes, "Constructing 'the Balkans' as a place where this happens implies therefore that the western 'we' is different because 'we' do not subscribe to this practice."[27] She argues that the idea of male ethnic aggression and female victimization underlay arguments both for and against intervention in Bosnia and cut across depictions of all ethnic groups in the conflict. For example, men of both Serb and Bosniak ethnic communities were described in unsympathetic terms in these reports. Serbian soldiers were described as "bearded," "filthy," "covered with blood," "drunken," "brutal," and "feral." At the same time, men of the Bosniak community were implicitly situated as unsympathetic patriarchs who would turn away from their abused sisters, wives, and daughters in addition to their own infant children.[28]

Labels for the babies reported and popularized by the press conveyed the impression that all sides in the conflict were behaving badly. Articles describe the babies as "children of hate," "products of barbarism," and "born of inhumanity" and demonize the rapists for their "barbarous" policy of mass rape. The rape victims' communities are condemned implicitly for "abandoning" "unwanted children" or allowing them to languish "unloved" in orphanages simply because they "represent a shame to society." Invocations of the "tragedy" of babies conceived through rape and then abandoned by local ethnic patriarchies figured ambiguously in both the calls for intervention and the fatalism that determined that nothing constructive was possible in Bosnia:

[A] large number of babies . . . will be abandoned this year by their young Muslim mothers, repeatedly raped by Serb soldiers. There has been widespread horror at this latest Bosnian atrocity: systematic rape by the Serbs with the deliberate intention of impregnating Muslim women with unwanted Christian babies.[29]

That child's existence reminds the world of the human tragedy that is still Bosnia—a tragedy which, despite the efforts of the United Nations, we are still powerless to end.[30]

Banks and Murray discuss the contradictions inherent in the emergence of the term *ethnic* as a modifier for depictions of the war in Bosnia: "On one hand, the Bosnian Muslims were Muslims, if of a rather secular sort, and therefore would normally be placed in a "feared other" category. On the other hand, they were also clearly the underdogs, the victims of ethnic cleansing, not its perpetrators."[31] Did imagining them as perpetrators of conservative religious-based crimes against innocent babies stabilize this contradiction in the Western psyche? Media narratives of rape babies framed Bosnian society as rural, patriarchal, and primitive; it was these assumptions about characteristics of the victim group, as much as about the genocidal logic of the perpetrators, that rendered explicable to a Western audience the abandonment of babies and rejection of their mothers.[32]

Dubravka Zarkov questions the construction of "rape victim identity" as rooted in an archetypal "traditional, conservative, rural Muslim Bosnia." She points to the assumption made by many authors that rape in Bosnia is somehow more heinous because of the patriarchal culture in which previously "chaste" women internalize shame at the crimes and risk rejection by their communities as a result of sexual violence. Critiquing this construct in the press and historical literature about the conflict, Zarkov asks,

> How different are Muslim women who cherish the importance of virginity, from Croat and Serb women who think the same? Are non-Muslim women less "chaste," and does rape hold fewer consequences for them, because of that? Is rape a lesser trauma for those women who do not think of marriage and children as their only future, or for those already married? Further, how different is the experience of rape of a religious Muslim woman from that of an equally religious Catholic or Orthodox woman? . . . Does rape have less traumatic consequences for women who are not religious? And why is the Bosnian Muslim community singled out as the one that stigmatizes and ostracizes raped women?[33]

According to Robinson, such stereotypes helped construct a notion of Bosnia as both in the heart of Europe and culturally foreign and backward, a frame that helped Western European bystanders indulge their sense of moral concern while remaining detached from the conflict as a European war. The view that Bosnians, as Europeans, were "just like us" was "juxtaposed . . . with the notion that Bosnia was part of an ongoing Balkan nightmare which had frequently erupted into chaotic, ethnic violence and any involvement should be kept to a minimum or better still avoided at all costs."[34]

Pathetic imagery of the "poor innocent" babies played into the media narrative of Bosnia-Herzegovina as a land in which atrocity was heaped upon atrocity, both integral to Europe and yet markedly different in terms of its status as a civilized nation:

Tiny Ivan, just six months old, is an outcast. A monster in the eyes of the troubled, war-driven community into which he was born. "There is evil in his genes," they say, nodding their heads and turning their backs on the innocent infant who cries out for love.[35]

Such frames obfuscated practical measures for securing these children's rights. The protection of the babies became embedded in an intervention narrative that called on Western states to pluck unloved children from the savagery of the Balkans to the safety of Western couples' waiting arms.

But there is some hope on the horizon for the children of this horror. The British Government has announced a major initiative to take the babies of Bosnia from the horrors of war and take them to Britain. It is a policy that women—like the mother of baby Emina—know is the only sure chance these children have of survival. Some of the babies will either die of neglect, or end up in orphanages. . . . Their only hope—a fragile hope in this vicious conflict—is to be airlifted to safety.[36]

Thus, this narrative figured in calls for intervention but also fed into British efforts to appear to provide assistance while refusing political and military solutions to the war itself. Non-Balkan countries, in this case Britain, are charged with "plucking" war babies from their fate in a "barbarous" country where "long-buried hatreds have been dragged to the surface."

By contrast, little coverage was given to grassroots efforts to counteract stigma against the babies, the courage and coping skills of women who embraced their children, or the fact that many rape survivors dealt with their trauma by taking up arms as snipers rather than wasting away as outcasts. The articles construct the children as objects of pity rather than subjects of rights for whose protection the state is responsible.

On the hunt for the worst story possible, reporters tended to put the saddest possible spin on what was usually a mixed bag of facts. In the case of Alen, Stacy Sullivan reported in 1996 that "the Muhićs' neighbors describe Alen as 'a great kid.' But many of them don't know his name. Some call him 'little Chetnik,' a derogatory term for a Serb." But in an interview I conducted in 2006, Alen's father told me,

A lot of journalists would write, for instance, they would write how that all over that town he's called little Chetnik, and that's not true. The town loves him, the entire town is crazy about him. It's only a very few people who gave us trouble.

Not only did such simplistic rhetoric draw attention away from the question of children as rights bearers, but it also helped to invoke a backlash in Yugoslav society against the possibility of foreign involvement in the protection of children for whom local adoptive families were not available.[37] As will be detailed in chapter 5, both the transnational Muslim community and the Bosnian government opposed the idea of exporting "Muslim" babies to be raised in the West.[38] According to some, the rationale behind keeping abandoned babies in situ was the hope that their birth mothers might later be persuaded to raise them, despite the fact that in some cases mothers who had been urged to raise their babies after attempting to surrender them had ended up killing their children.[39]

Such arguments were reported on, but seldom followed up on, by the international press. The responsibility of the newly recognized states in this region to fulfill their obligations under the Convention on the Rights of the Child and to make decisions based on the best interests of the child did not figure prominently in these stories. Correspondingly, as detailed in chapter 5, the human rights of children born of war were not prioritized by international humanitarian and human rights organizations in Bosnia during or after the war.

"Forced to Bear Serb Babies": Nationalist Propaganda and the Construction of Ethnic Divisions

> Serbian soldiers are being ordered to, literally, plant their seed among the people they revile, the Muslim women of Bosnia. . . . Peace has been shattered, and long-buried hatreds have been dragged to the surface; old scores being settled from the grim days of World War II and even earlier, times when the Serbs and Bosnians fought any number of such bitter vendettas.[40]

In addition to defining this region as implicitly different from the rest of Europe, reports of forced pregnancy in Bosnia were largely stories of *ethnic* crimes. This narrative did not entirely mesh with the reality for survivors of gender-based violence in Bosnia, but it did fit with the predominant media frame regarding the nature and rationale behind the conflict. Early on, the conflict was portrayed as resulting from hostility between discrete cultural groups and cast as a war not between different armed factions with specific politico-economic agendas but as a war between Serbs, Croats, and Muslims as entire peoples.[41]

Gregory Kent argues that such ethnic essentialism by the global press had adverse consequences. "Generalizations reinforced the notion of ethnicity as the initiating and sustaining force of the war, diminishing and contradicting political notions of top-down incitement and organization of violence. Simultaneously, it questioned the possibility of a continued multicultural Bosnia."[42] Yet as both Kent's analysis and several others show, much of the Western media adopted this frame. As *Washington Post* reporter Peter Maas argues, reporters became "addicted" to the habit of viewing Bosnia through an ethnic lens.[43]

Although it has been said that "journalism is the art of the cliché,"[44] it is arguable that there is nothing deterministic about this type of reporting: Journalists and editors make choices that either naturalize conflict or expose efforts to stem it. According to Dušan Reljić, "The media should at least attempt to orient its reporting style towards the creation of peace, instead of intensifying prejudices that in turn heighten conflict."[45] A handbook on war and peace reporting published in 1997 by the International Federation of Journalists states that "by practicing objective, fact-based reporting that avoids stereotypes or stirring up rumours, individual journalists and the media as a whole have a tremendous potential to contribute to understanding and bridge-building."[46]

In 2001, British news correspondents Annabel McGoldrick and Jake Lynch developed a manual for reporters with a specific list of suggestions for producing "peace journalism." They suggest that reporters avoid portraying conflicts in zero-sum terms, emphasizing essentialist divisions, adopting language that victimizes or demonizes, or reporting only the violence and horrors. Instead, they suggest, war reporters should "disaggregate the two parties into many smaller groups pursuing many goals," engage in "asking questions that may reveal areas of common ground," and ask victims "how they are coping and what they think."

As has already been well documented, media coverage of Bosnia in general fell short of these standards, and coverage of rape and forced pregnancy was no exception. Early on in the war, the Western media adopted the moniker *ethnic cleansing*, in use by the perpetrators of the worst atrocities and a throwback to Nazi notions of racial purity, to describe the forced displacement of civilians,[47] and the term *ethnic* to describe the cultural, religious, and political divisions in Bosnia was in widespread usage by August 1992.

As many authors have argued, this was a gross oversimplification of the conflict, whose origins lay largely in ethnic scare-mongering by nationalist leaders throughout the former Yugoslavia. Until the onset of the war, social cleavages were rarely articulated along religious or cultural lines but rather along political or rural–urban divides.[48] Significant portions of violent conflict during the war took place not across ethnic communities but within them, as different factions contended for control over the leadership.[49] Additionally, many nominal "Serbs" or "Croats" did not fight alongside Serbian or Croatian paramilitaries but defended besieged cities along with their Bosniak neighbors as, for example, fellow "Sarajevans."

Yet reporting of rape and forced pregnancy largely followed the "ethnic hatreds" script, casting the atrocities in ethnic terms corresponding to dominant Western understandings of who was to blame in the conflict. An indicator of this is the fact that the fifty-four news articles I obtained using Lexis–Nexis included 121 instances in which the perpetrators of rape are identified as "Serb" and 82 instances in which the victims of rape are labeled "Muslim," compared with 2 references to Croat rapists, 8 references to "Muslim" rapists, and only 12 and 16 references, respectively, to Serb and Croat victims of rape. In all cases mentioned, perpetrator and victim are of different ethnicity.

Such a narrative is misleading. Gender-based violence during the war certainly had an ethnic component, and in fact it constituted a means to construct ethnic boundaries, but the media coverage of these dynamics scarcely captured this complexity. For example, women were also assaulted by members of their own ethnic groups during the war. Feminists in the region documented the rise in domestic violence within each "ethnic" community at the onset of the conflict. According to Maja Korać, the SOS Hotline for Women and Children Victims of Violence documented a 100 percent increase in reported violence and rape of women in Belgrade during this time.[50] Politically active women, especially those opposed to the war, were especially at risk.

People in mixed marriages were also particularly vulnerable to sexual violence from within their or their families' "ethnic" group, but the rape of women in mixed marriages occurred according to a very different "ethnic" logic from that suggested by the media. For example, Croat soldiers were reported to have raped Croatian women married to Bosniak men in order to punish the women for marrying outside the group or to have raped Serb or Bosniak women married to Croatian men in order to punish their husbands for marrying outside the community.[51] These acts did represent the constitution of ethnic boundaries through the torture of women's bodies, and no doubt some children resulted from them. But they did not fit the conventional media frame. Rather than demonstrating the immutability of ethnic categories, these acts drew attention to the essential fluidity of ethnic boundaries themselves and the acts of power needed to enforce them. Consequently, they received little coverage in the media.

By contrast, narratives of babies as carriers of ethnicity across groups reinforced the notion that ethnic groups in Bosnia were clearly demarcated according to kinship, which, as suggested by the high rates of intermarriage before and during the war, was hardly the case.[52] Perpetuating and reconstituting this myth reduced the space for people committed to a fluid, multiethnic understanding of Bosnian identity. It also contributed to the notion that the babies belonged to the ethnic group perpetrating atrocities. But as Lisa Price details in her analysis of perpetrators, even rapists themselves may not have uniformly shared the view that Bosniak rape victims could be impregnated with pure "Serbian" children; the mindset facilitating war rapes was significantly more complex.[53]

Despite how it fed into and constructed the very sentiment it aimed to expose, as Rodgers argues, "Focus on the ethnic identity of the fetus . . . was common" in the global press as well.[54] Articles from both during and after the war are replete with passages such as the following:

The Yugoslav war crimes tribunal convened a landmark trial yesterday against three Serbs charged with running camps during the Bosnian war where Muslim women and girls were beaten, gang-raped and forced to bear Serb babies.[55]

Women are always raped in every war. That's not new. But here it is not only rape, but in the name of ethnic cleansing they are raped and being forced to become pregnant with the specific goal of forcing them to bear children of another ethnic group.[56]

A critical reading of these broadsheet press narratives suggests that rather than promoting an understanding of children's rights and how to secure them, stories of "Bosnian rape babies" helped to construct and naturalize very racial understandings of the conflict and of kinship that would make securing the babies' rights much more difficult. Indeed, whereas ethnic homogeneity was a myth of sorts before and at the onset of the war, during its course people in Bosnia increasingly came to identify with the ethnicities articulated in the local and global press. As Williams and Kaufman argue, this had important social consequences for people in mixed-ethnic families.[57] In chapter 7, I discuss how it has affected local constructions of these children's rights in postwar Bosnia as well.

In short, framing the conflict as essentially ethnic in character and essentializing the babies as packages in which ethnic messages are communicated between discrete, homogeneous warring groups helped construct the conflict environment as one in which liminality is inherently problematic—surely the worst possible environment in which to secure protection for children who are viewed as embodying "ethnic" multiplicity.

"The Product of Her Nightmare": Transnational Feminism and Women as War's Victims

> And rape. Just when you think you've read it all, you come across some new, sickening twist in the annals of violence against women. This time it is the politically motivated rape and enforced pregnancies of Bosnian Muslim women with the clear intent of destroying an ethnic group by shaming the women and forcing them to bear offspring of mixed ancestry. . . . And by the end of my Sunday night reading, I was left with these simple questions: Where are the women in the peace-keeping process? Why aren't they at the negotiating table?[58]

A third representation of babies conceived through wartime rape in Bosnia centered on the negative impact these pregnancies presumably had on their mothers, which emphasizes women's rights, not children's rights. As noted earlier, a number of scholars have traced the burgeoning awareness of violence against women as a global phenomenon, now a salient issue in international society, to widespread outrage over reports of mass rape in Bosnia.[59] According to Niarchos, an awareness of the rapes was also decisive in galvanizing international will to establish the International Criminal Tribunal for the Former Yugoslavia (ICTY) in 1993.

Unlike interview data collected by some feminist researchers during and after the war, dominant media accounts stressed the essential helplessness and victimhood of women, and this ended up having a powerful effect on transnational constructions of rape as an international crime. For example, whereas "rape victim" appears forty-nine times in my dataset, the more empowering term "rape survivor" is not used once. The Bosnian Muslim rape victim came to symbolize not just the plight of civilian women in war but the insecurity of women per se at the hands of men and male-dominated security institutions.[60]

Patricia Weitsman writes, "In scholarly and media portrayals . . . women are assumed to be passive actors in men's wars. . . . To be 'pawns' or 'caught in the crossfire' suggests that women have no agency themselves or are passive bystanders in wars fought by their husbands, brothers and fathers."[61] By defining women solely as "rape victims," the media imposed an unduly uniform understanding of the range of gender interpretations open to women and men in Bosnian society. First, not all Bosnian women remained in the civilian sector during the war: Female military units formed on all sides in the conflict, and women and girls played important roles as snipers.[62] Some took part in atrocities carried out in the many detention centers throughout the country.[63] Other women were active in civil society organizations, some opposing the war and creating cross-ethnic linkages, others in support of specific nationalist agendas.[64]

More specifically, by defining women as rape victims, the media negates the range of coping skills and strategies exhibited by rape survivors in Bosnia. Inger Skjelsbæk's interviews with rape survivors after the war contradict the assumption, widely promulgated in the press, that rape survivors were uniformly rejected by their male relatives, who saw them as damaged goods. To some extent, Skjelsbæk found, survivors were able to use the ethnic dimension of their experience as a source of solidarity with their male relatives, who may also have been victims of war crimes, and a number of women she interviewed were able to maintain trusting, honest, supportive relationships with male partners after the rape.[65]

However, the dominant media story was one of "weeping women," cast out by a shamed patriarchal society, and the existence of "rape babies" was viewed as the worst possible sequela for a wartime rape survivor, despite the wide variety of responses women exhibited toward these pregnancies. In many of these articles, the babies are situated not as human beings but as exemplars of their mothers' plight:

> Nine months ago Kata gave birth to Stipo, the product of her nightmare, and began a forced existence apart from the friends and neighbours she had known.[66]

> The unwanted children conceived in the rapes of some 20,000 women may be the most lasting scar left by Yugoslavia's bitter civil war.[67]

> The infant is the child of systematic rape, a living, breathing reminder of S.'s treatment during the Bosnian war.[68]

This depiction of the relationship between the babies and their mothers reflected constructions of mass rape by feminist scholars seeking to place gender crimes high on the agenda at the newly formed ICTY. This campaign was led by U.S. feminist legal scholars who fought to highlight the mass rapes among other crimes in the conflict and who identified forced pregnancy as a specific crime. A flurry of legal articles and briefs were published in leading law journals during this time and produced by women's advocacy organizations such as the New York—based Center for Reproductive Law and Policy; an entire special issue of the *Hastings Women's Law Journal* was devoted to mass rape in Bosnia in the summer of 1994.

Within the legal scholarship and activism that culminated in the recognition of gender crimes at the ICTY, two threads of argument highlighted the use of forced pregnancy in the conflict. First, forced pregnancy was seen in the broader context of the mass rapes in Bosnia. It functioned as an exclamation point to the argument that rape should be treated as a war crime and a crime against humanity. Writing about the psychiatric consequences of the rapes, Vera Folnegovic-Smalc emphasized the particular psychological damage to the women who were impregnated: "Suicidal thoughts are evident above all in the women who have become pregnant as a result of rape."[69] Rhonda Copelon wrote that "the fact of pregnancy, whether aborted or not, continues the initial torture in a most intimate and invasive form; and bearing the child of rape, whether placed for adoption or not, has a potentially lifelong impact on the woman and her place in the community."[70] Pregnancy may worsen the long-term impact of rape on a victim, it was argued, by eliminating any chance of maintaining acceptance by a husband or family through silence about the crime.[71] According to Anne Tierney Goldstein, writing for the Center for Reproductive Law and Policy, forced pregnancy "maximizes the pain of rape" because

> like rape, but to a greater degree, it increases and prolongs [the victims'] physical and emotional pain and makes it more difficult for them to resume any semblance of normal life. . . . Like rape, but to a greater degree, [it] is a means of demoralizing the victim and depriving her of personal dignity and family privacy.[72]

Second, forced pregnancy was addressed directly as a war crime and a crime in and of itself, because of its gravity and distinctiveness from rape. Copelon argues in her previously noted piece that "forced pregnancy must be seen as a separate offense" because to use forced pregnancy merely to articulate rape as genocidal obscures the extent to which it may occur in nongenocidal contexts.[73] Anne Goldstein and Siobhan Fisher each take up Copelon's call to deal with forced pregnancy explicitly, and each makes further distinctions between rape and forced pregnancy.

Goldstein, writing for the Center for Reproductive Law and Policy, argues that forced pregnancy may, but need not, be the result of rape. She recognizes that forced pregnancy may be covered by parts of the Geneva Conventions that do not necessarily entail rape, specifically "compelling a [civilian] to serve in the forces of a hostile Power."[74] Drawing on Goldstein's piece, Fisher articulates the specific and distinct barbarity of forced pregnancy and particularly the extent to which it by itself is genocidal.[75] Beverly Allen also devotes a chapter of her 1996 book to forced pregnancy specifically. Allen argues that forced pregnancy should be conceptualized not under the umbrella of "mere" war crimes or genocide per se but as a form of biological warfare that is prohibited under Article 3 of the ICTY as a violation of the laws or customs of war.[76]

As I detail in chapter 6, although both lines of argument make reference to the babies, they are never addressed in their own rights as victims of war crimes, crimes against humanity, or genocide. In the few cases where references are briefly made to the long-term impact of forced pregnancy on the children born of war, it is typically done to make a point about forced pregnancy itself rather than to draw attention to the specific needs of such children. This tendency results in a pattern of indifference toward child rights in these legal arguments.

For example, consider the context and extent of the following quotation:

> What would happen to [the Serb rapists] years from now, when the generation of babies created by this mass rape were adults? Would there not be a tidal wave of revenge? It all depends . . . on how the societies in which these children are raised represent the situation that produced them. And, from the point of view of the children, everything depends on whether their home societies accept the Serb ideology and consider them Serbs, and thus enemies, or whether they treat them as the innocent results of a policy for which they cannot be held responsible.[77]

This is taken from *Rape Warfare*, in which Beverly Allen constructs enforced pregnancy as biological warfare. At first glance the passage appears to articulate some of the intergenerational social dynamics affecting these children as they grow up either stigmatized or embraced by their mothers' community of origin. However, note the context in which she raises these concerns: Allen is situating rape warfare in the literature on means and methods of combat, ask ing whether forced pregnancy, like other forms of biological warfare, contains any possibility of a blowback effect. At first she says no, because "by definition, [Serb rapists] can never get pregnant themselves."[78] She then considers the possibility of vengeful war rape orphans. Allen's point about the manner in which the children are treated by the societies in which they are embedded is fundamental to addressing their rights, but she bypasses the discussion in order to focus on whether a strategic logic behind the rapes could be discerned in order to prosecute Serb policymakers.

Adrien Wing and Sylke Merchan also wonder in passing about the fate of the children:

> One can only speculate as to how a generation of such children will fare, living among people who have just concluded a brutal war in which the purity and indeed the very survival, of nationalities has been held so consciously in the fore.[79]

Combining an anthropological perspective with legal analysis, these two authors are thinking harder about the use of identity in conflict and the manner in which identity politics are manipulated to wound or destroy the spirit of a cultural group. They provide a salient context for addressing both the tenuous status of children born of ethnic war and the impact of their existence as variables in an ongoing relocation of ethnic and civic identity in postwar contexts. But beyond these lines, they fail to discuss children born of war as ontological beings in their own right or place their speculations in the context of human rights law.

> The woman is placed in the unique position of either abandoning a child that is half hers or raising a child that is half her rapist's. All of her options entail anguish; the more one considers her situation, the more difficult it becomes. On the one hand, the baby was conceived in violence and hatred. On the other hand, it has grown inside her for nine months and is itself innocent of wrongdoing. A woman may have mixed feelings about the baby, and find that she is unable either to wholly love it or wholly despise it. Once it is born, the woman must either try to repress her loathing and revulsion and raise the child with love, perhaps with every feature of her assailant imprinted on the child's face as a constant reminder of her violation, or else she must give in to her revulsion and part with an innocent child that is her own flesh and blood. If her culture has now branded her unmarriageable because of the rape, she may also be giving up the only child she will ever have.[80]

The construction precludes consideration of the babies themselves as human subjects (note the use of the pronoun *it* in the passage) or as victims. It underscores and naturalizes the unwantedness of the child on the part of the culture into which he or she is born rather than questioning the patriarchal agenda behind it.[81] This combination of "natural" hate for the child and identification of the child with the enemy may have also contributed to indifference among writers of this period toward the fate of the children. This indifference manifested itself in the general lack of attention by scholars to evidence of abandonment, neglect, or abuse of the children and outright justifications of infanticide such as Allen's remark, "Many attempt to kill their babies at birth in a reaction that, speaking in terms of the mother's psychological well-being, might even be considered healthy."[82]

A more poignant example of the indifference to infanticide engendered by this discourse is to be found in literary representations of Bosnian rape camps. In her novel based on testimonies of war rape survivors, former war journalist Slavenka Drakulić describes her protagonist's reaction to witnessing an infanticide:

> They come for her in the night to help deliver a baby. A girl from the camp has gone into labour in one of the destroyed houses. . . . The mother leaves S. to keep an eye on the girl and, together with another woman, goes out to the back of the house. S. thinks she can hear the dull sound of a shovel against the earth. . . . They bury the new-born child in the hole they dug in the dark. They place stones on top of the shallow grave. The mother comes back and gently strokes her daughter's cheek. Don't be afraid, sweetie, she says, it's over. It's better this way. . . . S. cannot go back to sleep all night. The sight of child-birth has upset her. The same could happen to any one of them, any one of the girls from the "women's room." To give birth to a child conceived by rape would be more disgraceful than betrayal for them, a fate worse than death.[83]

There is no room in Drakulić's narrative for concern over the fate of the child himself. The lead character later carries a child to term and considers herself weak for being "unable to finish the child off with her own hands."[84] Although her character keeps the baby in the end, Drakulić describes this as not a particularly hopeful ending, saying in an interview printed as an appendix to the book that "the consequences of accepting a child of rape are grave."[85]

In short, although the Bosnian rapes signaled a watershed in international understanding of women's human rights in armed conflict, news reporting did little to connect the children's rights movement to the issue of wartime gender-based violence. The frame appropriated by women's groups and feminist writers, and developed into legal arguments about sexual violence, also drew heavily on imagery of the babies bodies' as attacks on women. The babies born of rape are described as part of the problem afflicting their mothers; hate toward the babies is assumed and naturalized; threats of infanticide or abandonment are whitewashed or treated as an ordinary and inevitable outcome of "ethnic cleansing." Such constructions are hardly consistent with a child rights view of this issue.

A Child Rights Frame?

The implicit counterfactual argument in my analysis is that a child rights frame might have primed human rights and humanitarian actors to take other measures and to put more consistent pressure on the government of Bosnia-Herzegovina to fulfill its treaty obligations and ensure that the children's human rights were not violated. What would such a child rights narrative have looked like?

Studying a sample of print press coverage from this period drawn from the Lexis–Nexis database, I looked in particular for passages where children were described not as signifiers of ethnic atrocity or maternal trauma but as human beings entitled to protection against stigma, discrimination, and infanticide. There were only a few instances in which the point of reference appeared to be the babies' best interests and even fewer that invoked the language of human rights, which the government is responsible to protect.

Most of these passages centered on three issues: whether women should be permitted to abort their fetuses, given that Pope John Paul came out in February 1993 as saying that the women should care for "these beings" inside them;[86] whether the babies' best interests were served by keeping them in the country, where they might suffer stigma; and whether, in the case of foreign adoptions, it was ethical to streamline the process, insofar as it could result in improper vetting of prospective parents. Journalists covering these types of debates helpfully juxtaposed the dominant discourse as it tied into nationalist, economic, or domestic interests of particular parties to the best interests of the children:

Babies must not be used to earn easy credit for politicians or to gratify the transitory impulses of well-meaning people.[87]

Aganović does not believe that the children should remain in the war-torn region. "From a psychological point of view, for the future of these babies, they must be adopted," he said. "And the best thing is to send them far away from here."[88]

Note, however, that these are expressed as moral or political dilemmas, not questions of child rights per se. The Convention on the Rights of the Child is not invoked. The term "best interests of the child," though implicit in these passages, is not used in these articles. Experts on child rights are not interviewed as sources. One editorial opposing the streamlining of adoption practices appears more concerned with avoiding domestic consequences: "Cutting corners will only store up trouble for the future and probably cost the taxpayer more in the long run."[89]

In the smaller spate of articles that appeared after the war, inklings of a more rights-based discourse begin to appear in some of the reports. For example, Toomey invokes the responsibility of states for the situation of children born of war when she draws attention to "Samira," a ten-year-old orphan "caught in a legal limbo" since the war, and to a number of disabled children born of war still institutionalized in Croatia, whom the Bosnian government refused to repatriate and care for.[90] Bećirbašić and Secic emphasize the lack of attention by the Bosnian government to the socioeconomic situation of the children and their mothers after the war. Both these articles emphasize not simply the horror stories from the war but the present situation and, in particular, the lack of assistance to these families from the governments who are charged with providing a protective environment for these children. As Kate Holt and Sarah Hughes argue, the babies and mothers have been "forgotten by the state."[91]

Postwar, we also begin to see a more sophisticated kind of narrative, a more nuanced, less sensationalist focus that touches on the complexity of the child rights dimension, interconnected to the status of the women who gave birth to the babies. Some articles pay closer attention to the agency of survivors, diverging from the standard ethnicized script of the earlier wartime period. Toomey's article pays close attention not just to women who preferred to abandon their children but also to a survivor who chose to raise her daughter, emphasizing the best practices by Medica Zenica that assisted this family and attempting to capture the mother's "complex relationship with her child." Bosnian filmmaker Jasmila Žbanić also worked closely through Medica with a similar family to create the feature film *Grbavica*, attempting to capture not the horrors of the war but the more complex, everyday economic and psychological struggles of the mother and her preteen daughter in the aftermath.

Interviews with the authors of these articles also suggest a more human rights–focused approach, both in substance and procedure, than the frenzied reporting of the war years. This is reflected both in the complexity of the articles themselves and in the reporters' own narratives in interviews about the rationale behind their project and their hopes for how the coverage might elicit change. .

> We were looking for a strong story, something that would matter. . . . Our government doesn't recognize this as war condition. The war stopped years ago—these politicians were always talking about women and children when we wanted military intervention, but after the war nobody seems to care.

> We got interested in the subject in October last year when we worked with a couple of articles concerning the war-children born by Danish women, who had had relationships with some of the more than 250,000 German soldiers that occupied Denmark during World War II. During the research in this topic we got to think about the mass rapes in Bosnia and we wondered why we had heard and seen nothing about the women and their children since the end of the war.

Additionally, these writers clearly took care to "do no harm" through the fact-finding process; for example, several of them refused to share information on their sources with me when asked, out of concern for their respondents' anonymity. Two Danish journalists researching this topic in summer 2005 described the lengths they took to avoid retraumatizing informants: reading more than 3,000 pages of source material, choosing not to focus "on the past and the awful details of the rapes" but to describe the families' present situation, and consulting in advance with experts on torture counseling in their own country on "how to do an interview [just in case] we got in touch with either women or children—what should we avoid talking about, what danger signals should we look for, and so on."

An ethical responsibility toward their informants is also suggested by the efforts these reporters made to give back to the affected communities. Many articles in this period concluded with opportunities for readers to send donations to specific families or civil society organizations. Perhaps this indicated that there is a different type of journalist who gravitates toward stories about marginalized populations in the aftermath of war rather than in the heat of a conflict. But there are also far fewer such stories after the war, when, as Toomey laments, "the plight of these women is no longer a fashionable cause." Nor, she might have added, is the plight of the children.

Ultimately, most of these articles take as their starting point the human rights of the mothers rather than the children. When international law is mentioned, it is the emerging jurisprudence around gender-based violence to which the authors refer. Similarly, Jasmila Žbanić's film *Grbavica* ends when the child finds out about her background, and the director told me, "That's for the next generation to answer that question. Not my generation." Raymonde Provencher's documentary *War Babies* focuses substantively on the babies, but primarily through the voices and with the consent of mothers, not the children.[92]

Too often the assumption that meeting the needs of women will meet the needs of children is not borne out. The case of a child left in an institution for seven years, then retrieved by his mother, is cast in one news article as "an uplifting ending, but it sheds light on the tragic experience of the many women." When I interviewed a counselor at Vive Žene in Tuzla about this case, she countered this media portrayal, suggesting that the mother had a sense of closure, but it was not a happy ending as far as the boy was concerned. In fact, he resented being removed from the only home he'd ever known, and there were serious emotional difficulties between him and his birth mother as a result of the abandonment he had experienced.

These examples demonstrate the fallacy of assuming that women's and children's needs are synonymous. Beneath these disagreements lies an important dialectic about the meaning of child rights to different actors, and in particular what it means to promote the rights of these children. Important debates exist in the movement about how to define children, at what age they can exercise genuine agency, and where the many rights enumerated in international law sit in a hierarchy of importance.

Applied to children of war, open questions abound. Does the right to be free of discrimination refer only to formal discrimination by the state or also to the myriad acts of sociopolitical exclusion that can characterize a person's navigation through childhood? Does the right to identity mean the right to *any* identity, the right to a *particular* identity, or the right to define one's identity freely without discrimination? How does the right to identity tie into the right to participate meaningfully in the cultural life of the community, if for cultural reasons an individual child is made to feel unwelcome in her community of origin? Does the right to a family mean the right to *some kind of* family, or is a relationship with a birth parent, however dysfunctional, the default position? If this is the case, does this extend to a literal right to access to available information about one's biological roots, even if the birth parent doesn't want to divulge this information? Does the right to participate and speak on one's own behalf (in fact-finding studies, for example, or in documentary films) necessarily mean children should be consulted about sensitive issues they may not want to think about? Is it appropriate to allow adults around them to serve as intermediaries? And at what age can a child legitimately be expected to choose between these conflicting priorities?

Digging deep below the veneer of child friendliness that is presented by most of those who claim to govern in local and global spaces, my fieldwork exposed the complexity of these questions and their salience, once raised, in the consciousness of local and international actors alike. This complexity is unpacked in the chapters that follow. However, none of it was captured in media or scholarly treatments of what went on in the war zones of Bosnia, during and after the war.

CONCLUSION

I have argued in this chapter that three sets of tropes—one that ties into nationalist propaganda, one emphasizing women's victimization, and one positioning Bosnia as beyond the "civilized" West—characterized the media's coverage of mass rape and rape babies in the former Yugoslavia during and after the war. My examination of the media also demonstrated how rare suggestions for protecting the babies themselves as rights-bearers were in this coverage. The exceptions were grandiose proposals to "airlift" babies out or export them to "loving British couples" for adoption rather than pressuring the Bosnian government to ensure their protection through formal means consistent with the Convention on the Rights of the Child. By discounting local governments' capacity to exercise their responsibilities under international law, the media drew attention away from these responsibilities and delimited human rights organizations' attention to the issue as a human rights concern. Nascent discussions about what children's rights are in the context of war babies continue to receive little coverage or analysis in the mass media.

As Smillie and Minear point out, "The media are not a humanitarian instrument as such. . . . There is only so much disaster news that the media can and will handle at one time."[93] Therefore much of this analysis confirms important critiques of wartime coverage of mass rape. One reporter I interviewed, when asked "why this story?" replied simply,

> Because we're vultures. . . . It's a story, a poignant story, it's a story that if I read I will probably read it to the end, because we all love children, we all feel

for victims of violence, which includes rape, it's a tear jerker. It's as simple as that. There are many other stories you could tell because they would be helping people but you wouldn't be able to get them into a newspaper. So this is the criteria that I think most of us work under.

But this tendency to sensationalize had costs. First, as I show in chapter 5, the neocolonialist narrative actually encouraged aid groups to shy away from the issue, discounting the validity of recognizing stigma against children born of war as a bona fide child rights concern falling within their mandate. Second, chapter 6 demonstrates how situating children of rape as signifiers of gender trauma resulted in new international legal concepts that limited the space for thinking about the unique obstacles these children face as subjects of human rights law. Third, as explained in chapter 7, the way in which these babies figured into ethno-nationalist discourse has profoundly limited the space in which to discuss or even investigate their human rights situation in postconflict Bosnia.

Consequently, neither aid organizations nor child protection officers in Bosnia-Herzegovina or international postconflict justice mechanisms have adequately considered, much less resolved, the important debate about what *rights* can mean with regard to such people. As I will show, this is not because international institutions, civil society organizations, or postwar governments are staffed by people who care little about vulnerable children. It is because each of these professional communities relies on a language and set of concepts that make it easy to overlook children born of war, even when they are hiding in plain sight.

5.
"PROTECTING CHILDREN IN WAR,"
FORGETTING CHILDREN OF WAR
Humanitarian Triage During the War in Ex-Yugoslavia

The prime motivation of our response to disaster is to alleviate human suffering amongst those least able to withstand the stress caused by disaster.
—ICRC, *Principles of Conduct for the International Red Cross and Red Crescent Movement and NGOs in Disaster Response Programmes*, 1

No one's ever followed it up. It's been an issue that women have been raped, but then what happened to their children, they just disappeared into history.
—Focus group participant, Columbia University, 2004

FOR FOUR YEARS AFTER THE WAR broke out in the former Yugoslavia, humanitarian relief was the international community's primary response to the conflict.[1] Western European nations viewed the violence in Bosnia-Herzegovina as regrettable birth pangs, a civil war that would quickly run its course if outsiders avoided taking sides. The UN Security Council had authorized coercive military operations in Kuwait, northern Iraq, and Somalia shortly after the end of the Cold War, but these types of missions were already suffering from a crisis of confidence by 1993. The United States pulled out of Somalia after eighteen Rangers were killed, mutilated, and dragged through the streets of Mogadishu, and President Clinton promulgated a presidential decision directive in 1994 that limited U.S. involvement in foreign wars not in the national interest. UN peacekeeping, which had worked well in earlier conflict zones characterized by a ceasefire and territorial frontiers between warring factions, seemed inadequate to the complex emergencies of the early 1990s. Western publics watched the siege of Sarajevo unfold on their television screens, but there was little political will to force a solution.[2]

What the international community could and did do was send relief to assist the civilian victims of the war. Bosnia quickly became the humanitarian ground zero of the early 1990s. Funding per person in the former Yugoslavia was twice that sent to the Great Lakes region of Africa; funding for all other regions of the world was much lower.[3] So urgent was the crisis perceived to be that the UN High Commissioner for Refugees (UNHCR), mandated primarily to deal with legal claims for displaced people crossing borders, entirely remade itself as an organization to take on the role of lead humanitarian agency inside Bosnia. Along with the International Committee of the Red Cross (ICRC) and a plethora of nongovernment organization (NGO) partners, whose shipments were protected by military troops from twenty nations under the auspices of a UN peacekeeping operations, the UNHCR delivered 27,460 tons of food, medicines, and other supplies in Sarajevo between July 1992 and January 1993 alone.[4] Aid convoys worked from there to deliver supplies to refugee centers and besieged villages throughout the country, risking their lives in negotiations with the warring sides for access to civilians of all three ethnic groups. According to Thomas Weiss and Cindy Collins, more than 3,000 humanitarian workers were in the region by 1995, providing life-sustaining assistance to 4 million war victims.[5]

Protection of and assistance to war-affected children in Bosnia was a high priority for international aid organizations. References to war-affected children figured prominently in diplomatic rhetoric and Security Council debates over how to respond to the crisis. Many of the organizations operating in the region, such as Save the Children and the United Nations Children's Emergency Fund (UNICEF), had a specific mandate to help children in particular. Others began mainstreaming child protection programs into their programming. For example, UNHCR established a new post of senior coordinator for refugee children at its headquarters in 1992 and issued its first guidelines on care of refugee children in 1994.[6]

Bosnia also catalyzed the world's attention to gender-based violence in war zones as a humanitarian catastrophe. Whereas humanitarian relief had previously been primarily about providing shelter and distributing food and medicine, aid organizations began collecting prevalence data on gender-based human rights abuses and emphasizing reproductive health needs in camp and post-trauma counseling. According to Julie Mertus, "The case of Bosnia was a turning point in international recognition of protection for women in conflict and in attempts by governments and aid workers to solve the problems of women and girls."[7]

Despite the attention paid to children and war and to women and war as a result of this particular conflict, the humanitarian sector paid little direct attention to protecting children born of gender-based violence in Bosnia. Although aid agencies recognized that babies were being born and possibly abandoned, and although some early concern was expressed about how to respond, the humanitarian community quickly determined this was not a priority. This did not change after the war.

This chapter examines the humanitarian sector in Bosnia during the war and explores why it responded as it did to the issue of children born as a result of rape. It argues that the selective attention of aid agencies to vulnerable groups can be driven as much by political judgments and pragmatic organizational concerns as by a careful assessment of who is the most vulnerable in specific contexts. Indeed, this is particularly the case when conflicts exist between validating one vulnerable group's claims and helping another.

I begin with a sketch of the humanitarian sector and its activities in the former Yugoslavia. I examine the sporadic attention paid to the issue of babies born of mass rape and describe the factors that drew attention away from this issue. I conclude by tracing the imprint on more recent conflicts left by the relationship between child rights and gender violence, and I explore this imprint further in chapters 6 and 7.

PRINCIPLES VERSUS PRACTICE: THE HUMANITARIAN INTERNATIONAL IN BOSNIA-HERZEGOVINA

The term *humanitarianism* is often used to describe activities as disparate as feeding the poor and sending "good guys" with guns to a crisis zone. According to a popular textbook on humanitarian affairs, the humanitarian imperative is "an individual belief that wherever there is human suffering, the international humanitarian system must respond, regardless of political considerations."[8] Even if one defines it as noncoercive efforts, leaving out any consideration of armed humanitarian intervention, humanitarian action still encompasses quite a wide variety of efforts to relieve human suffering. These include the provision of medical assistance and food to war victims, tracing of family members who have become separated in crisis zones, and direct efforts to prevent further victimization of noncombatants in wars, such as appealing to prison camp guards or lobbying weapon-bearers to respect the rules of war.[9]

Broadly, humanitarian activities can be categorized into two types: assistance, which seeks to respond to the effects of human suffering, and protection, which seeks to mitigate the human rights abuses that lead to suffering in the first place.[10] Examples of humanitarian assistance include delivering supplies to the displaced and providing medical care to the sick or wounded. Humanitarian protection might include advocacy efforts or practical measures to prevent abuses from occurring, such as an NGO vehicle placed in front of a threatened family's house. Protection can also mean helping people escape when abuses are likely to occur. In Bosnia, aid convoys were used to evacuate besieged civilians, just as they were used to deliver food. Some organizations protect human rights by facilitating governments' understanding of their legal obligations.[11]

Humanitarian principles are enshrined in two sets of international treaties that govern the behavior of warring parties with respect to enemy noncombatants. Just as the UN Charter sets limits on when states may resort to war, the Hague Conventions, often called the law of armed conflict, place limits on how wars may be fought: which weapons combatants may use against one another and what constitutes a legitimate target. In particular, the law of armed conflict prohibits the deliberate targeting of civilians. The Geneva Conventions delineate rules governing how noncombatants, including civilians, prisoners, and the sick or wounded, may be treated once they are captured or otherwise in the power of the enemy. Since the mid-1970s, these two threads of law have increasingly blurred together. Together they enshrine the principles that even wars have limits, that those not or no longer taking part in conflicts have a right to be treated humanely and to receive relief, and that independent, neutral aid organizations have a right to offer such assistance.

The term *international humanitarian community* is generally used loosely to describe all actors engaged in providing such relief across borders, and it distinguishes these powerful players from local NGOs and religious groups that mobilize to assist their own communities during conflicts. As Ian Smillie and Larry Minear write, "This arena has a few saints, a great many dedicated humanitarian professionals, and not a few hustling entrepreneurs, fly-by-nighters, freebooters and purveyors of snake-oil."[12]

Abby Stoddard defines the humanitarian international as "the network of key implementers, donors and international organizations (IOs) involved in humanitarian assistance."[13] *Donors* generally refers to state governments contributing official resources for humanitarian relief, such as the Canadian International Development Agency or its U.S. counterpart, the U.S. Agency for International Development. International organizations include specialized agencies of the United Nations, such as UNHCR and the World Health Organization, and other organizations whose members are governments. It also includes the 260 NGOs whose members are private citizens and whose primary goal is to deliver aid to crisis-affected populations.[14] The biggest of these are the Committee for Aid and Relief Everywhere, Doctors Without Borders (known in the humanitarian sector by its French acronym, MSF), the Oxford Committee for Famine Relief, Save the Children, and World Vision.[15] Despite their idealistic mandates, these organizations are businesses that rely for their survival on contracts from multilateral agencies and governments.[16] The International Red Cross includes both the ICRC and its national chapters; the ICRC is often said to constitute a cross between an NGO and an IO.[17]

In most conflict zones, these central players are joined by as many as 200 smaller NGOs, some parachuting in from other hotspots for a slice of the donor money being thrown at a conflict, some founded specifically because one or more citizens wanted to do something for a particular population. Medica Zenica, an NGO particularly known for assisting female war victims, was founded by Monika Hauser, an Italian businesswoman working in Germany who identified post-trauma care for displaced women in central Bosnia as a pressing and unfulfilled humanitarian need.[18] Between 1993 and 2002, Medica Zenica provided counseling to 3,845 people, gynecological services to 27,692 patients, and educational support to more than 600 children and adults.[19] Medica Zenica's model of holistic, nonpartisan, need-based response to women war victims has remained a model of best practice and been exported to a number of other conflict zones, including Afghanistan.[20]

Although the majority of literature on humanitarian action identifies this policy domain most closely with influential Western-based organizations such as MSF and the ICRC, large amounts of relief also flow from Muslims worldwide through Islamic charities designed to channel *zakat* contributions.[21] Some 6,000 Islamic charities worldwide channel billions of U.S. dollars per year to crisis-affected Muslim populations.[22] Although it is true that some of these "charities" have served as fronts for financing terrorist groups, in general this threat appears to have been exaggerated. By 2007, Britain's Charity Commission had conducted only twenty inquiries into suspected links with terrorism out of more than 1,000 Islamic trusts and charities in the United Kingdom; half of those inquiries had been dropped.[23] Similarly, although forty Islamic charities are on the U.S. government's terrorist watchlist, the government has failed to convict a single charity of financing terrorism.[24]

NGOs in the Islamic sector vary widely in terms of their operating principles. Some are actively religious: They recruit staff on the basis of sect, target primarily Muslim populations, and proselytize as part of their programs. Others might be better considered faith based. For example, the UK-based Islamic Relief defines its mission statement in terms of Islam and has designed its microcredit programs according to the principles of Islamic finance, yet it does not include efforts to proselytize and is careful to provide aid in particular countries without concern for the religion of the beneficiary.[25]

The Islamic aid sector in Bosnia was a significant source of funding for Bosnian Muslims. At the close of the war, 20 percent of the NGOs operating in the country were Islamic.[26] Saudi Arabia's High Relief Commission was originally established specifically to disburse humanitarian funds to the Balkans, sending more than $800 million by 2000. Other Arabian Gulf countries, particularly Kuwait and the United Arab Emirates, were similarly generous. According to Burr and Collins, by 1997 Muslim countries had sent "more than $1 billion in military and humanitarian aid to Bosnia."[27] Unlike Western governments, which persisted in a blanket arms embargo for the entire conflict despite the fact that this worked decidedly in favor of the better-armed Bosnian Serbs, some Muslim majority governments, particularly Iran, Afghanistan, and Sudan, shipped not only supplies and construction crews but also weapons. Some now argue that today's *mujahideen* networks in Europe, for which Bosnia-Herzegovina has become a key transit point, have their origins in the humanitarian crisis.[28] Although many humanitarian NGOs did become complicit in the militarization of humanitarianism, as have Western NGOs in some contexts, it is certain that civilian Muslim aid agencies in the region also genuinely assisted numerous families.[29]

Although actors in the humanitarian sector differ widely in the way they prioritize their goals, most share a general commitment to certain humanitarian principles. The most important of these are the principles of impartiality and neutrality. *Neutrality* means that the focus of humanitarian action is to relieve suffering, not to take sides in the conflict. At one level, this means that aid work is ostensibly nonpartisan; it is not to be directed toward a resolution of a conflict in the favor of one or the other actor. At another level, it means that humanitarians are to respond to human suffering because people are in need, not to advance political, sectarian, or other extraneous agendas. Neutrality is not simply a moral principle for humanitarians in conflict zones. It is also an operational strategy that helps aid agencies access civilian populations by providing a framework for negotiations with belligerents on all sides of the conflict.[30]

Impartiality likewise has two elements. First, it means nondiscrimination: All victims shall be assisted, irrespective of religion, ethnicity, sex, political affiliation, or any criteria other than need. For example, although the media story in the West suggested that Serbs were the aggressors and Muslims the key victims in Bosnia, Western aid agencies aimed to assist victims of all ethnic groups. Second, it means that the provision of life-saving assistance should be proportional to the need. A UNHCR field manual describes the relationship between these principles in the following words: "Humanitarian assistance should be provided without distinction. Relief must address the needs of all individuals and groups who are suffering, without regard to nationality, political or ideological beliefs, race, religion, sex or ethnicity. Needs assessment and relief activities should be geared toward priority for the most urgent cases."[31]

In conflict zones, this means a humanitarian imperative to assist consistently rather than selectively.[32] It also means, in specific conflicts, prioritizing the most vulnerable people. Thus humanitarian law has specific provisions for pregnant or nursing women, and children under five and older adults are understood to be particularly vulnerable to deprivation, so they are often prioritized. In short, children exemplify the humanitarian imperative because of their innocence and vulnerability. The principles of neutrality and impartiality suggest that all children must be assisted and that first priority should be given to those most vulnerable to direct threats. On the face of it, one might then assume that protecting infants at risk of infanticide would be a significant priority.

Yet politics intervened. In actuality, the principles of impartiality and neutrality are difficult to achieve in many conflict zones.[33] For one thing, aid workers know that strict adherence to humanitarian principles and action can feed conflicts.[34] The system of humanitarian relief works well when warring parties fulfill their obligations under humanitarian law, avoiding civilians, treating prisoners humanely, and allowing the passage of neutral humanitarian actors. But in Bosnia, the war was over territory, and targeting civilians directly was quickly seen as an effective way to clear and hold valued land.[35] In such a situation, humanitarian evacuations, for example, could actually contribute to ethnic cleansing. And a neutral approach that fails to distinguish between aggressors and victims can be tantamount to complicity in atrocities. In fact, MSF was founded by physicians who quit the ICRC in protest over its "neutral" position during the Biafra conflict in Nigeria, which they saw as exacerbating an unfolding genocide. As Jose Mendiluce, chief envoy for UNHCR, said during the conflict, "You don't reply to fascism with relief supplies, and you don't counter ethnic cleansing with reception centers for the displaced."[36]

A second problem is that the principles themselves may come into conflict with one another.[37] In Bosnia, Bosniak civilians were at risk in greater numbers than Bosnian Serb and Croat civilians. An impartial approach would have meant providing proportionally more aid to Bosniaks. However, Bosnian Serbs argued that this would constitute siding with the Bosniaks, and so to maintain an appearance of neutrality, aid organizations often cut deals with the Serbs for additional supplies to ethnic Serb civilians.[38]

But perhaps most importantly, there is sometimes a perceived tension between protecting some groups and protecting others. For example, adult men and older boys were some of the most vulnerable civilians in the Bosnian conflict because they were most likely to be summarily executed; a truly impartial approach would have meant prioritizing their protection. In reality, however, aid agencies feared being seen as nonneutral if they attempted to protect adult men who were viewed by the other side as being fighters, so women and children benefited disproportionately from protection measures.[39]

As I show in the next section, ultimately children born of war rape were overlooked by humanitarians because of a similar perceived conflict, between assisting the babies and acceding to the desires of other vulnerable groups in the conflict: raped women and cultural groups targeted for ethnic cleansing. This was the result of preexisting narratives, beyond humanitarians' control, that defined the babies as tools of genocide and put barriers in the way of those who advocated for them against victim communities at whose hands they suffered.

CHILDREN BORN OF WAR AS A HUMANITARIAN CONCERN

At a glance, it appears as if aid organizations forgot children of rape during the war almost entirely. For example, UNICEF, the organization with the clearest child rights mandate in emergencies, produced a 1994 situation report that referred to a variety of other protection needs for children in Bosnia-Herzegovina but eclipsed the issue of safety for newborns conceived in rape.[40] Another illustrative example is a set of guidelines issued by UNICEF in February 2002, titled *Principles and Guidelines for the Ethical Reporting on Children and Young People Under 18 Years Old*. The Press Centre was responding in part to concerns, documented in chapter 3, that journalists operating in conflict zones were contributing to stigma and trauma of young respondents in the way they conducted interviews and reported on war zones.[41] The document lists an extensive set of principles and strategies for protecting child respondents. A particular concern was that children not be stigmatized on the basis of media coverage:

> Do not further stigmatize any child; avoid categorizations or descriptions that expose the child to negative reprisals, including additional physical or psychological harm or to lifelong abuse, discrimination or rejection by their communities.

Yet although the document listed several categories of child UNICEF wanted journalists to be particularly careful with, including victims or perpetrators of physical or sexual abuse or exploitation, HIV-positive children or children of

HIV-positive parents, or those charged with crimes, it does not mention children born to rape victims. Nor was stigma against children of rape addressed by any of the same organizations that were actively beginning to grapple with stigma against rape victims and against returning child abductees in other contexts. As a practitioner put it in a focus group,

> There is very little data: We have good data now on the consequences of sexual violence for women, but looking specifically at what happens to the children, I've not seen it.

Yet digging a little deeper, this turned out to be not simply a case of institutional blindness. It was not that aid organizations had not recognized the risks to these babies in the Bosnian context or that some attention was not considered. Rather, humanitarian organizations operating in the region took stock of the situation and consciously decided not to make protection of war babies a humanitarian priority.

Several international fact-findings studies produced early in the war either paid lip service to the babies' existence or specifically considered the humanitarian response to babies born of rape. One was a European Commission study led by Danish diplomat Anne Warburton. Between December 1992 and January 1993 Warburton and her team visited the region and met with religious leaders, field staff of international agencies and local organizations including women's groups, and a small number of individual victims. The resulting Warburton report is the source of the oft-cited "EC estimate" of 20,000 Muslim women raped during the conflict, but the study does not describe how the authors arrived at this estimate. A single paragraph deals with pregnancies resulting from rape and mentions abandonment of babies and citizenship difficulties presented by the lack of legal provisions between Croatia and Bosnia to cover adoptions. Although the report provides a detailed set of recommendations for responding to the physical and psychological needs of rape victims, it says nothing specific about how to protect the babies.

A second, more systematic study was also carried out during the same period, this one under the auspices of the UN Commission on Human Rights, and made much stronger recommendations to policymakers. The Mazowiecki report emphasized its concern to "avoid, at all costs, the stigmatization of, or trafficking in, babies who are born as a result of rape" and expounded at some length on the importance of changing adoption laws to allow married women to surrender babies of rape without the consent of their husbands.[42] Citing the provisions regarding adoption in the Convention on the Rights of the Child, it also pays lip service to the best interests principle and urges policymakers to consider how to facilitate the adoption of the babies.

Humanitarian agencies in the field grappled with the question early in the war. UNHCR issued a situation analysis in 1993 on women and children that included a section on abandoned babies stating, "While we have as yet no idea of the expected number of babies born to victims of sexual assault, it is clear that there must be some contingency plan to ensure that whatever steps are taken are in the best interests of these children."[43] A study conducted jointly by UNICEF, UNHCR, and Defense for Children International (DCI) addressed children of rape under the category "unaccompanied children."[44] The Center for Reproductive Policy analyzed these children's rights in the context of meeting women survivors' mental health needs.[45] The ICRC mentioned the need to "account for the prospects of" such children in a 1995 document on the protection of civilians.[46] The International Social Service produced a pamphlet outlining questions pertaining to the international adoption of such children.[47]

Clearly, in the 1990s humanitarian players took stock of the vulnerabilities of children born of war and their capacity to protect them. Yet no consensus seems to have emerged among international humanitarian actors over precisely how these children's needs should be addressed in humanitarian programming, other than vague statements that they should not be stigmatized.

Instead, organizations issuing guidelines about children born of rape settled on a strategy of passing the buck to local civil society. The reports described here all emphasize the need to empower local actors to define and meet these children's needs as they saw fit. The Mazowiecki report states that "the efforts of local communities should be identified, respected and supported by the international community."[48] The International Social Service document also emphasized the need to support local capacities but reminded child welfare advocates and agencies to engage in oversight with respect to this population: They should "ensure that unaccompanied infants are not warehoused for political reasons" and "offer assistance to the local authorities with a view to helping them meet the present and future needs of the infants and children involved."[49]

In other words, humanitarian actors ultimately fell back on the sovereignty and "cultural appropriateness" arguments rather than answer the more difficult question themselves of what their own role should be in protecting the babies' rights as frontline providers of reproductive health care and assistance to refugee children.[50] Despite some early concern over the babies, by 1994 a consensus had emerged in the humanitarian sector that the risk to these children had largely been exaggerated and that local governments were most appropriate to deal with any remaining protection issues.

Explaining the Programming Gap

What drove these conclusions? One argument commonly given by those to whom I spoke was the sheer difficulty of gathering accurate data on the number of babies and the types of harms to which they were susceptible, in order to formulate a coordinated response. Practitioners were well aware that accusations of forced pregnancy were being inflated by all sides. Some women abandoned their babies, but others wanted to keep them. Unlike refugee children, whose numbers could be counted and whose needs were viewed in simple terms, children born of rape constituted in some respects a hidden population whose specific needs had to be assessed on a case-by-case basis. In a conflict zone, where events were moving quite quickly, the structure of the problem itself imposed significant disincentives to create a one-size-fits-all response. At the same time, however, this is an insufficient explanation for inattention to war babies, because the same problem faced humanitarians who meant to assist rape victims themselves, but it did not stop them from trying.

More important, I argue, was a reluctance among practitioners to question the wishes or motives of other populations perceived to be victims themselves: women and minority ethnic groups. The babies were conceptualized by all involved as consequences of human rights violations, and humanitarian practitioners' frame of reference was chiefly those violations themselves, not the future harms that (tragically but understandably, it was sometimes suggested) might come to the babies. Addressing infanticide would have meant confronting traumatized mothers and extended families. Speaking out against stigma perpetrated by a conservative Bosniak society seemed to mean criticizing a cultural group that many perceived to be suffering from genocidal attacks. Questioning the Bosnian government about its capacity to protect children who had been conceived by the enemy as war strategy seemed politically incorrect when that government itself was desperately attempting to fight a defensive war under an arms embargo.

As if the humanitarian community's own normative sensibilities were not impediment enough, there was significant local pushback when outsiders did attempt to press claims on behalf of the babies. A team of women from the World Council of Churches visited the region in December 1992 to find out what they might do to help. In their report *Rape of Women in War* they documented the impatient reaction of one woman to the possibility of help from outsiders: "She thinks we are making too much fuss about the children of rape. Who supports invalid children? The children with Downs syndrome, multiple sclerosis, etc? They are neglected and need help."[51] When asked about international adoption by a reporter in 1993, Jelena Brasja, director of the Roman Catholic charity Caritas in Zagreb, was quoted as saying defensively, "We have a centuries-old culture here and we can manage to bring up these children. . . . We are not savages."[52]

The defensiveness of local Bosniaks was fed by the type of sensationalist media reporting on the issue documented in the last chapter, from which aid agencies worked hard to distance themselves. Many practitioners I spoke with referred distastefully to journalists who "blew things out of proportion" or gathered information in a manner insensitive to basic humanitarian principles. In such a context, it can be harder for aid agencies to broach a culturally sensitive issue without becoming associated with a hegemonic and counterproductive media narrative.

These cultural obstacles interacted with institutional norms among the Western humanitarian sector that mitigated against certain policy options. As noted in chapter 4, one of the key media narratives was international adoption as a humanitarian response. But for humanitarian organizations, foreign adoption or evacuation of children out of war zones is generally frowned upon.[53] There has been a long history of exploitation of war orphans, and as a result, the humanitarian community generally seeks to protect and assist children in situ, with an emphasis on reuniting families and, when adoptions are necessary, to assist the state in finding a local solution.[54] This norm was very much reflected in the many references by humanitarian players to the fear of baby trafficking.[55]

Aid agencies had a particularly negative response to Britain's policy of streamlining red tape in order to quickly export Bosnian "rape babies" for adoption by British couples. Tim Yeo, then the junior health minister, promoted this policy as a humanitarian response to the crisis. His proposals, which were reported in *The Guardian* in January 1993, were criticized by humanitarian organizations given that his government was far less welcoming to female refugees from Bosnia who sought to emigrate *with* their babies.[56] However, the British press lauded his proposals as an undeniably humanitarian impulse and reiterated his claim that a "large number of Bosnian babies . . . will be abandoned this year by their young Muslim mothers," replicating an ethnic perspective on a highly complex issue and an assumption that the issue was primarily one of scale and of abandonment.[57]

Because the "thousands of unwanted babies" frame set foreign adoption as the key barometer against which to measure the validity of some humanitarian response, agencies that concluded that the need for adoption had been overstated tended to shrug off other possible responses as well. In their March 1993 report, UNICEF, UNHCR, and DCI argued, "The world . . . expected that large numbers of infants would be available for adoption in the former Yugoslavia. . . . In reality, contrary to the world's expectation, very few infants in that category are to be found. . . . It would seem that the women are dealing with the matter themselves and that outside agencies are intrusive and unhelpful."[58]

In short, the assignment of blame against Serbs for victimizing women and Bosniaks powerfully shaped aid agencies' preferences when it came to framing the human rights of babies conceived by "the enemy." This explains why aid organizations consistently erred on the side of promoting mothers' rights and deferring to the local society when it came to solutions for babies born of rape. For example, the UNICEF and DCI report that detailed the many risks to children born of war ultimately concluded, "The best approach for the outside world to help these children would be to assist local support systems as required and requested. At all times the mother's wish for secrecy and privacy must be respected."[59]

Once this decision took shape, proposals to develop specific programs and shelters for the families were quickly abandoned because it was perceived that they would only draw attention and exacerbate stigma. Despite calls for public education efforts to promote social acceptance of the mothers and children, aid agencies did not generally undertake such efforts. Nor did they work to evacuate the children from the country. Rather, they provided emergency obstetric care where needed and facilitated the anonymous placement of the babies in institutions and with the Bosnian Centers for Social Work that handled adoptions. Aid workers decided that by explicitly not identifying the babies and by clustering them into the broader group of unaccompanied minors, they could mitigate stigma. Once this was done, however, the subject of stigma against the children as a category began to drop off the humanitarian agenda. Aid agencies no longer asked themselves what they should do to protect or monitor the babies as a group, for they were no longer able to identify them as a group.

The lack of a specific policy on children of rape did not mean that no children of war received specific assistance from the humanitarian community. Some were assisted as part of larger groups; and on a case-by-case basis aid workers assisted specific babies and their mothers. For example, despite initially being warned by social workers and doctors that there was no institutional assistance available for families who adopted newborns, the Muhić family was able to access both a stipend for orphans through the state-run Centers for Social Work and the same type of general humanitarian assistance available for other war victims. In addition, Muharem Muhić was able to barter his labor to aid organizations in order to get by:

At that CSW, I was getting special food that had a priority for orphans and things like that. So monthly we got a little packet with sugar, coffee, oil, biscuits, milk. A small packet but regularly, every month. Plus we got like the rest of the community some humanitarian help, flour and things like that. So then I connected myself to an org called MSF. They were helping through the hospitals. They arranged with me to do some work. Since they weren't paying any money they were giving some food or detergent, sugar, oil and such, things like that. And somehow we managed.

Some aid workers I spoke with told stories of initiating "practical protection" measures on a case-by-case basis, despite the absence of a formal policy. One former UNICEF representative told me of a request by a young woman with a baby during the Sarajevo airlift to be evacuated from the country, which would have required a deviation from the technical criteria for medical evacuations:

She wanted to keep the baby but didn't feel she should have the baby in the environment in Sarajevo; she wanted to go to relatives in Germany. The dilemma: Was she in a health condition that requires evacuation? No, but at the same time she did have a claim. We discussed whether to make the case to the peacekeepers that she should get out; eventually we did get her out. In the end I've always wondered what happened to the baby and to her. This case was a happy case; we know there were other cases.

Besides these ad hoc responses by the major organizations, local organizations such as Medica, supported by the international community, were able to assist a number of families in a more holistic fashion. However, their model was not adopted by aid organizations operating throughout the country, and they reached a limited number of war victims relative to the need. Moreover, although some babies received assistance through their mothers in programs such as Medica, few specific measures were taken to implement basic steps for their practical protection against stigma, against abuse or neglect by their mothers, or against the state. Folding assistance for the babies into humanitarian measures aimed at mothers meant that some children fell through the cracks, including those rejected or abandoned by their birth mothers.[60] Adopted children did not qualify for particular assistance, nor did their parents receive counseling to assist them in dealing with threats or stigma from the community in cases where the child's origin was known.

In sum, after some initial reflection on the matter, Western aid organizations settled on a strategy of supporting state institutions in placing children born of war as anonymously as possible; they did not track or concern themselves with what happened from that point on. They made efforts from time to time to assist a particular family but had no general policy regarding protection in this area. As one aid worker put it, "We try to deal with cases on a one-to-one basis but we haven't come up with a longer term solution for a much larger problem; we have not dealt with it broadly." Beyond the soul searching of a few isolated reports early in the Bosnian war, organizations dealing with child protection did not even consider their responsibilities toward children of rape as a specific category, but rather they hoped to meet their needs in the context of wider programming for unaccompanied children, children in institutions, and children displaced with their mothers.

A Comparison: The Islamic Sector

The logic behind the Western humanitarian response can be illustrated by a comparison to the Islamic humanitarian sector. A much more formally institutionalized response to children born of war came from Islamic organizations operating in the Bosnian arena. Whereas Western IOs and NGOs largely demurred on the subject of children born of war, the six Islamic NGOs still operating in the region by the time I landed in the field in 2004 had embraced them specifically as a category of concern. According to my interviews, their initiatives during the war included opening safe houses, initiating antistigma campaigns, and seeking to intervene on a case-by-case basis to support women in raising their babies and encourage families to accept and protect the women and children. After the war, they engaged in ongoing financial support to the families of the type consistently denied to families such as the Muhićs by Western humanitarian organizations.[61]

The particular attention given to children of rape by Islamic organizations might be partly explained by the symbolic significance of children born to Bosniak rape survivors to Muslim perceptions of the conflict. As the head of the Islamic community in Bosnia told me in an interview, "You see, the aggressor's plan on this hasn't succeeded. Because they wanted to trigger a chaotic situation in a moral sense. We are conscious of that and [because we protected our women and accepted the children] we did not allow that to happen to us."

It is also a result of the particular Islamic emphasis on orphans. The Prophet Muhammad was an orphan, and pious Muslims allude to a saying of the Prophet that whoever looks after orphans will be favored by Allah in paradise.[62] Thus the care of orphans is an emblematic emphasis of Islamic charity. For example, the British NGO Islamic Relief distributes stipends to 4,000 orphans worldwide, and 467 in Bosnia-Herzegovina alone, linking Muslim donors to specific families.[63] Because children born of war are considered orphaned by virtue of not having a male breadwinner, Islamic charities have paid them more systematic attention than IOs and Western secular NGOs. The Islamic humanitarian sector in Bosnia-Herzegovina was also less influenced by Western norms regarding adoption or discourses distinguishing "orphans" from "unaccompanied children."[64]

But perhaps most importantly, the Islamic NGOs were not constrained, as was the Western humanitarian sector, by concerns with reproductive rights for female rape victims. Most opposed abortion services for female war victims after 120 days of pregnancy, even in cases of rape. Thus, whereas hospitals and medical clinics throughout Bosnia and Croatia and reproductive health specialists working for Western NGOs would perform late-term abortions for rape victims, Islamic organizations emphasized that the rape survivor "is to carry, give birth to, raise and take care of that baby."[65]

Nor were they as constrained by a desire to appeal to local cultural norms to avoid seeming imperialistic, because in many ways they perceived themselves to be carriers of those very norms.[66] Such NGOs may indeed have encountered less resistance from some Bosniak rape survivors and the Bosnian government as imperialist outsiders as they constructed programs for babies of rape and their mothers. Although safe houses for rape survivors and their children initially established by Western NGOs had a low success rate, I heard stories of similar houses run by Muslim NGOs, including Merhamet, where women presumably found some solidarity and a sense of religious purpose that may have helped them overcome their trauma.[67]

In an era when the care of rape victims was rapidly becoming a marker of progressive transnational feminism and when the global Islamic community was increasingly framed by the West as impeding resolution of gender-based inequalities, it is an irony that the most meaningful humanitarian response to children born of gender-based violence came from Islamic organizations. Whereas the Western humanitarian community was content to subsume children of rape within larger categories of war-affected children and hope for the best, Islamic NGOs designed specific policy initiatives to make certain these children and their mothers were able to access assistance. That they were viewed as more authentic in this regard than Western humanitarian players confirms insights from Sally Engle Merry's recent study of human rights implementation: Merry argues that successfully translating international law into local justice depends on translating norms into the vernacular of specific cultural contexts.[68] They were not constrained, as Western organizations were, by discourses constructing children of rape as weapons against women, ethnic groups, and civilization.

However, this does not mean that the Islamic approach was completely consistent with global child rights laws or that it was not also shaped by these very constructions. In fact, although Islamic programs to aid war babies and their mothers were not impeded by the discourse of transnational feminism, they were fundamentally tied to ethnic constructions of rape and of the war.

The best evidence of this is that Islamic assistance to orphans in Bosnia seemed designed primarily to reach children born to Muslim victims. I heard little recognition in the interviews I conducted, even among organizations whose recipients came from all ethnic groups, that similar needs may exist among ethnic Serb or Croat rape survivors. Even among the families it served, the Red Crescent's orphans program was limited to stipends, and the director I spoke to lamented the lack of a more holistic approach that would include skill training for mothers and assistance finding jobs. According to one respondent, "Many women because of this go to a bad way. We urge women to take care of their child, that this is a problem for God, and that this will be a problem for the child. But for us it is enough to give some money, allow the mother to come talk to us if she has a problem." Even during the war, when such programs were provided, I was told they amounted to only 20 percent of the budget.

Because the purpose of the program was as much to reconfirm a sense of Muslim victim identity and ensure that the children would be raised as members of the community, it is no surprise that child rights themselves were often a secondary concern. For example, the orphans program itself requires families to meet a complex set of criteria. To qualify as an orphan, a child must typically have lost not his mother but his father.[69] Because the fathers of these babies cannot be presumed dead, and the mothers certainly cannot be expected to supply a death certificate, in Bosnia such children are considered orphans with "missing fathers." For this category, the Red Crescent requires a letter from the government stating that the father is missing. In the case of children born of war rape, this requirement is waived. However, the organization's staff attempt to verify the woman's story by "asking around" to make sure there is no father.[70] Such queries of neighbors and friends could have the effect of drawing attention to the child and mother, reducing incentives for the mothers to seek assistance for their children. They may also signal to the community that the child may qualify for aid, a fact that in other contexts has been known to promote jealousy and backlash from other war-affected people whose families are not so "lucky." Although such projects have certainly provided individual families with some sustenance, it is questionable whether they have contributed to reducing stigma against children born of war in Bosnia.

At any rate, no Islamic organization I spoke to had conducted any studies evaluating the success of their programs in protecting children against stigma. The assumption seemed to be that if mothers were willing to raise their children, they must "accept" them, and that the key was to make certain their basic needs were met. It was even better if they could be married off; one Islamic leader told me,

> I was actually influencing some young men, good religious men, if they want to have the greatness in front of God's eyes, to actually marry such a woman, and there were situations like that. To this day these are very good marriages, with children, living normally, even though in their eyes there is never true happiness. Because the soul's wound is different than the bodily wound.

Yet Islamic NGOs in Bosnia were ill equipped to deal with psychosocial work, such as attachment difficulties between mother and child: Only in 2006 did Islamic Relief establish its first psychosocial programs in the country.[71] Admittedly, they did not see this as their comparative advantage, for as one informant told me, "There are so many other women's NGOs already in Bosnia-Herzegovina." Moreover, some of my respondents argued that their ability to do work in this area is limited by the priorities of their donors: "If you want 1 million *konvertible marks* to rebuild houses, no problem, but 1 million KM to help widows deal with psychological problems, the mental side of human suffering, well, donors don't see this as such a priority."

CONCLUSION

The humanitarian international has had more than a decade to absorb the lessons of dealing with the fallout of mass rape in a conflict zone. One effect of this experience has been much more attention to sexual violence through humanitarian programming since the early 1990s. The UNHCR and other humanitarian agencies issued guidelines on the treatment of rape survivors in 1995;[72] there has been raised awareness about problems of sexual violence in refugee, postconflict, and displaced settings;[73] various "lessons learned" conferences have aimed to disseminate best practices on sexual violence prevention and treatment;[74] the ICRC is addressing rape in its dissemination practices;[75]

major human rights organizations now actively document the use of rape in conflict zones;[76] and the World Health Organization has created a research initiative on sexual violence.[77]

But attention to children born of rape is still lacking, both in Bosnia-Herzegovina and in the broader humanitarian network. Information about identifying the protection needs of children born of war has not been incorporated into medical worksheets for refugee workers; attention to this form of stigma has not been included in training for child protection workers. This resulted from a desire, during the war, to avoid policies that implicitly shifted the focus away from women and ethnic groups as victims of war rape and promoted an imperialist narrative of savagery in the Balkans. Aid organizations trusted in local society to act in the best interests of the children.

So by the time I arrived in the field in 2004, Bosnia's children of war had fallen completely off the radar screen of international organizations doing relief and postconflict reconstruction in Sarajevo. Practitioners told me the issue was too complex, too taboo, too sensitive, too sensational, too hard to assess. Some argued that concerns were blown out of proportion. Some were convinced that children were generally safe with their mothers, and supporting mothers and Bosnian civil society—the true victims of the war—would be the best way to assist babies as well. As before, earlier constructions of wartime wrongs created a context that shaped the permissibility of rights claims against adults in a local context. As I show in the next chapter, this was no less the case when it came to punishing the perpetrators of war crimes.

6.

"FORCED TO BEAR CHILDREN OF THE ENEMY"

Surfacing Gender and Submerging Child Rights in International Law

Behind all law is someone's story: someone whose blood, if you read closely, leaks through the lines. . . . The question . . . is whose experience grounds what law?
—MacKinnon, "Crimes of War, Crimes of Peace," 141

I ARRIVED ON THE DOORSTEP of the International Criminal Court (ICC) on July 3, 2007, five years and two days after the court came into force, on the first day of the month after the sixtieth day after the sixtieth government ratified it.[1] My hope was to interview someone from the prosecutor's office about the likelihood of including indictments for forced pregnancy into any charges leveled against members of the Khartoum regime, said to be behind campaigns of extermination and genocidal rape in the Darfur region of the Sudan. Stories of women and girls forcibly impregnated with "Janjaweed babies," some of whom were reportedly killed or stigmatized in the refugee camps of western Darfur and Chad, had helped galvanize international attention to the humanitarian crisis in the region and small waves of interest in the vulnerabilities of the babies by aid organizations in the region. The subsequent investigation into atrocities in Darfur was an early opportunity for the new court to leverage new language regarding gender crimes. I was curious about the extent to which this was happening and about whether by 2007 the consciousness of ICC prosecutors about the crime of forced pregnancy had come to include concern for the babies born as a result.

Judging by how difficult it was to get an interview with anyone from the ICC once I explained the topic of my book to a public relations officer, it seemed unlikely that such concerns were on the radar screens of the international civil servants staffing the new court. Those I was able to access, first by pestering by phone and e-mail and later by showing up without an appointment and finagling my way into a briefing for Emory University students, insisted that the right person to speak to was someone from the Gender and Children Unit. Although this sounded promising, at least as long as one assumed (as I did not) that gender issues and child rights were synonymous, I insisted on speaking to someone who also dealt more generally with investigations and prosecutions. (The litmus test for gender sensitivity in any institution is not whether there are a few gender experts on staff who "get it" but whether anyone else does.)

On paper, the ICC is one of the most gender-inclusive multilateral institutions in the global system. Achievements of the Rome Statute in terms of gender-sensitive jurisprudence include recognizing gender discrimination as a form of persecution, providing for gender balance in court personnel, and offering gender-appropriate resources to witnesses.[2] Largely because of the dedicated advocacy of women's organizations during the treaty negotiations, the Rome Statute also includes a comprehensive list of gender crimes, including the first codified definition of the crime of forced pregnancy in international legal history.

But the concept seems unlikely to ever be used in the court, much less to give voice to babies conceived for the purpose that they shall be unwanted. When I finally met with a representative from the Office of the Prosecutor, I was told, "That goes well beyond our area of expertise." As of 2007, three other "situations" were being investigated by the court, but none of the crimes under investigation included forced pregnancy, nor would "bush babies" or "Janjaweed babies" be a concern if they did, according to my interviews.[3] The ICC's Gender and Children Unit focuses on preparation of witnesses, but despite efforts by women's groups, by 2007 the ICC had failed to appoint a gender legal advisor who could consult with the Office of the Prosecutor about which crimes might be investigated in a given situation.

Indeed, as an appeals lawyer at the ICC explained to me, the rules of the court specifically prohibit investigators from going to look for evidence of specific crimes, particularly those for which it is necessary to demonstrate the perpetrator had a particular intent. Instead, the court focuses on establishing the gravest and most easily judiciable offenses in a particular case. These appear unlikely to include forced pregnancy, and if they did, the frame of reference would be the female rape survivor, not her child. Wrongful procreation claims aside, long-term harms to children of rape "are not within the reach of the court," according to the Gender and Children Unit. This is in large part because forced pregnancy has been defined as a crime not against children but against female rape victims, for whom the existence of the child itself is part of the trauma of war.[4]

Language—or its absence—is of crucial importance in constructing or foreclosing the possibility of new human rights claims. I argue in this chapter that the international criminal regime missed an opportunity to promote the rights of these children as part of its response to gender violence precisely because of the function images of the children played in constructing gender violence as a weapon of war. Rather than the long-term harms they face being front and center alongside those of their mothers, the babies were situated as tools of genocide, weapons of biological warfare, members of the perpetrating group, and signifiers of their mother's trauma. Thus the human rights of children born of war were framed off the international agenda long before the Rome Conference, first in the early legal arguments through which scholars situated rape as a crime of war and second in the jurisprudence of the earlier ad hoc tribunals, the criminal courts for the former Yugoslavia and for Rwanda. By the time the ICC came into force, the idea that forced pregnancy is a crime against a woman, not against a child brought to term, was well established in international law.

This interpretation of forced pregnancy not only resonated with feminists but fit the framework of international criminal law, which emphasizes harms done by enemy forces during wartime rather than (for example) secondary victimization of women or children at the hands of their own communities.[5] These understandings are now reflected in the evolving structure of the law and in its institutions, including the ICC and the International Criminal Tribunal for the Former Yugoslavia (ICTY). So it is no surprise that suggestions by activists that babies born of rape might themselves deserve restitution makes little sense today to career civil servants working within the tribunals. I conclude by considering whether punitive justice makes sense when taking into account the human rights of children born of war.

CRIMINALIZING FORCED PREGNANCY IN INTERNATIONAL LAW AND SOCIETY

Fifteen years ago, rape in war was still treated as a sordid but inevitable byproduct of armed conflict, barely condemned and rarely prosecuted. Today, sexual violence in various forms has been codified in treaty law, is condemned, and forms the basis for war crime indictments in various international institutions. This change in consciousness occurred largely because of the tireless efforts of feminist legal scholars outraged by the atrocity reports of rape in the former

Yugoslavia and the availability of a forum to press these claims in 1993: the newly formed ICTY.

The ICTY was originally conceived largely as a political substitute for meaningful intervention to stop the atrocities.[6] It was plagued from the start by the absence of key staff, budget shortfalls, and disagreements between the major powers.[7] It has been criticized for the glacial pace at which trials proceed, for the fact that several of the most important indictees remain at large, for failing to prosecute the North American Treaty Organization for alleged war crimes under its jurisdiction, and for possibly exacerbating ethnic tensions rather than promoting reconciliation. At a keynote address to the Association of Genocide Scholars in Sarajevo in 2007, I watched Bosnian intellectuals attack chief prosecutor Carla del Ponte for doing too little, too late, to prosecute the most serious crimes.

Yet the very creation of the court was a landmark in the evolution of international jurisprudence. It was the first such instrument to be created in response to mass atrocities since the end of World War II and the first opportunity to clarify international humanitarian law at the global level since the negotiation of the Additional Protocols to the Geneva Conventions in 1977. For example, the court's judgments reflect an expanded understanding of crimes against humanity and of command responsibility, contributing to customary law and future jurisprudence in these areas. In the fifteen years it has been at work, the ICTY has indicted a total of 161 people, and as of May 2009 it had completed proceedings with regard to 117 of them, with 44 cases ongoing.

The ICTY has also been progressive on gender issues compared with previous war crime tribunals, with sensitivity toward the views of women both in its substantive decisions and in its rules of procedure. This was far from inevitable.[8] The original statute for the ICTY, thrown together by the UN Security Council, barely mentioned sexual violence among crimes under the court's jurisdiction. Only after a flurry of feminist scholarship and activism in the early 1990s did the ICTY prosecutors and judges come to understand rape as a bona fide war crime.[9]

It is hard to overstate the significance of this achievement. After all, ancient scholars argued openly that rape was a normal, if regrettable, part of armed conflict and was to be expected by the women of the conquered.[10] By the Middle Ages, women acquired some legal protection under the Ordinances of War, promulgated by Richard II at Durham in 1385 and by Henry V at Mantes in 1419, which made rape during war a capital offense. However, the ordinance did not apply to cities taken by siege and was seldom enforced.[11]

In 1863, the Lieber Code, a military code for the Union Army, prohibited rape on penalty of death. The multilateral Hague and Geneva conventions, drafted at the turn of the century and updated after each world war, also pro-vided protection against rape. Yet as Susan Brownmiller notes, the nineteenth and twentieth century saw a huge increase in the scale of rape in armed conflict (as well as other atrocities against civilians), and the presence of legal sanc-tions for rape was not translated into international legal action.[12] Despite well-documented and publicized atrocities against women during World War I and World War II, the International Military Tribunals in Nuremberg and the Far East never addressed rape explicitly. Rather, the tribunals subsumed rape un-der the general category of "ill-treatment of the civilian population."[13]

Worse, the basis for criminalizing rape in these contexts reflected the very attitude that made it such a useful tool of war. Specifically, it was a crime against "honor, dignity or family rights," and the rape of women was associated with carrying off men's property. Such a conceptualization stands in contrast to the way in which late-twentieth-century feminists sought to redefine rape, as a crime against the bodily integrity of individual women, carried out in the larger context of deeply patriarchal societies. In an influential essay titled "Sur-facing Gender," leading feminist scholar Rhonda Copelon argues,

> Where rape is treated as a crime against honor, the honor of women is called into question and virginity or chastity is often a precondition, . . . and while the concept of dignity potentially embraces more profound concerns, stand-ing alone it obfuscates the fact that rape is fundamentally violence against women. . . . This failure to recognize rape as violence is critical to the tradi-tionally lesser or ambiguous status of rape in humanitarian law.[14]

The establishment of the ICTY in 1993 provided an opportunity for women's advocates to challenge previous constructions of war rape by advocating for language in the ICTY Statute that would rank rape as a grave breach of the Geneva Conventions alongside summary executions, torture, and biological experiments. Feminists interested in exposing and correcting the shortfalls in international humanitarian law immediately recognized in the court a site for clearly articulating the impact of armed conflict on women and girls, exposing the law's inadequacy and gendered underpinnings, and reformulating it so as to approximate justice for war victims regardless of gender.[15]

But this progress came at the expense of attention to the secondary harms associated with wartime rape, including those faced by children born as a re-sult. Indeed, the very manner in which rape was constructed as a war crime played a role in framing the children off the international agenda. In the next section, I provide a critical genealogy of the criminalization of war rape in inter-

national law and then demonstrate how these frames depended on and reproduced a particular understanding of the babies.

Putting Rape on the International Agenda

Understanding the space in which women's advocates had to maneuver as they
sought to criminalize war rape in the 1990s requires a grasp of basic concepts in
international criminal law, which distinguishes between several types of crime.
"War crimes" are grave breaches of the laws of war as codified in The Hague
conventions, which regulate what combatants may do to one another, and the
Geneva Conventions, which regulate what combatants may do to members of
the enemy population who are not or are no longer participating in hostilities.
These include wounded or sick enemy soldiers and sailors as well as enemy
civilians and prisoners of war.[16] By contrast, the term *crimes against humanity* means widespread and systematic attacks against any civilian population.
They need not take place in the context of an armed conflict and can include
human rights violations by a government against its own citizens. To amount
to "genocide," wide-scale human rights abuses must be carried out with the
intent to destroy a national, ethnic, racial, or religious group as such. Even the
most heinous crimes against humanity do not meet these criteria if it cannot be
shown that the perpetrators intended to contribute to the destruction of one of
these types of group. These distinctions, each of which arose from a particular
historical trajectory, had an important bearing on strategies women's advocates
used to situate the rapes in Bosnia in the context of international law and their
use of references to the children conceived through rape in particular.

Originally, rape was mentioned only once in the ICTY Statute and only as a
"crime against humanity,"[17] which, as Dorean Koenig points out, would require
"proof that the act was part of a widespread or systematic attack against a civilian population."[18] In the context of Bosnia, rape certainly could be viewed as a
crime against humanity on these grounds; however, feminists argued that the
gendered nature of the crime should be made explicit in the language of the
statute. For example, Catherine Niarchos wrote, "It would be insensible to fail
to recognize rape, in war or in peace, as a form of gender discrimination. . . .
Either by amendment to the current conventions or by declaration, international humanitarian law should be revised to reflect this concept."[19] Similarly,
Copelon stated that "the expansion of the concept of crimes against humanity
to include gender is part of the broader movement to end the historical invisibility of gender violence as a humanitarian and human rights violation."[20]
These concerns were later realized in the jurisprudence of the court, whose

judgments reflected the view that rape could implicitly constitute a war crime as well as a form of enslavement.[21]

Feminist writers also sought to broaden the ICTY's jurisdiction over sexual violence by defining rape as a war crime as well: To qualify as a war crime, or "grave breach" of the Geneva Conventions, an act must be committed in the course of an armed conflict, and it need not be systematic or widespread.[22] Thus, "rape on a wide scale would be prosecuted as a crime against humanity; a single case would be prosecuted as a war crime."[23]

Rape is a grave breach on several accounts, feminists argued. Although rape is not listed explicitly among the crimes considered grave breaches, it is encompassed under Article 2 of the Geneva Conventions as "inhumane treatment" and "willfully causing great suffering or serious injury to body or health."[24] Additionally, scholars insisted rape be viewed as a form of torture when carried out by an agent of the state,[25] and Koenig included "unlawful confinement of a civilian" as applicable in the context of the rape camps in Bosnia.[26]

Finally, it was also argued (controversially) that rape had been used as a tool of genocide during the conflict.[27] Initially, accounts of the human rights situation in Bosnia addressed rape and genocide as distinct issues, but several writers moved toward emphasizing the intersection between the two crimes, drawing on the previous understanding that rape is used in war largely as a form of psychological warfare against groups. This understanding of the strategic logic of war rape was articulated by Brownmiller in 1979 and reiterated in her 1994 essay: "Rape is considered by the people of a defeated nation to be part of the enemy's conscious effort to destroy them. . . . Men appropriate the rape of 'their women' as part of their own male anguish of defeat."[28] According to Ruth Seifert, "If the aim is to destroy a culture, [women] are primary targets because of their cultural position and their importance in the family structure."[29]

It was a short leap from understanding rape as psychological warfare to understanding it as one tool among many to destroy an ethnic group. "Rapes spread fear and induce the flight of refugees; rapes humiliate, demoralize and destroy not only the victim but also her family and community; and rapes stifle any wish to return," wrote Alexandra Stiglmayer in her introduction to the collection of essays *Mass Rape: The War Against Women in Bosnia-Herzegovina*. Catharine MacKinnon's chapter in that volume described rape as genocide on three counts. First, "the war is an instrument of the genocide; the rapes are an instrument of the war";[30] second, "rape as genocide [as in] rape directed toward women because they are Muslim or Croatian";[31] and third, "rape as ethnic expansion through forced reproduction."[32] Beverly Allen concurred with MacKinnon both in the use of the term genocidal rape and with her descriptions of different patterns of rape that function as genocide in multiple ways.[33] Though nervous about conflating rape and genocide because it risked obscuring the horror of "common" rape, Copelon nonetheless concurred that "from the standpoint of these women, [rape and genocide] are inseparable."[34]

Forced Pregnancy as a Specific Crime

In making such arguments, feminist legal scholars emphasized the forced pregnancy campaigns that had been documented during the war. Evidence of a systematic policy of forced pregnancy punctuated and supported all these claims as feminists sought to firmly embed gender crimes within the statute of the ICTY. The pregnancies that resulted from the mass rapes were seen as exacerbating the grievousness of rape and were capitalized on in constructing rape as a crime against humanity, a war crime, and a tool of genocide. This was the case regardless of whether forced pregnancy was viewed as intentional policy or as a byproduct of rape.

However, forced pregnancy was also articulated during this period as a crime in and of itself, distinct from rape. As a war crime, forced pregnancy—either through its association with rape or by extension—can be encompassed under several grave breaches. It is a form of sexual assault, it is an inhumane act, and it is an "indecent assault" under Article 76(1) and a "humiliating and degrading assault" under the Additional Protocols to the Geneva Conventions. Forced pregnancy "willfully causes great suffering or serious injury to body or health" because pregnancy and childbirth are potentially injurious or fatal.[35] In addition, great suffering may encompass both moral and physical suffering, of which forced pregnancy was constructed as an example.[36] Additionally, forced pregnancy constitutes "compelling a civilian to serve in the forces of a hostile power," which is prohibited by the Third Geneva Convention of 1949, and it is a violation of honor and family rights, which Goldstein reconceptualizes in terms of a woman's self-determination and personal dignity rather than a man's property rights.[37] When carried out by the state, it is also an act of torture under Article 1 of the Torture Convention because childbirth, even when not forced, is physically painful, and the emotional impact of impregnation maximizes the trauma of rape.

As a crime against humanity, forced pregnancy must be shown to be widespread or systematic but not necessarily both. Several authors describe forced pregnancy in this way.[38] Fisher incorporates forced pregnancy under "other inhumane acts," drawing from the Nuremberg Charter, Article 6(c).[39] Goldstein characterizes forced pregnancy as a potential form of "enslavement" prohibited under Article 5(c) of the Nuremberg Charter on the basis that it entails the exercise of a power "attaching to the right of ownership."[40]

In constructing forced pregnancy as genocide, activists stressed several different aspects of the crime. If rape were genocidal without forced pregnancy (by reducing the marriageability of victims and the cohesiveness of the victimized community), forced pregnancy made rape more visible and explicit, symbolically branding victims and precluding silence or denials.[41] Additionally, insofar as rape victims are members of the victimized group, the pregnancies as serious bodily or mental harm to them are genocidal.[42]

According to Siobhan Fisher, the pregnancies themselves also serve a direct genocidal capacity because they interfere with the reproduction of the victimized group: "When reproduction is used to proliferate members of one group and simultaneously to prevent the reproduction of members of another, it is a form of destruction."[43] According to Fisher, forced pregnancy interferes with group reproduction in three ways: "First, women may be psychologically traumatized by the pregnancy and unable to have normal sexual or childbearing experiences with members of their own group. Second, women who are raped and bear the children of the aggressors may no longer be marriageable in their society. Third, the women, simply because they are pregnant with the children of the aggressors, cannot bear their own children during this time—their wombs are 'occupied.'"[44]

Insofar as the pregnancies deliberately interfere with a group's reproduction, they are covered by the Genocide Convention under Article 2, a claim echoed by Jennifer Green and her colleagues.[45] They go even further, also arguing (paradoxically) that forced pregnancy additionally constitutes "forced removal of children from the group." (The contradiction is glaring. To be forcibly removed *from* the victimized group, the children must be members *of* the group, but if they are members of the group, then births within the group have been facilitated, not prevented.)

Through such intellectual and semantic gymnastics, forced pregnancy was constructed both as a component of rape as crime and as a specific crime itself, under the rubric of war crimes, crimes against humanity, and genocide. Despite the disagreements or conceptual ambiguities within these legal arguments, when taken together they played an important role in placing gender crimes on the agenda of the ICTY and subsequent international legal institutions. But despite the strengths and successes of these arguments, all articulate forced pregnancy as a crime against women only, eliding children born of the rapes from consideration; in fact, all rely on specific and problematic representations of these children in their definition of forced pregnancy as a crime against women and against cultural groups. In the next section, I address two linguistic devices that marginalized child rights in this discourse before turning to an analysis of the effects of this marginalization on emerging international law.

Children Born of War in Forced Pregnancy Discourse

> Women are raped frequently, perhaps numerous times each day. . . . Some captors say their intention is to impregnate the women, to make "Chetnik babies." . . . The women were examined by gynecologists. If found to be pregnant, they were segregated, given special privileges, and held until their seventh month when it was too late to obtain an abortion; at that point, they were released.[46]

As exemplified in this quotation, forced pregnancy was constructed by legal scholars as a conscious policy to force women to conceive and bear children. But in the construction of forced pregnancy as a crime, children were never discussed as victims of potential human rights violations themselves. Instead, they were invoked as evidence of atrocity.

Two discursive patterns appear across this literature that impede thinking about the babies through a human rights lens and help to explain the absence of attention to them in international judicial mechanisms. First, these issue entrepreneurs defined forced pregnancy in such a way as to make a focus on more than one victim of the crime quite difficult. Second, the children's identities themselves were often essentialized, casting them as non-Muslim (a social construction that placed them outside the group against which genocide was being committed) or, in some cases, as literally Serb, thus identifying them with the group viewed as perpetrators.

These discursive tendencies, whether intentional or inadvertent, relied on arguments about the political significance of the children, which resulted in an emerging set of norms inadequate to address the rights of those children as individuals.

Articulating Forced Pregnancy

Until the concept was finally codified in the Rome Statue of the ICC in 1998, the legal literature on forced pregnancy lacked a coherent terminology or definition for the crime. In fact, a number of analytically distinct concepts were embedded in the single term *forced impregnation*, which was often used in earlier writings on the issue.

The first component typically described is the act of rape and conception itself, the second is the prevention of access to an abortion, and the third is the actual birth of a child.

Consider the following description of forced impregnation: "Croatian and Muslim women are being raped, and then denied abortions, to help make a Serbian state by making Serbian babies."[47] Two concepts are listed here: rape with intent to impregnate and denial of abortions. MacKinnon places both acts under the same label to argue that forced impregnation is genocidal. Goldstein at first attempts a more careful definition: "Forced impregnation can be defined as an impregnation that results from an assault or series of assaults on a woman perpetrated with the intent that she becomes pregnant."[48] But later, in arguing why forced impregnation should be seen as torture, she writes, "The woman who is *forced to carry a rapist's child to term* is . . . humiliated and violated."[49] In short, she combines all three concepts under the umbrella term *forced impregnation*.

There is a conceptual error here. Where abortion is available, the crime of rape with intent to impregnate ("forced impregnation") is distinct from the crime of preventing abortion access, or "enforcing" a pregnancy. This became a point of contention during the Rome negotiations when the Interfaith Coalition opposed allowing condemnation of rape to be conflated with an argument in favor of abortion access for rape victims. But the distinction is also crucial when thinking about the child of rape through a human rights lens. Because the right to life for an unborn child is still contested in international law, human rights law can be brought to bear only on children who have been born; certainly not all rape-related pregnancies are brought to term. Making a space to bring children's rights into the equation arguably required that some distinction be made between forced pregnancies that result in live births and those that do not.[50] Instead, forced impregnation was equated in one context with rape and in another with abortion rights. The language of abortion rights applied to a situation in which both women and *born* children are involved focused attention on women's reproductive freedom and *unborn* children's rights and away from the born child. The conflation of these various concepts precluded an analysis of children's rights altogether, defining the act primarily in terms of the mother and the debate in terms of fetal rights.

Eventually, the status of born children as factors in the equation was erased through the gradual adoption of *forced pregnancy* (as opposed to *forced maternity*) in international legal discourse. In the Vienna Declaration, it is "forced pregnancy" that is condemned; this term was also used by Catharine MacKinnon when she invoked the Alien Tort Claims Act and sued Radovan

Karadžić, then traveling to the United States on diplomatic business, on be-half of several rape victims then residing in the United States.[51] In 1998, after a heated debate with religious conservatives that nearly derailed the conference, a limited definition of forced pregnancy was included in the statute for the new ICC. As I show later in this chapter, this language was chosen not in contrast to a broader conception of forced maternity, which could have focused on chil-dren's rights as well,[52] but in contrast to enforced pregnancy, or the prevention of abortion access to raped women.

Essentializing Ethnicity: The Babies as Serbian, Non-Muslim, or Perpetrator

As noted earlier, constructing forced pregnancy as genocidal entailed linking the crime to any or all of the following genocidal acts: intent to destroy, in whole or part, a national, religious, ethnic, or racial group; killing, causing serious harm, or inflicting conditions calculated to bring about the group's destruction; imposing measures to prevent births within the group; or forcibly transferring children of the group to another group.[53] Whereas children were ignored in the detailing of forced impregnation as a war crime and a crime against human-ity, overt references to children of rape were made throughout efforts to frame forced impregnation as genocidal in the 1990s. But by situating the child out-side the group against which the genocide was being committed, such refer-ences distanced the idea of the child born of war from the image of a victim and categorized the child instead with the ethnic group perpetrating the genocide.

In most of the writing on forced impregnation, the babies are referred to in some way as non-Muslim: "Croatian and Muslims women are being raped . . . to help make a Serbian state by making Serbian babies,"[54] "a woman who is forcibly impregnated must perform . . . the gestation of her captor's child,"[55] and "impregnat[ing] women with children of another ethnicity . . . [is a] measure 'intended to prevent births within the group.'"[56]

Categorizing children born of war as members of the rapists' ethnie reified the highly contradictory Serb logic that led to the policy of forced pregnancy, a mistake that Beverly Allen noticed: "The Serb policy of genocidal rape aimed at pregnancy offers the specter that making more babies with a people equals killing that people off. This illogic is possible only because the policy's authors erase all identity characteristics of the mother other than that as a sexual con-tainer."[57] Allen argues that many feminist analyses reproduced this mistake by failing to recognize it and thus "also erased all the victims' identities but the sexual."[58] But in her critique, Allen explicitly identifies the victim as the mother and defines the mother alone as the battlefield on which the war of identities is fought. However, the logic of Serb ethnicity for the baby also erases half of *the child's* identity and precludes her inclusion in the group against which genocide is being committed.

By extension, identifying the child born of war as Serb categorizes her or him as a member of the perpetrating group. Allen's subsequent argument reducing the child of rape to a tool of biological warfare serves as an example: The fetus "attacks" women's reproductive systems, causing "atrocious physical pain, mental suffering and often death," she writes.[59] According to Allen, such babies remained in the group not as members and co-victims but as parasites, "unplanned children . . . taxing the target population for years, if not generations, to come."[60]

Allen is not alone in treating children born of forced pregnancy as one of the enemy. Siobhan Fisher writes, "The forced carrying of a child of the enemy can certainly be interpreted as an injury to human dignity."[61] The papacy, which opposed feminists on whether "enforced pregnancy" should be considered a crime, ironically concurred on the ethnic status of the children: "The women should transform these acts of violence into acts of love by accepting *the enemy* within them."[62] Of course, although they are misleading, these statements are not completely false: In strict biological terms the child is ethnically half her father's as well as her mother's. But Fisher continues, for example, in her reasons for considering forced pregnancy genocidal: "The women, simply because they are pregnant with the children of the aggressors, cannot bear their own children during this time—their wombs are 'occupied.'"[63] Here, the child is not just part Serbian; she is explicitly *not* Muslim; she is not her mother's own child. According to Goldstein, a forcibly impregnated woman "is incapable of conceiving and bearing a child of her own ethnicity."[64]

The construction of the child's identity in feminist discourse reified both the false logic of genetics that brought about the pregnancies and a patriarchal assumption that any child born of rape automatically will be perceived as "other," rejected, stigmatized, and unwanted by the culture that claims the mother's reproductive identity. For Wing and Merchan, assigning a Serb identity to the child is not necessary for denying him or her inclusion in the Muslim group. They refer to the children as non-Muslim but not necessarily Serb: They are in an "ethnic/religious limbo . . . some unrecognized 'mixed' ethnicity that is not likely to be accepted among Muslims or Serbs."[65]

On the surface it seems puzzling that numerous feminist scholars would reify, rather than question, the patriarchal and nationalist agenda that is manifested in a rejection by one ethnic community of children born to genocidal rape victims. However, these patterns become more intelligible given the gendered structure of international law itself. The goal of these writings was to situate forced pregnancy as genocide. Given the limits of existing international law on genocide, two possible bases for doing so were prevention of births and forcible transfer of children.[66] Either legal strategy was contingent on the assignment of the child to one group or the other. Rather than articulating the inadequacy of international law to deal with such cases, scholars assigned a blanket identity to children of rape according to whichever linguistic strategy would fit the requirements of the Genocide Convention.

To prove that forced pregnancy prevented births within the group, an analyst would need to prove that the child born was not a member of the group. On a genetic basis, this required delegitimizing a maternal genetic link, which reified patriarchal notions of kinship. But if the child is not a member of the group, having never been accepted by it, how could the child also be "forcibly transferred from the group to another"? Green et al. argued that forced pregnancy was genocidal on both accounts within the same sentence.[67] Wing and Merchan used feats of semantic inconsistency, claiming first that the "resulting child will never be considered an ethnic Muslim, thereby preventing the birth of a Muslim child" and then that "the event of the birth of such a non-Muslim child resulting from rape transfers that child *from* the Muslim population to the non-Muslim population."[68]

As the 1990s wore on, understandings of forced pregnancy in international law drew on the notion that such children's existence pollutes ethnic communities. The ICC definition emphasized forced pregnancy as a crime against groups by limiting the definition to cases in which pregnancy occurred "with the intent to alter the ethnic composition" of a target community. Recent scholarship on the advances for women exemplified in the ICC Statute reified forced pregnancy as an actual expression of ethnic pollution (rather than an expression of such *intent*), engraving children of rape in international law as belonging to the ethnie of their rapist fathers. For example, in her otherwise excellent analysis of the implications of the new rape and forced pregnancy definitions at the ICC, Kristen Boon writes,

> The legal harm in forced pregnancy is that women are kept pregnant by means of confinement, violating their rights to bodily integrity and privacy. The effect of this condition is that these women are forced to carry and often give birth to babies of a different ethnic group.[69]

Similarly, the landmark Akayesu judgment at the International Criminal Tribunal for Rwanda referenced forced pregnancy as a hypothetical violation of the Genocide Convention:

In patriarchal societies, where membership of a group is determined by the identity of the father, an example of a measure intended to prevent births within a group is the case where, during rape, a woman of the said group is deliberately impregnated by a man of another group, with the intent to have her give birth to a child who will consequently not belong to its mother's group.

Such international legal constructions have been significant in attuning international courts to the gendered nature of war crimes, but an unintended side effect has been to exacerbate and reify the patriarchal logic that assigns a child ethnicity through patriarchal descent. The general inattention to this problematique suggests the continued acceptance of the idea, in international law and institutions, that children exist to reproduce group identities rather than as human beings with claims on communities and states.

In many respects this is an extension of a particular feminist critique of genocidal rape discourse. For example, as Rosalind Dixon points out in her defense of the exclusion of genocide from the Kunarac indictment at the ICTY, advances in international criminal law have not included attention to secondary victimization of female rape victims at the hands of their own communities. Dixon argues that defining rape as genocidal based on its harm to a group's men and their patriarchal culture "fundamentally obscures the double harm to women of primary and secondary victimization. In Bosnia, many women were not only raped by the 'enemy' but beaten and cast out by their fathers and husbands. They were not only forced to carry an unwanted child, but denied any right to establish a familial connection or bond with that child by a rigid (patrilineal or ethno-religious) concept of purity."[70] Dixon concludes that to treat these harms as genocidal against a particular male-dominated group only further denies women's experiences; she might also add that it denies and excludes the experiences of the children created by such acts.

In the next section I elaborate on this set of claims. Besides the general occlusion of secondary harms in international humanitarian law, situating children of war rape as members of "the enemy" made it singularly unlikely that the specific harms to which they would be subject should receive attention in reformulations of humanitarian law, and in fact the documentary record demonstrates that this is the case. There are few examples in these writings addressing the effects of conception by forced pregnancy on the children born as a result. Typically, mention of the children as subjects of human rights or victims of a new kind of war crime was avoided: They were not addressed as victims of war crimes, crimes against humanity, or genocide in the legal literature. Correspondingly, although they are invoked as evidence of atrocity against women in the sexual violence trials of the ICTY, no consideration has been given in ICTY jurisprudence to the possibility that rapists be held to account specifically for the harms they knowingly inflicted on these children.

FROM DISCOURSE TO PRACTICE: CHILDREN OF THE RAPES IN THE ICTY TRIALS

The commitment to prosecuting rape under the ICTY did not go unrealized. According to Karen Engle, 20 percent of all cases brought before the court have involved allegations of sexual assault,[71] and three landmark cases focused specifically on rape, with one set of convictions hinging exclusively on evidence of sexual assault for the first time ever in a war crime tribunal.[72]

Unlike the ICC, the ICTY Statute did not establish that court's jurisdiction over the crime of forced pregnancy, nor has the crime been prosecuted by the court. However, although the term *forced pregnancy* is used nowhere in the transcripts or judgments of the three main sexual violence trials at the ICTY, references to a policy of forced pregnancy were used in establishing the *mens rea* (intent) requirement for a finding of guilt in the most famous of these cases, *Prosecutor v. Kunarac, Kovač and Vuković*.

These three men were Bosnian Serbs from the town of Foča in the Republika Srpska, where they and others oversaw the detention, torture, gang rape, and sexual enslavement of Bosniak women and girls between April 1992 and February 1993.[73] Though not charged with masterminding any grand policy of systematic rape, they were framed at The Hague as ethnic cleansing's foot-soldiers. As Judge Florence Mumba of Zambia stated in presenting her judgment, "Political leaders and war generals are powerless if the ordinary people refuse to carry out criminal activities in the course of war."

The Foča case was thus among the "thematic" cases at the ICTY involving lower-level perpetrators, but it proved significant. Dragoljub Kunarac, a commander in Foča, was identified early on by ICTY investigators as being mentioned in many of the interviews by rape victims from that area; he was indicted on charges of not only rape but also command responsibility for his subordinates. He eventually surrendered voluntarily to French Stabilization Force troops, and two of his subcommanders, Radomir Kovač and Zoran Vuković, were also taken into custody and charged with rape.[74]

The prosecution presented testimony by several victims of rape and by military generals who spoke to the nature of command responsibility in armed conflict. The defense argued variously that the Bosniaks had started the war, that any sexual contact between soldiers and female civilians at Foča was not rape, that if rapes had occurred they were not part of any widespread or systematic attack on civilians, that Kunarac was not in a position of command responsibility over his soldiers when not on duty, and that ultimately, because women at Foča had not been killed, these crimes did not rise to the gravity typically addressed by international humanitarian law.[75] In the end, the court rejected these arguments, both in the trial chamber and on appeal, finding the men guilty of war crimes and crimes against humanity and sentencing Kunarac, Kovač, and Vuković to twenty-eight, twenty, and twelve years in prison, respectively.

The Foča judgment is considered a watershed in international gender justice for several reasons. It was the first conviction in an international tribunal to define rape as a form of enslavement[76] and the first international trial in which the defendants were convicted and sentenced solely as rapists rather than concurrently with other, presumably more significant crimes.[77] It was also the first conviction for rape not simply as a war crime but also as a crime against humanity, "authoritatively affirm[ing] that rape in armed conflict is a crime against humanity under international humanitarian law."[78]

Forced pregnancy was not addressed in the trial as a specific crime. However, an important part of the trial proceedings involved various efforts by the prosecutor, Dirk Ryneveld, to underscore impregnation as evidence of rape at Foča. For example, Ryneveld questioned former detainees on whether specific women had become pregnant as a result of rapes that occurred at Foča:

Q. Were you also afraid that you might have become pregnant?
A. Yes, of course I was afraid. That was always in my mind, but I was lucky. When I went for a medical examination in Novi Pazar, I found that I was not pregnant. So I thanked God for not making me pregnant.
Q. Do you know whether the other women were also afraid that they were pregnant?
A. Yes. They were all afraid of that, and they would all talk to each other, "God forbid that this should all happen." And I was the first to say that had I been pregnant, I would have jumped into the river or committed suicide, because I just couldn't take it.
Q. Do you know with any—do you know for sure, with certainty, whether any of the other women had become pregnant?
A. I don't know.[79]

Efforts were also made to underscore the abortions sought by women impregnated in Foča during this period. For example, it was emphasized that forty abortions were alleged to have "shockingly" been performed on women who were exchanged across enemy lines.[80] In highlighting these aspects, the prosecutors appeared to intend to demonstrate not only that rape and forced pregnancy had occurred but also that the women were uniformly rejecting the children, an assumption consistent with the dominant discourse of genocidal rape.

Attorneys for the defense consequently spent much effort attempting to debunk "rumors" of abortions among the detained women:

Q. Did any of the individuals on the list before you become pregnant?

A. No.

Q. Who told you that some of them had abortions?

A. I don't know.

Q. I don't understand. What don't you know?

A. I don't know what they did, how they did it. I don't know. I wasn't interested in that. It wasn't—how shall I put it?—it wasn't—I don't know. It wasn't easy for me at all.

Q. I have to refer you back to the statement you gave, page 6 of that statement, paragraph 3. The sentence begins: "I know that many of the women became pregnant. I heard that in Montenegro some of them had abortions. I don't know where all the women went to." You say you know.

A. I know that.

Q. How do you know?

A. Well, I heard it talked about, that when—and when they went to Montenegro they had to go to the doctor and have themselves examined.

Q. But you don't know; you know that from the stories that were told?

A. Yes. They went off whenever they went off, to Turkey or wherever. I don't know. I never heard of them or saw them after that.

MR. JOVANOVIC: [Interpretation] Your Honours, I have no further questions. Thank you.[81]

The rejection of the "child of the enemy" is also reflected in the emphasis placed on stories of women allegedly abandoning newborns, as in the following:

Q. In your statement, you mention some events linked to the hospital in Foča.

A. Oh, yes. In our hospital, there were quite a number of abandoned children, quite a number of Muslim children, orphans also. We had a Muslim child who used to live there before the war, and he was a favourite of ours. We carried toys and food for him. And there were some Muslim women in hospital to deliver babies, and we went to visit them because the hospital—those of us who lived nearby, and we took toys and food for them.

Q. I didn't quite understand you. You said that Muslim women who were about to give birth had left and the children stayed behind. Could you explain that?

A. There were some such cases.

Q. That mothers abandoned their children?

A. Yes.

Q. Thank you.[82]

This set of rhetorical practices is consistent with dominant constructions of what Zarkov calls wartime rape-victim identity.[83] Wartime rape survivors are constructed by the media and nationalist discourses as having internalized the shame and disaffection toward their children "of the enemy" that would lead them to seek to abort or abandon their children. There is little space in such a narrative to account for survivors who chose to connect with their newborns and in so doing reject the dominant constructions of their child's ethnicity and their own lack of agency in the aftermath of rape. Such thinking illuminates the practice of treating abortion and abandonment data as indicative of rape (although abortion rates often rise in wartime because of wartime conditions in general).

This is not to say that many women who survived the Bosnian camps did not genuinely want to abort or surrender their babies, either because of the trauma of rape or because they had internalized dominant discourses about their ethnicity. What matters here is that the lack of consideration given in this setting to questions about the status, fate, or future of those children. Their existence was highlighted in the court proceedings in the service of a different agenda: to elaborate crimes against a national group and against women as reproductive vessels tainted by the seed "of the enemy."

The prosecution's emphasis on the alleged intent to produce "enemy" children was particularly prominent in arguments about the nature of the rapes. In opening statements, Ryneveld stated, "You will hear that Kunarac kicked [Witness 48] and dragged her out. She was taken to a room at Hotel Zelengora, where both the accused Kunarac and the accused Vuković raped her that night. She was then told that she would now give birth to Serb babies."[84] Later, the prosecutor prompted this witness in particular to disclose remarks made by the accused as to whether she should become pregnant:

Q. Did Kunarac say anything to you?

A. Yes. He said it was a pity that others should rape me. That he thought I looked like a Montenegrin. That he thought I looked good.

Q. Did he say anything about you having Serb babies?

A. Yes, yes. He said that we would no longer have Muslim babies, that we would only give birth to Serbs, and that there would be no Muslims in Foča anymore.[85]

These aspects of the testimony were particularly crucial in the judges' decision that the rapes had been part of a systematic pattern to humiliate the women as part of the war effort. The initial judgment included a statement that "you personally raped Witness 183 and . . . further mocked the victim by . . . saying she would carry Serb babies and that she would not know the father."[86] The trial judgment states that the *mens rea* for discrimination was based on the derogatory comments made about Muslims as the rapes took place: "Kunarac, for instance, told 183 to look a Serb in the eye when he was raping her, and Kunarac also told Witness 48 that she would bear Serb babies."[87]

This testimony was part of the prosecution's effort to link the individual rapes to the broader ethnic cleansing of Bosniak Muslims. In order to prosecute these rapes not simply as individual war crimes but as crimes against humanity, the prosecution needed to show that the rapes had taken place in the context of a "widespread or systematic attack on a civilian population." Because the defense argued that even if rape were proved, "the accused would have done so out of a sexual urge, not out of hatred," the burden of proof was on the prosecution to demonstrate the racialized character of the rapes and their connection to the wider conflict.

Although attorneys for the defense appealed the initial judgment in part on the basis that "the Trial Chamber erred in reaching the conclusion he had committed the crimes with a discriminatory intent solely on the basis . . . that, when he raped women, the Appellant told them they would give birth to Serb babies," the Appeals Chamber rejected this claim, stating that this evidence "provides a firm basis for the Trial Chamber's finding that the Appellant committed crimes for a discriminatory purpose."[88] Thus the racialized language with which the rapists justified their actions and the argument that pregnancies were an intended outcome of the rapes underpinned the legal arguments criminalizing these acts and developing the case that they should be prosecuted as crimes against humanity.

Campbell observes that the concept of crimes against humanity takes as its referent not humanitarian law violations against individual human beings but "a collective subject, 'humanity,' which it constitutes through a positing of universal norms of 'humanity.' . . . These crimes challenge the moral and legal foundations of international society because they violate the very notion of universal 'humanity' which founds it. . . . Rape as a crime against humanity involves not only a physical and psychic trauma to the subject but also a symbolic trauma to 'humanity.'"[89] Therefore it is important to note the excision of children as rights bearers from the definition of this crime. Obfuscating particular harms stemming from these crimes (such as secondary victimization of women or their children of forced maternity) in order to focus on others (in this case, the dehumanization of civilian populations) has a bearing on the salience attached to certain consequences of war and feeds into the marginalization of certain concerns from the agenda of the human rights regime. Thus, although the Foča conviction is rightly seen as an important advance in war crime jurisprudence, it also demonstrates the limits of the progress made in international criminal law in terms of conceptualizing the full spectrum of consequences of gender-based violence in armed conflict.

FORCED PREGNANCY AND THE EVOLVING STRUCTURE OF INTERNATIONAL CRIMINAL LAW

This brings us back to the ICC and its presumably progressive provisions on gender-based violence and children's rights. On one hand, the Rome Statute included numerous provisions favorable to women's human rights, including expansive definitions of gender-based violence, gender-sensitive rules of procedure, and a quota system for selecting staff and judges. Child rights were also mainstreamed into the work and self-image of the court: Representatives I spoke to in 2007 pointed proudly to the fact that the first indictee, Thomas Lubanga Dyilo of the Democratic Republic of the Congo, had been indicted primarily on charges of child recruitment. At the same time, the Lubanga indictment suggests the limits of the court's gender jurisprudence: The charges did not include specific reference to the abduction of girls for sexual slavery or other gender-based crimes documented in areas under his control during the conflict.[90] These kinds of seeming contradictions are explained by the effect of women's advocacy on the court and the underlying structure of international law and politics in which both the court itself and gender justice advocates must operate.

The ICC and the advances in humanitarian law represented by the ICC Statute were very much creatures of the international community's experience in

Bosnia and Rwanda. The idea of such a court was not new. It had been raised when the League of Nations was created and again when the UN replaced the League of Nations in 1945. Tiny Trinidad and Tobago lobbied for the court again in the 1980s, hoping for help with their transnational crime problem. But the court itself was established only at the turn of the twenty-first century.

It was the conflicts in Bosnia and Rwanda that galvanized the international community to create a standing international tribunal capable of trying the world's worst war criminals, those guilty of genocide, crimes against humanity, and war crimes. By the mid-1990s, governments around the world had increasingly come to see the ad hoc tribunals established in the wake of the Rwandan genocide and Bosnian war as costly, ineffective, and cumbersome. They had also become concerned about the license taken by international judges in progressively interpreting the very broad statutes for these tribunals. The establishment of the ICC not only would satisfy the international community's desire for international justice at less cost and with more consistency but would represent an opportunity to rework humanitarian law through multilateral consensus rather than through what some had come to see as judicial activism.[91]

Cognizant of these concerns, government officials who knew they might someday be called to account took care, during the July 1998 Rome Conference and its earlier Preparatory Committees,[92] to codify the definitions of crimes as precisely as possible. Delegates from 160 countries met in Rome in July 1998 to haggle over the final version of the document. During these final negotiations, the status of forced pregnancy in international law was a topic of heated debate that nearly derailed the conference. The debate demonstrates both what was at stake in this codification process and the absence of child rights concerns in the discussions.

On the question of whether to include and how to define such a crime, the Women's Caucus faced a formidable opponent in the Interfaith Caucus, a conglomeration of religious groups consisting of Catholic and Muslim country delegations and a few conservative nongovernment organizations. Religious conservatives accused feminists of conflating forced pregnancy (as rape, prevention of abortion, and childbirth) with the international abortion debate. The term *enforced pregnancy*, which had previously been used interchangeably with *forced impregnation* became the feminist buzzword for rape with intent to impregnate that included the process of detaining women until abortion was impossible. Women's advocates argued that the term would not necessarily imply that abortion restriction was a human rights violation; as the Women's Caucus for Gender Justice put it: "It is difficult to understand how the debate about the crime of enforced pregnancy has become a debate about abortion. National laws which criminalize the termination of pregnancy are not violations under international law and thus would not come within the ICC's jurisdiction."[93] But for the interfaith network, led by the pope, the term symbolized *primarily* restricted abortion access, which it was unwilling to construct as a crime even in order to criminalize genocidal rape.

At no point in the debate were the consequences of forced pregnancy on children born as a result considered. Although Michael Goodhart argues that the concept of wrongful birth could be applied to such children, insofar as a rapist conceiving them for the purpose that they should be outcasts is violating the "right to have rights" under the Universal Declaration, such concerns were not raised in the Rome negotiations.[94] Rather, the debate centered on human rights violations against women on one hand and the right of states to regulate reproduction on the other; questions about the consequences of forced pregnancy on children born as a result were framed off the agenda altogether. A human rights lawyer told me, "The intent [of women's activists] was never to deal with this category of child, but to focus on the crime against the woman herself." This view was confirmed by a member of the Women's Initiative for Gender Justice in The Hague, which liaises with the ICC and other tribunals advocating for an inclusion of gender concerns: "It's stronger to keep the crime of forced pregnancy as a crime against women, as opposed to women and children."

The compromise definition was widely touted as a landmark by women's activists,[95] but is in fact remarkably limited.[96] Designed to capture situations analogous to the rape camps of Bosnia, it does not cover pregnancy incidental to rape rather than intended, such as the 2,000–10,000 children brought to term after the Rwandan genocide, or intentional impregnation without subsequent detention. The Rome Statute ended up defining forced pregnancy in terms of the intent to alter ethnic communities through reproductive interdiction rather than in terms of the harm caused either to the female victim or to the child brought to term as a result.[97] According to the statute, the term "means the unlawful confinement of a woman forcibly made pregnant, with the intent of affecting the ethnic composition of any population or carrying out other grave violations of international law." This definition was then qualified by the statement that the language of the statute could not be interpreted to affect domestic abortion laws. Questions of whether the perpetrators should be held responsible for the effects of conception on children born as a result were inconsequential to the debate; forced pregnancy was not treated as an issue for children. The perspective that but for detention by the perpetrating forces these children would not be brought to term at all is reflected in descriptions of forced pregnancy as an "aggravating harm" of rape[98] and the insistence by women's advocates that prevention of abortion access be a constitutive element of the crime.[99] It is also consistent with American pro-choice advocacy that stresses the particular importance of abortion access in cases of rape and with the acceptance of this argument by a large proportion of people who otherwise oppose abortion rights.[100]

For their part, Catholic and Islamic states seemed less concerned with the protection of children conceived as a result of rape than with setting an international precedent that could provide leverage to activists opposing domestic anti-abortion legislation.[101] Although the pope had come out early in the war with a controversial statement stressing the innocence of the babies and the responsibility of the community to protect them, child protection concerns clearly did not underlie religious advocacy in 1999 at Rome, for little in the discourse of conservative delegations centered on getting language into the document that recognized the long-term harms suffered by such children at the hands of the communities into which they were born.

Instead, conservative states seemed motivated by maintaining sovereign control over domestic policies affecting the family in general, a position already honed at the earlier Cairo and Beijing conferences on population and women's rights. The concern of this coalition to enshrine traditional notions of "family" in the statute was also reflected in heated disputes over the inclusion and definition of the term *gender*.[102] Although some rhetoric at the conference was couched in terms of the sanctity of fetal life, the resulting document says nothing with respect to born children of rape, preserving instead a limited right of state sovereignty over national abortion laws.

It is too early to know what effect this particular framing will have on jurisprudence at the ICC. Although feminist commentators consider it a significant victory that language regarding forced pregnancy made it into the statute, it is not at all clear that the court will pay significant attention to gender crimes. According to a lawyer I spoke with, the strategy of the court is to seek out easy and uncontroversial cases, avoiding "sensitive" subjects such as forced pregnancy; and investigators at the court confirmed the view that there were no plans for the ICC to take on an "activist" role in developing international law as had the ICTY.

Institutional obstacles also exist to prosecuting forced pregnancy through the ICC. Trial lawyers and investigators I spoke with in The Hague explained that, for one thing, the ICC has a policy of reducing the number of charges so as to conclude trials quickly, avoiding some of the criticisms of the earlier ad hoc tribunals.[103] The court is intent on indicting people only for crimes they are likely to be able to easily prove; the main goal for any young international institution is to solidify its own credibility. In investigating a range of crimes in any given scenario, the Office of the Prosecutor will focus not on every allegation but on those considered most grave and most representative of the conflict zone in general. Representativeness is measured in terms of the number of reports regarding a type of crime in a particular context. This means that crimes such as forced pregnancy, wherein victims have a disincentive to report, are likely to go unprosecuted.[104]

Potential prosecutions for forced pregnancy face another set of obstacles: the very fact that the crime itself, as codified, applies only in cases where a rape was carried out with explicit intent to impregnate so as to affect the ethnic composition of a target group. A trial lawyer at the ICC explained to me, "Prosecutors don't like 'specific intent' crimes. For instance, we all want to prosecute genocide, but when it comes to the point of establishing specific intent, things get difficult; you need objective facts about what someone was thinking, which you may or may not have."

Nor can ICC investigators go into a war-torn context aiming to gather the sorts of facts that might verify particular patterns of crimes that may have been reported in the press. Rather than making the strongest case for the prosecution possible, the court's job is to provide the most objective account for the judges. This places strict limits on the fact-finding methods ICC investigators can use in the field. Rather than asking the types of probing questions that might bring out the truth about a rape or a child born of rape, ICC investigators limit themselves to open-ended questions such as "What happened to you that day?"

Consequently, it is not surprising that those doing investigations in Darfur have not uncovered specific allegations of forced pregnancy. It is quite often the case that victims of crimes about which a strong taboo exists will not offer information unprompted about their experiences. With such a set of operational norms, ICC investigators are likely to uncover primarily the types of abuses about which victims feel most comfortable speaking publicly. All this means that forced pregnancy is unlikely to be prosecuted by the ICC in the near future.

Even if forced pregnancy charges are leveled in future cases regarding Uganda or Darfur, there is a great deal of skepticism that the existing terminology could ever be legally applied to children born of genocidal rape. As one staffer put it,

Yes, they're treated as rebel kids. . . . Some of them get beat up, . . . mistreated, . . . but I don't see how you can make the case on that. We always go after the clearest cases. So making these more tenuous arguments, we just don't really bother with that.

In fact, the official I interviewed at the Gender and Children Unit actually laughed when I asked about holding perpetrators of rape accountable for secondary victimization of survivors and their babies. For now, questions of what justice means for children born of war crimes, crimes against humanity, or genocide remain nonissues for international legal institutions.

CONCLUSION

The arguments that placed gender crimes on the international agenda advanced humanitarian law in important respects; yet in many ways they re-enshrined the group, the nation, as the unit of analysis when it comes to measuring war crimes. On one hand, whereas wartime rape has traditionally been dismissed as an inevitable byproduct of war,[105] recent scholarship and jurisprudence have illuminated the systematic and strategic use of rape as a means of torture,[106] of terror,[107] and of psychological warfare before, during, and after armed conflicts.[108] Forced pregnancy has been constructed as a war crime and a crime against humanity; when carried out with the intent "to alter the ethnic composition" of a target group, it has also been considered genocidal.[109] This new awareness has had important ramifications for international law, with rape convictions issued by ICTY, with the International Criminal Tribunal for Rwanda defining rape as a tool of genocide, and with steps toward reconceptualizing rape in war as a gender-based persecution for the purposes of asylum.[110]

On the other hand, in some respects these advances also reproduced the gendered underpinnings of international law, which emphasized children as vessels of cultural reproduction and as property of families and kin groups. The recent codification of forced pregnancy in international law is limited to cases in which the perpetrator intends to alter ethnic communities through reproductive interdiction. In other words, the language by which forced pregnancy has been codified and invoked in international institutions reifies, rather than questions, the status of women and children as property of ethnic groups, reinforcing the notion that children are primarily signifiers and women bearers of group identity rather than individuals in their own right.

This is particularly puzzling given the efforts of feminist legal scholars in the past decade to recast and ungender international law.[111] By privileging children's role as signifiers of group identity above their status as rights bearers, dominant constructions of forced pregnancy reify the very assumptions from which genocidal rape campaigns originate. This discourse of genocidal rape situates such children's existence as a grievous harm and naturalizes hate crimes against them.

As Engle notes, it is a political irony that feminist articulations of war rape dovetailed so conspicuously with the frames of religious conservatives, both constructing these children as "of the enemy" and sidelining the rights of born children in disputes over women's reproductive self-determination. In so doing, both re-enshrined conventional assumptions about the patriarchal family as the constitutive unit of international law. The doctrine of child rights encourages us to think past these metaphors and focus on the child as a human being. But the child rights regime bumps up against older ways of visualizing children in war, with unfortunate results.

Women's activists consistently and perhaps correctly argue that the purpose of gender jurisprudence in humanitarian law institutions such as these tribunals has never been, and should not be, to address the needs of babies who result from sexual violence. In the words of one gender justice activist, "We would probably stay focused on forced pregnancy as a crime against the woman, as opposed to it being a crime against the unborn child. . . . We wouldn't want to go down that path. We know where that discussion leads. . . . It would be a complicated strategy." So the puzzle is not why gender specialists have been unattuned to the ways in which gender crimes affect children but why child rights specialists have been so as well, despite calls from certain organizations that they pay attention to this issue. In chapter 8 I demonstrate how their preferences too have been shaped by these gender discourses.

Debra DeLaet has carefully considered whether existing postconflict justice mechanisms, either punitive or restorative, are adequate for bringing justice to children born of war. She argues that punitive justice mechanisms, including war crime trials, present many contradictions when conceiving of war's victims in such a broad sense.[112] Trials emphasize individual punishment, but the individual perpetrators of bodily integrity violations against infants may include traumatized mothers themselves, and taking a punitive view toward such acts, she argues, could contribute to a broader marginalization of the children themselves. In seeking to hold war rapists accountable for these longer-term harms, international law would risk criminalizing the birth of a child itself.

Although Goodhart's "wrongful procreation" concept would circumvent this conceptual issue, it is unclear whether trying war criminals for their callous efforts to deprive children of rights would promote ultimate justice for the babies or their mothers, absent broader efforts to transform the inequitable social contexts in which such people find themselves.

Based on the history of punitive justice to date, DeLaet's claims seem to make empirical sense. Tribunals have been sites for submerging, rather than surfacing, war babies' human rights, as they once submerged the rights of women war victims. It is unclear whether any of the currents that made international criminal law more responsive to women's concerns will emerge so as to harness the same institutions in the service of children. When I asked Carla del Ponte about this issue after her keynote address at the July 2007 meeting of the International Association of Genocide Scholars, she replied that it had been important enough simply to get women's concerns into the court's judgments. An ICTY lawyer from the prosecution told me after a fascinating dialogue, "I'm not sure there is a human rights answer to these kinds of questions." In the next chapter, I explore the efforts within Bosnia to make sense of that very question—whether there is a human rights answer—in the aftermath of the war.

7.

"THESE CHILDREN (WHO ARE PART OF THE GENOCIDE), THEY HAVE NO PROBLEMS"
Thinking About Children Born of War and Rights in Postwar Bosnia-Herzegovina

We know that these children are much loved, and as far as you know they don't have any problems, except that this one the whole family gave up on her.
—Interview, civil society activist, Bosnia-Herzegovina

For *sure* they have problems compared with normal children: discrimination. I don't think that they have any rights in our society. They don't have much space, to grow up, to see, to learn. I don't believe that they even know that they have rights.
—Interview, civil society activist, Bosnia-Herzegovina

EARLY IN MY FIELDWORK IN 2004, I interviewed the ombudsman for children's rights for the government of Bosnia-Herzegovina. Sitting in his office over coffee with my interpreter, I went through my customary list of questions. I asked him to tell me about the work of his office and how it tied into other postconflict governance issues. I asked him specifically what he knew about the situation of children born of wartime rape and what his office was doing to ensure that they were protected in the postwar environment.

The ombudsman seemed willing to talk to me and interested in my work but very apathetic about whether the issue of children born of war fell under his mandate. He had no problem answering questions about his current agenda. At times, he was able to link children of war rape to other aspects of his agenda, such as unaccompanied children who have lost their property rights (war babies might fall into that category, he suggested), education issues, or foster families. He referred me to women's organizations working with rape survivors, such as Vive Žene. At one point in the interview, he stressed the importance of continued international attention to the Balkans, emphasizing that working on the issue of war children could indeed be useful in keeping the international community's attention. He whipped out a map of world religions, showed Bosnia as a meeting point of civilizations, and described the Balkans as a litmus test for multiethnic democracy.

But he refused to even speculate about children born of war in the absence of facts, and he pointed out that the facts out there are easily manipulated. He seemed skeptical of anecdotal data but also cynical about the possibility (or political utility) of collecting more rigorous data. He was also concerned about the political uses to which such data might be put and skeptical about the kinds of claims one might make on behalf of such children. He repeatedly pointed out that the lack of employment of these children's mothers was no different from unemployment in general.

His office generally issues investigations in response to complaints. The ombudsman pointed out that "there has never been a complaint on behalf of these children." Although this could be the case for many reasons (those who might speak on the children's behalf don't see the need, those who might see the need are unaware of the role of the ombudsman's office and complaint process, or for some reason no one is willing or able to lodge complaints), my respondent considered this proof that the children had no problems: "What would the complaint be about?" he asked.

"Economic support," Jasna, my interpreter, suggested.[1]

"Everybody would like more of that, but there is a separate welfare process that people can apply to."

"Harassment."

"Well that's a possibility."

As it turned out, the ombudsman's office can also initiate its own investigations. I asked what kind of topics were selected for investigation. His general answer was that you pick topics where fact finding is reasonably feasible and where knowing the facts can actually make a difference in terms of advocacy. For example, he pointed to concrete cases in which teachers were using hate speech and intimidating students. In this kind of clear-cut case, the ombudsman's office can exert pressure, and pressure makes a difference. "There are practical problems: You want to pick an issue where your effort will actually be translated into some good," he said.

However, this was not the reason that Bosnia's war babies had not been investigated. The ombudsman made the reason clear: "*We didn't think of this issue*. But, if we had, I doubt if we would have focused on it specifically: It is too big, too complex. To find these children, analyze their situation, the economic, the psychosocial, longitudinal work, so many different dimensions. And after all *that*, what are you going to do about it?"

The ombudsman's comments illustrate some broader patterns that help explain the inattention to Bosnia's children of war since the conflict ended. Among others, the relationship between the local government and the international organizations operating in Bosnia has created both opportunities and constraints for efforts of this type. But more importantly, the way in which children born of war function in postwar nationalist narratives matters greatly in shaping the space in which their rights can be discussed in a particular postwar society. And both local and international human rights organizations in Bosnia have been highly ambivalent about the value of such efforts, in part for parochial reasons and in part because no agreement exists on what children's rights mean when applied to such children or how to negotiate the seeming tradeoffs with other human rights issues. This, in part, is what the ombudsman meant when he said the issue is "too big, too complicated." In this chapter I first discuss the meaning of human rights in general and show how the postwar Bosnian context makes it difficult to translate human rights principles into practice. I then elaborate on each of these additional patterns—nationalism and contestation within civil society—to explain why it is particularly hard to translate international rights standards into justice for children of war in this country.

HUMAN RIGHTS AND POSTCONFLICT POLITICS

Despite efforts by nongovernment organizations (NGOs) to promote what is now called a human rights culture that would guide the behavior of all citizens, the concept of human rights boils down to a set of claims made by individuals against states.[2] To evaluate how well the process of translating human rights commitments into the enjoyment of rights by children born of war has worked in Bosnia, therefore, we must take a look at postwar Bosnian government policy and at pressures from civil society, or the lack thereof, to reform that policy.

In the context of Bosnia, it's important to distinguish human rights from humanitarian law, whose principles were enumerated in chapter 6. Humanitarian law applies in time of armed conflict. It regulates the treatment of foreign noncombatants (civilians, prisoners of war, and war wounded) by the military forces of a given state. By contrast, human rights law regulates the relationship between the citizens of a state and the state itself and therefore applies not only during armed conflict but also, importantly, between wars.

Today, human rights are said to be universal, applying to all humans by virtue of membership in the species, irrespective of culture, religion, race, sex, age, birth, or other status. They are said to be inalienable, meaning it is impossible to give up or lose one's rights. They are standards, not laws, meaning that it is up to governments to convert them from abstract moral statements into legislation with teeth. A fundamental difference therefore exists between the *possession* of rights in these abstract terms and the *enjoyment* of rights, which entails an important set of both positive and negative actions on the part of authorities.[3]

The concept of human rights was intended primarily to protect individuals from abuses committed by public officials and secondarily to enumerate guarantees that states were to provide for human welfare.[4] But the concept of human rights has moved far beyond these initial underpinnings, thanks to the creativity and agenda-setting influence of a wide array of transnational civil society groups.[5]

For example, originally inhering in the individual, human rights are now sometimes articulated as belonging to entire groups, such as the right to cultural self-determination.[6] At times these "third-generation rights" can conflict with the rights of individuals within groups, such as women and children.[7] Similarly, Alison Brysk has shown how activists have leveraged new claims on behalf of individuals suffering not at the hands of states but in the "private" domains of the home, the workplace, or the medical establishment.[8] And Joel Oestreich has documented the way in which human rights has come to be appropriated as a responsibility not just by state signatories to the key treaties but also by international organizations committed to implementing "rights-based programming" and promoting a "human rights culture" among individuals at the grassroots.[9] These dynamics suggest both the cultural power of the language of rights and the difficulties in translating these lofty principles into practice.

In theory, here is how international human rights standards are supposed to work. Governments sign multilateral treaties, often at the behest of a range of transnational activists, committing themselves to abide by a set of rules agreed upon through consensus by delegates at an international convention.[10] They then go through a process of domestic ratification of the treaty, which can vary depending on the political system in question. In the United States, ratification of treaties takes place in the U.S. Senate. In the former Yugoslavia before 1990, a similar process occurred in the Federal Assembly.

Once a treaty has been ratified, it is binding on the state, which means the state is obligated to implement its provisions through domestic legislation. Compliance with a treaty first means passing laws, converting international commitments into domestic legislation that criminalizes or mandates certain behaviors. For example, U.S. legislation enacted in 1994 provides for the prosecution of U.S. citizens who commit torture as defined in the UN Convention Against Torture, which the United States ratified in the same year. The state must then actually enforce the laws—in this case, punishing people who torture.[11]

Treaties also generally obligate states to monitor and report on how effectively such legislation is implemented and on the levels at which individuals consequently enjoy these rights within their borders. In theory, states are expected to report yearly to the UN Committee on Human Rights on how well they have discharged their treaty obligations.

Of course, implementation can and often does break down at any of these stages. But where it does, a state's commitment to a treaty empowers transnational human rights advocates to "name and shame" that state for failing to comply with its provisions.[12] Even when powerful states are indifferent to their treaty obligations and immune to pressure from abroad, the process of treaty ratification alters the domestic political agenda within countries and makes litigation possible, putting states in the position of needing to justify their actions.[13] Surprisingly often this can bring about real change in state policy and, eventually, behavior. For example, it is because of international human rights standards that Britain no longer allows corporal punishment in its public schools.

When a new state is created or secedes from a previous government, it inherits the international obligations of its predecessor. The Convention on the Rights of the Child (CRC) was ratified by what was then Yugoslavia on January 3, 1991. Under international law, the successor states of ex-Yugoslavia, including Bosnia-Herzegovina, inherited these obligations; Bosnia-Herzegovina duly ratified the CRC on March 6, 1992, shortly after declaring independence.[14] The provisions of the CRC most relevant to children born of war include Article 19, which protects children against abuse, maltreatment, or neglect; Article 7, which affirms children's right to know their parents; and Article 6, which guarantees an adequate standard of living, social security, and health care.

To date, although all children *possess* these rights, there is mixed evidence of activity by the government of Bosnia-Herzegovina to implement these standards in such a way that children born of war can be as certain as other children to actually *enjoy* these rights. Although a system was in place to channel abandoned babies into adoptive homes, no monitoring has taken place to ensure that these children's vulnerabilities have been minimized in the postwar period. Although the government does not formally discriminate against such children, it has not made positive efforts to ensure that they are protected from mistreatment, neglect, or abuse at the hands of the communities in which they are being raised. A national office for the protection of child rights exists, but the ombudsman for that office had not even considered the situation of children born of war by 2004 when I visited the country. Not surprisingly, a few journalists by 2003 were characterizing these children as forgotten by the state.[15]

Three aspects of the postwar political context provide a permissive environment for such "forgetting": the extreme decentralization of the political system, inattention to gender issues, and the agenda-setting influence of the expatriate communities in Bosnia-Herzegovina.

Political Decentralization

Providing a context in which human rights may be enjoyed is the responsibility of the state, but Bosnia-Herzegovina is one of the most decentralized states in the world. The war in ex-Yugoslavia was ended by a treaty hammered out at an airbase in Dayton, Ohio, that stabilized the borders of the country and provided for a set of postwar institutions aimed at creating a peace that the different warring parties could live with.

In practice, the Dayton Peace Accord divides the country into two statelets along ethnic lines, each of which has its own distinct administrative structure. The central government has very little power other than to make foreign policy, in particular because its legislative structure provides veto power to members of each constituent "people." A presidency, collectively held by co-presidents from each of the three ethnic groups, is not to execute legislation or provide for the common defense but rather simply to represent the country abroad.[16] Robert Hayden describes the central government as "essentially a customs union with a foreign ministry."[17]

This means, for example, that the federal government negotiates and signs human rights treaties but has little power to implement them. Policies that would affect individuals' ability to enjoy human rights are administered at the "entity level." The Muslim-Croat Federation, an entity encompassing Bosniak and Croat-held areas of the country, was divided administratively into ten cantons so as to create a power-sharing arrangement acceptable to Bosniak and Croat leaders.[18] The Republika Srpska (RS) is a "state within a state" with its own constitution, parliament, written language, and, until very recently, its own army.

Both entities nominally have constitutionalized extremely progressive human rights standards, but a huge gap exists between letter and practice. The Muslim-Croat Federation's constitution, which dates to 1994, enshrines "the highest standards of human rights and freedoms," but the responsibility for human rights and social welfare in the Federation is held jointly by the cantonal and federal governments, an arrangement that encourages both parties to pass the buck to one another.[19] As for the RS, its social welfare provisions include health care for children, women, and older adults; employment for all, with sufficient leisure time; and minimum social services for all. But as Bose wrote in 2002, "The social reality of the RS is that the unemployment is usually estimated at 60% and as much as 90% of the population is said to live in poverty."[20]

Although the Dayton Accords envisioned and promoted a multiethnic society and reconciliation between the previously warring groups, Bosnia-Herzegovina today is far more ethnically stratified than before the war. Once a proudly mixed city of Serbs, Croats, Muslims, and Jews, by 1997 Sarajevo had become 87 percent Bosniak Muslim, with most of Sarajevo's Serb population relocated to Western Europe, Serbia, or neighboring Pale.[21] The language known as Serbo-Croatian under Josip Broz Tito has now nominally devolved into three separate languages, Serbian, Croatian, and Bosnian, demarcated by slight shifts in vocabulary and accent. This is reflected in the geography of postwar Bosnia: The lettering on road signs shifts to Cyrillic when one crosses the border from the Muslim-Croat Federation into the Bosnian Serb–dominated RS. According to Coles, even the national currency has ethnic variations: "Notes issued in the *Republika Srpska* feature Serb writers and those issued in the Federation feature Muslim and Croat authors."[22] And as many of my informants lamented, the curriculum in the ethnically segregated classrooms continues to cover history, and particularly the history of the war, through very different lenses.

The combination of decentralization of the national government and the assignment of citizenship according to ethnicity in the two-entity system has had direct, negative effects on some children born of war.[23] Christine Toomey documents an example in a *Sunday Times* article: An institutionalized child growing up in what is now the RS remains essentially stateless because the authorities deny the circumstances under which she was born:

> While some children have savings accounts set up in their name, to which various charities make occasional donations, Samira does not. Because the Serb-controlled municipality where her mother was born will not accept responsibility for her, she still has no national identity number, necessary for a bank account to be opened in her name. Legally, she does not in effect, exist.[24]

Low Salience of Women's and Children's Issues

In postwar Bosnian politics, as in many postconflict zones, women are greatly underrepresented, and issues concerning children and women are typically subordinated to "more pressing" concerns.[25] As Madeleine Rees argues, those who negotiated the General Framework for Peace in Bosnia and Herzegovina were nearly all men, and "gender issues never surfaced in the drafting process."[26] Important reconstruction issues such as who gets contracts to assist returnees,[27] who qualifies for postwar jobs,[28] and how government benefits are allocated all reflect what feminists call masculinist assumptions and priorities—those that serve the interests and agendas of men in power. Victims of gender-based violence, and their children, remain on the margins.

An example of how this played out in government policy is the postwar law on civilian war victims. A government fund was set up to provide benefits to survivors of the concentration camps and other civilian victims of the war. However, in order to be eligible for such benefits, civilian victims had to demonstrate that they had been wounded or traumatized. Victims of rape and their children seldom qualified because many had been unable or unwilling to document the physical trauma of rape in the immediate aftermath of the crime, and unlike the visible wounds of landmine victims, for example, rape survivors' trauma was often psychological. Until 2006, such survivors were unable to access government resources or the social status of "civilian war victim" unless they could demonstrate that they were "60% disabled" by the rape.[29] The secondary harms stemming from social stigma are not addressed at all.

Besides such general policy failures, the general inattention to the gender dimensions of the postconflict environment by those engaged in social policy has contributed to the lack of attention to children born as a result of sexual violence. The explicit policy of the Bosnian government has been *not* to monitor the status and fate of these children. Although this is justified as a way to protect children from stigma by not identifying them, in fact it has simply impeded assessments of their situation or responses to their programmatic needs. It also enables the government to make the case that they do not exist as a social category or have real problems. Government officials frequently referred me to women's civil society groups, although it is the state that is responsible for ensuring that human rights are implemented within a country. This sort of buck-passing is predicated on the idea that the state cannot be held responsible for protecting individuals against societal problems.

In short, an official policy of denial seemed to be in place during the period of my fieldwork. This pattern was confirmed by surveys carried out under the auspices of the United Nations Children's Emergency Fund (UNICEF) in summer 2004, which found government officials reluctant to discuss the issue and found no evidence that the government was addressing the children's vulnerabilities. The Center for Social Work in Sarajevo officially denied the existence of such children in Sarajevo canton, although women's NGOs in Sarajevo had case files on several such children. One can interpret these kinds of denials in a positive light, as a deliberate decision to maintain confidentiality for the children and mothers by refusing to cooperate. The tradeoff is that such secrecy makes it impossible to monitor or assess government protection of the children and makes it easy for the government to look the other way.

National and Transnational Relations

Another defining factor in the postwar political landscape is the foreign presence in the country.[30] Bosnia-Herzegovina remains heavily influenced by the outside world, both institutionally and ideationally. In fact, John Carlane argues that the crucial division in postwar Bosnian society is not between government and civil society but rather between local and international organizations.[31]

From 1996 to 2005, between 20,000 and 60,000 soldiers from the North American Treaty Organization (NATO) and fifteen non-NATO countries were stationed in Bosnia-Herzegovina, buttressed by a significant number of civilian contractors employed by the U.S. military. In addition to the international military presence, three other major international organizations were present in the country: the Organization for Security and Cooperation in Europe, which monitors elections and promotes democratic reforms; the Office of the High Representative, which oversees other civilian aspects of the transition; and the United Nations Mission in Bosnia-Herzegovina, which until 2002 coordinated the work of the various UN agencies in the country and included an International Police Task Force to oversee police reform. In addition, there are an assortment of international organizations and NGOs, employing thousands of expatriate and local staff.

The role of the international tribunal and international organizations will be explored further in subsequent chapters, but here it is also important to point out the hierarchy between the local and international that the postwar expatriate economy has generated. For example, as Kimberly Coles details in a recent analysis, very different governance structures exist for expatriates and local Bosnians in the post-Dayton order, such that "while enveloped in a discursive and institutional space of union and integration, the on-the-ground practices of internationals create difference and exclusion."[32]

One notices this hierarchy upon arrival at Sarajevo airport, where a separate customs line exists for international staff, who need only an ID rather than a passport, and the much longer line for all others passing into Bosnia. Similarly, Coles describes the parallel institutional structures that govern the banking, security, transportation, and health sectors for internationals in Bosnia. In addition, international troops, civilian police, and contractors enjoy immunity from crimes committed in the country, such as rape or trafficking in women.[33]

This institutional segregation contributes not only to a sense of hierarchy and difference between the international sector and Bosnians but also to bitterness among locals and resistance to rights-based discourses seen as imperialist and hypocritical, such as those pertaining to children.[34] When I conducted a follow-up interview with my interpreter at the conclusion of her work with UNICEF on a fact-finding study, she told me, "International organizations . . . just create projects they can get money for to keep themselves busy, but I don't think we really see any of this. I think these people are just coming here to fill their own quotas, to accomplish their own goals. So I think the real, honest interest is lacking, not only in UNICEF, but in the international community in general."

However, the West is not the only resented international influence in ex-Yugoslavia: The Muslim Middle East also exerts what many Bosnians view as a colonial presence in the country. A poignant example of this influence is the construction of conspicuous Middle Eastern–style mosques in the place of indigenous Bosnian mosques destroyed by the war (Figure 7.1). In the countryside and around Sarajevo, Bosnians point to these structures as ugly examples of outsiders intruding into their cultural domain (Figure 7.2). "You Westerners give aid in exchange for democracy; the United Arab Emirates gives aid in exchange for mosques," one of my interpreters once told me. Cab drivers

FIGURE 7.1
Old-Style Bosnian Mosque, Barscarsija, Sarajevo

FIGURE 7.2
Postwar Mosque Outside Sarajevo

shuttling me from the airport on my many visits pointed to the new "King Fahd" mosque, claiming it had been identified as a terrorist stronghold but that "this has nothing to do with Bosnia." On the way from Sarajevo to Zenica, one passes a brilliantly postmodern Kuwaiti mosque with rainbow stained-glass minarets in an otherwise heavily rural landscape. It bothered my driver that I was interested in stopping to take a picture of it. He reacted as if it were an alien sentry implanted on the territory of his homeland. "It's is the ugliest thing I've ever seen," he said.

In addition to mosques, the Bosnian landscape has been flooded with ex-patriates from the Middle East, particularly from donor governments such as Saudi Arabia, Pakistan, and the United Arab Emirates, whose humanitarian donations to Muslim-majority areas often rival those of Western organizations. Anders Stefansson has documented the nervousness of local Sarajevans when confronted with a Middle Eastern immigrant community they view as "muja-heddins," which he argues are "looked upon as the most threatening and cul-turally different group by both Sarajevan Bosniaks and members of minority groups. . . . The financial assistance [from the Muslim world] is perceived to be spent for wrong and politically extremist purposes, like building mosques, religious schools, and promoting Islamic values, instead of using their wealth for more secular purposes, such as (re)construction of houses, public schools and factories."[35]

The relationship between a local postwar government and the transnational actors operating in its territory matters in shaping the political space for press-ing human rights claims. In the Bosnian case, government relies in many re-spects on Western international organizations to set the human rights agenda.[36] Although the ombudsman for children's rights resisted focusing on a complex issue such as war babies, he also told me that if someone else, such as an in-ternational organization, were able to do the research to determine that the problem both exists and could be manageably solved, he'd be very interested. "If any survey is done and someone comes up with statistics—there is x% of women, children affected—then you can go to the authorities to do some-thing," he stated. Similarly, an official from the Ministry for Social Policy told me, "Without data we can't deal with this category of children or even figure out how to prioritize them. We need time, space, resources, and we have much bigger priorities."

In this milieu, the failure of international organizations to lobby the govern-ment specifically in regard to the needs of these children is a partial explanation for this policy vacuum. My interviews with the staff of different international institutions operating in postwar Bosnia revealed an absence of awareness or focus on children born of war. Some were indifferent: The International Committee of the Red Cross officer I spoke to in Sarajevo argued that her organization's "emphasis was on war victims: What we do with children involves children of the missing, as well as dissemination of humanitarian law in schools." Representatives from the United Nations High Commissioner for Refugees seemed confused and unprepared for the question: "I've never heard such a situation. . . . My opinion is these women are not here in Bosnia-Herzegovina. I really don't know, no one speaks about it." Others were more blunt: "We don't know, no one's bothered to find out, and no one's doing anything."

However, it would be too easy to assume that attention from advocacy organizations, given other factors at play, would have been sufficient to change this outcome. An important exception to the general rule, discussed in chapter 8, was UNICEF's attempt in 2004 to conduct a fact-finding study on the issue. But that organization quickly ran up against resistance from entities within the government. Ultimately, the complexity of negotiations with the government over how to edit the report contributed to UNICEF's decision not to publish it at all.

Thus, although a government may be in a position to pass the buck to the internationals, using their inattention to an issue as an excuse for inaction, it can also resist the promotion of certain issues by international players when desired. As I show in chapter 8, the fear of encountering such resistance is one of the key rationales members of the international community give for avoiding the issue of children born of war. By avoiding "sensitive" issues, they can maintain a sound working relationship around other problems with advocacy partners.

"A PARTICULARLY SENSITIVE ISSUE"

So what makes this issue so "sensitive"? In addition to the general problems of decentralization, gender blindness, and the distribution of power between the government and international community, I argue that international actors were constrained, and government ambivalence normalized, by two other important factors. First, the way in which children born of war function in postwar nationalist narratives matters greatly in shaping the space in which their rights can be discussed in a particular postwar society. Second, both local and international human rights organizations in Bosnia have been highly ambivalent about the value of such efforts, in part for parochial reasons and in part because no agreement exists on what children's rights mean when applied to such children or how to negotiate the seeming tradeoffs with other human rights issues.

In this section I elaborate on each of these patterns to explain why it has been so hard to translate international rights standards into justice for children of war. I conclude with a discussion of two recent Bosnian films whose production and release illustrate the interplay between these dynamics.

The Role of Postwar Nationalism

What constitutes a "sensitive" issue can mean different things in different contexts, but in Bosnia-Herzegovina part of what makes war babies such a hot-button topic is the way in which it is bound up in postwar renegotiations of identity. Rape and children of rape figured prominently in discussions of what it means to be Bosnian and of religion, gender, and family policies during and after the war. In this sense, the assignment of blame for previous atrocities inhibits the articulation of new rights claims.

It is typical to describe the war in Bosnia as a conflict between different ethnic groups over the identity of their nation. And indeed, nationalist sentiment was an important sustaining factor and has fundamentally shaped the postwar sociopolitical landscape. But as Benedict Anderson long ago argued, nations or ethnic groups do not exist independent of the many symbolic and communicative acts that tell us they exist; they are "imagined communities" that become real to the extent that those within and outside the group act as if the group is real.[37] Therefore, articulating and policing boundaries around national or ethnic groups is itself a political process that becomes heightened particularly during wars, when the "community" is most threatened existentially, and in the aftermath, when war-torn communities must both make meaning of the former conflict and wed new forms of national identity to a state-building process that presumably will forestall future wars.[38]

In the former Yugoslavia, it was elite appeals to exclusivist national identities that enabled and exacerbated a conflict in a land where multiple religious communities had coexisted peacefully for forty years.[39] In particular, Serbian Communist Party leader Slobodan Milošević is often blamed for blending Serbian myths, legends, and poems suppressed under the previous Tito regime to create a sense of persecution among ethnic Serbs, to justify carving Bosnia up and joining ethnic Serb majority regions with the Republic of Serbia.[40] Histories of the war often point to Milošević's infamous rally in 1989, in which he drew on a specific interpretation of the 1389 Battle of Kosovo Polje to rally ethnic Serbs around the banner of Serb nationalism.[41] Later, General Ratko Mladić made a similar speech referencing the 1389 battle just days before the July 1995 attack on the town of Srebrenica.[42]

But as David MacDonald had demonstrated, politicians on all sides used ethnic ties as a rallying cry, stoking a sense of righteous victimization within their own group: "History was reinvented in the 1980s and 1990s, in order to paint each nation as a long-suffering victim of ancient, predatory enemies, bent on their destruction. . . . A Manichean morality pervaded both sides, in which the other was unequivocally evil, and the self could do no wrong."[43] Alija Izetbegović himself used nationalist rhetoric to cultivate a sense of besieged Muslim religious identity.[44]

Far from being an accurate or inevitable interpretation of historical reality, as Western commentators such as Robert Kaplan suggest, these narratives were skillfully constructed by politicians who stood to profit from an ethnic war. Ethnic groups on all sides competed for international sympathy as the biggest victims in the region, and in order to motivate troops to continue fighting, a sense of siege and difference was cultivated between people who had once thought of themselves as friends and neighbors.[45]

The effect of this, and of the war itself, has been to activate and cement ethnic identities among even urban populations in the former Yugoslavia in ways that were inconceivable before the conflict.[46] It is not that ethnoreligious identity was meaningless before the war.[47] To the contrary, as Helms explains, "National (ethnic) differences were maintained and even reinforced through census categories and carefully balanced power-sharing mechanisms that reserved positions in governing bodies for members of each . . . nationality."[48] But such bounded communities coexisted, with high degrees of intermarriage in some areas, because of social norms of tolerance and neighborliness. These were systematically reconstructed by nationalist politicians after Tito's death. For example, by 1994 polls showed that 89 percent of ethnic Serbs in Serbia viewed ethnic Serbs favorably, but 75 percent disliked Muslim Slavs and 74 percent disliked ethnic Croats.[49]

It is very typical for images of both women and children to figure prominently in nationalist imagery during and after wars, and it was no different in the Bosnian case.[50] Instigators of conflicts often use derisive imagery of "the enemy's women" to denigrate the male leaders of the enemy group.[51] In the years before the Serb crackdown on Kosovar Albanians, for example, Kosovar Albanian women were characterized as "baby factories" engaged in a strategy of overpopulating the province with Muslim children.[52] At the same time, the need to defend or protect women of one's own community becomes a rallying cry during war. This protection is justified through reference to women's role as symbols and bearers of national culture. Yet their perceived role as cultural symbols representing national territory is precisely what makes women vulnerable to violence, including rape, during conflict.

Women's rights are also often curtailed by their own "nations" during wars. In return for militarized protection against harm from "enemy" men, women are encouraged by their own governments to behave in such a way as to be worthy of "their" men's sacrifice and, through pro-natalist policies, to bear and sacrifice additional sons for the nation.[53] Thus narratives of patriotic motherhood become politicized during wars. While criticizing Albanian women for having too many children, Serbian nationalists glorified Serbian women as "mothers of the Serb nation," and they restricted access to abortion and contraceptives.[54] Because women's bodies are often imagined to be symbolic of ethnic territory, marriage across ethnic or national lines is frequently denounced during identity conflicts. Such narratives circumscribe the ability of women to participate in or, in particular, to speak out against armed conflicts.[55] In Croatia and Serbia, feminist peace activists were vilified as "witches" and "whores" and received death threats for betraying the nation by opposing the nationalist policies ostensibly designed for their own protection.[56]

As Elissa Helms points out, much of the literature on destructive nationalism in the former Yugoslavia has focused on Bosnian Serb and Croat nationalism, but Bosniak nationalism has been equally gendered during and after the war. Similar to his Serbian and Croatian counterparts, Alija Izetbegović called for women to embrace motherhood and traditional gender roles on behalf of the Bosniak nation. Testimonies of war rape have been appropriated in Bosniak postwar consciousness as attacks on the nation rather than on individual women, which explains why the state has allocated very few resources to support female survivors. And rape has been characterized by postwar discourse in the Federation as something that Serbs did to Bosniaks rather than a crime of men against women. As a result, these crimes became part of an essentialist postwar narrative about Serb psychology as inherently primitive and aggressive.[57] This narrative disregards the fact that Bosniak soldiers also committed rapes, that violence against women also occurs within ethnic communities, and that many Serbs risked their lives to oppose war and gender violence.[58]

Implicit but seldom theorized in gender analyses of nationalism is the role of children in particular, rather than women, as signifiers of national identity. If women's predominant role in wartime national culture becomes mothering sons for the military, it is ultimately their children's bodies on which the concept of the nation is etched. Women's reproduction is controlled because of the symbolic significance of the children they bring to life; if the women are bearers of national culture, the children represent national continuity itself. It is as much for this reason as because of international norms protecting innocent noncombatants that the targeting of children in armed conflict is often understood as symbolic of the worst atrocities. Some commentators associate genocide in particular with efforts to eradicate groups by targeting children, and women's immunity from attack has traditionally been couched in terms of their role as caretakers of children as much as through their presumed noncombatant status.[59]

As with women, however, this symbolic valorization of children is not always consistent with a framework that privileges all children's rights or needs. Alison Brysk highlights the tension between three sets of global processes in which children are framed alternatively as commodities, persons, or patrimonial subjects whose "primary social function is to reproduce identity." Brysk argues that children's role as "bearers of group identity for the family, ethnie or nation . . . trumps their rights or needs as individuals."[60]

This dynamic is very much borne out in the case of mixed-ethnic children in Bosnia, and children born of war to an even greater extent. Whereas before the war intermarriage was common and children of mixed backgrounds were proud symbols of Yugoslav multiethnic coexistence, ethnic identity in postwar Bosnia is far more stratified.[61] This has limited the ways in which it is legitimate for all people, including children, to imagine their religious, ethnic, and national identities.[62] Children whose emerging political consciousness does not coincide with dominant narratives of national belonging struggle to situate themselves comfortably vis-à-vis mechanisms of citizenship and identity.[63]

In the postwar period, pan-Islamists associated with President Izetbegović's Party of Democratic Action outspokenly opposed mixed marriages on the basis that Muslim women should instead bear children "for the nation." Mixed marriages were described as "frustrating" children and sending a "destructive message."[64] Young Bosniaks were encouraged to marry Muslims only, for the sake of their children and the Bosniak nation. Intermarriage was even characterized as "worse than rape" in one article.[65] As Helms explains, "The threat to the nation was clear: if Muslims, and especially women, did not marry within the fold, the nation would lose them and the children they produced."[66]

My interviews with different people in Bosnia-Herzegovina revealed three narratives about Bosnian identity that suffused questions about children born of war. A 2004 visit to a hospital in Sarajevo provides an illustrative example of these. Although I was seldom greeted with suspicion or hostility during fieldwork in Bosnia, one such incident occurred when I arrived to ask a social worker there about babies born to rape victims during the war.

The woman's first question to me reflected her disdain for foreigners' interest in such issues: "What does a rich American care about children here in

Bosnia?" I deflected this by explaining that I was not there as an American but as a mother, concerned with children everywhere. During the discussion that followed she spent some time recounting the trauma of her own experience working in the hospital during the war, the details of the sexual violence survived by the women in her care, and the horrific ways in which the "Serb aggressor" had used Muslim women's bodies for the campaign of genocide. Later, when my interpreter prompted her with questions about what had happened to the babies, she assured me that they had all been adopted "by the best Bosnian families" and were experiencing no troubles in the world. However, she could not point to any evidence to this effect.

This incident reflects some postwar social currents that have narrowed the space for articulating the comprehensive needs of children born of war through a human rights framework. First, babies conceived by Bosniak rape victims themselves continue to be constructed very much as symbols and reminders of Serb aggression against a seemingly unproblematic Bosniak community.[67] Conversations about *dijeca silovane žene* rarely include references to mixed-ethnic children resulting from rapes by Croat and Bosniak soldiers during the war; the narrative in the Federation, where I conducted interviews, is one of ethnic Serb rapes against Muslims.[68] Second, similar to feminist observations about the appropriation of women's suffering as symbolic of trauma to the nation, the referent point is often not the rights or experiences of the child but the violation of women's bodies and, through them, the purity of the Bosnian Muslim community. For example,

The children are part of the genocide because rape was an aspect of the genocide. Most women raped were Bosniak.

We, the Muslims, in a special way lived through that violence that was done unto our women. . . . Today the question is not resolved, the permanent status of these women and their children."

In some ways, this pattern is consistent with evidence gathered in other postconflict settings, such as postwar Germany, where women raped by the Red Army after the fall of Berlin were able to secure exceptions to Germany's anti-abortion law; or Bangladesh, where women were forced to abort or to surrender their babies for foreign adoption.[69] In such contexts, children born of wartime rape symbolized an assault on the national community, and their presence was minimized or pushed underground in the interest of building a coherent postwar order.

In Bosnia, despite a similar understanding of the symbolic character of the rapes, the policy response to the issue is significantly different and more progressive than either of the cases described earlier. Whereas women were encouraged to abort rape-related pregnancies in Germany, and Bengali babies were forcibly exported to India, Canada, and the United States for adoption, Bosnia-Herzegovinan authorities have adopted the opposite policy, identifying such children as Muslim and encouraging the Bosniak community to accept and raise them as Bosniaks, that is, Muslims. This was also reflected in the government's decision to refuse to allow any children orphaned by the war to be adopted out of the country.[70]

The emphasis in Bosnia on a religious policy response to the problems facing these children is exemplified by the statement of a representative of the State Commission for the Collection of Facts on War Crimes. When asked about children of the rapes, he referred immediately to the efforts made by the Islamic community in Bosnia to reintegrate Bosniak rape survivors. "We appealed to the Islamic community," he told me, "because 95 percent of rape victims were Bosnian Muslims, so stigma was very obvious, very much alive. Asked them [religious authorities] to explain to women how they should act. That it was not this sinful act but a result of aggression. . . . These children as well should be cared for and treated in the same way as any child. Sadly this has remained an unresolved area. It's very complex."

Compared with a policy of "putting babies in dustbins" documented by D'Costa in the Bangladesh case, such efforts appear strikingly focused on child rights. However, a number of factors suggest it is the consolidation of Bosniak identity as a response to aggression, not the children's rights per se, that is privileged by this approach. As Joana Daniel-Wrabetz writes, "The ban on international adoption . . . in accordance with religious principles laid down by the Muslim community, was motivated not only by the hope that relatives of these children would take care of them, but also by the desire to repopulate the country."[71]

Also, although the government is clearly invested in the idea that it took a liberal approach to the babies, it has not followed up with any efforts to ensure that they are accepted and protected in postwar Bosnia. Until very recently, rape survivors, including those with children, were not entitled to remuneration from the government. In addition, the space in which children's multiethnic origins can be discussed or rendered socially acceptable remains very limited. As one humanitarian worker told me, "Essentially this approach guarantees rights for children only as long as they are Muslims."

The emphasis on the Muslim upbringing of such children should be understood in the context of a wider effort to Islamicize the meaning of the war. Xavier Bougarel has written extensively on what he calls the "cult of the *šehidi*" (Muslim soldiers who died defending Bosnia).[72] The veneration of Bosniak soldiers as *Muslim* soldiers (a move not welcomed by all Bosniaks) is reflected in the proliferation of *šehid* cemeteries and the establishment by the Party of Democratic Action of special foundations for families of *šehidi*. To be a child who has lost a father during the war confers not only special social status but also potential financial benefits. However, there is no comparable status for female combatants or civilian women who were tortured or raped during the war. And the elevation of religious martyrs in war memory forecloses other forms of heroic narrative: The child of the Bosnian Serb who defended Sarajevo as a secular Serb or an Orthodox Christian fits uneasily with the new narrative of what it means to be Bosnian, as does the fatherless child or the child of mixed ethnic heritage.

Today, rape survivors who chose to raise their children face a dilemma of what to tell the child who asks about his or her father; war rape survivors face the additional challenge of fitting their story to the sociopolitical context in which the child is developing a social identity. A common strategy used by Bosniak rape survivors has been to tell their child that the father died as a *šehid*. Such women themselves often turned toward religion as a coping mechanism and because it increased the support of the community. Strategies included insisting on traditional Muslim naming ceremonies for the child, encouraging the child's identification with Islam, and making up stories of husbands killed in the war. However, documentation would be required to translate this story into economic benefits, and social workers involved with one such family expressed concern that this strategy would backfire when the child eventually learned the truth:

It needs to be considered that the child is informed about the extent of the crimes and types of genocide committed on the territory of Bosnia and Herzegovina as well as the fact of who are the perpetrators. Considering that she is now living as a "child of martyr" and that she has been accepted as such in the local setting where she currently lives, child reactions are unpredictable if she finds out the truth about her real origin. Will she be able to live with the knowledge of the truth? Will she be able to forgive her mother for the lies? What is she going to say to the people who know her? Are her friends still going to accept her? Will she take her own life?"

Nor has much consideration been given by the government to cases in which the child's best interests are simply not served by remaining in the custody of his or her traumatized birth mother. Instead, the establishment discourse promulgated by the government and Bosniak religious authorities assumes that the child belongs with the mother, the mother has a duty to raise the child, and the community should assist in making this happen, through marriage if possible.[73] Like the social worker's insistence that the children were doing "perfectly well" in the absence of any evidence to that effect, this narrative secures not children's well-being but a conception of the national community that situates Bosniaks as having overcome atrocity to set a moral example for other ethnic nations in the region. As Helms explains, "Calling for men to marry pregnant rape victims meant re-claiming both the women and the children for the nation."[74] Such a narrative makes it difficult for nationalist leaders to consider ways in which their own policies may have undermined the security of these children and their mothers.

Finally, Bosniak identity after the war has been deeply shaped by the experience of abandonment by the international community.[75] Contemporary efforts to follow up on the "products of barbarity" after the war can therefore seem belated and hypocritical to Bosnians. Women's activists rightly ask, "Where was the support for women during the war, when they might have been protected from rape in the first place?" That Bosnians were left to fend for themselves then buttresses arguments today that the sitting government knows best how to protect these babies and should not be questioned by outsiders.

This ties into a critique of international child rights discourse articulated by Vanessa Pupavac that the regime pathologizes the global South.[76] In response to what can be framed as paternalism, the postwar government can all too easily deflect criticisms of its current policy with respect to the babies. Such a government can also draw selectively on certain interpretations of the "best interests" principle to forestall arguments that active monitoring of such families should take place. Therefore, as I discuss in the next chapter, rights-oriented organizations in field situations must pick battles carefully with postwar governments, particularly those that can claim to have been the victim in the former conflict.

CONTESTED RIGHTS CLAIMS IN POSTWAR CIVIL SOCIETY

The second constraint on speaking out for children born of war is the ambivalence of local civil society organizations in Bosnia-Herzegovina. When I arrived in the region in 2004, it was difficult to find any local organizations involved in either children's or women's rights actively lobbying the Bosnian government to monitor or protect these children. One activist reported indifferently, "We are not very familiar with that subject because . . . we didn't have a place for that in our plan of action. So that is the reason we aren't very serious in that area." As I show in this section, the construction of rights for other groups—those who made it into local activists' plans of action—contributed to a general avoidance of this topic.

Before the war, NGOs as such did not exist in Bosnia-Herzegovina, partly because of the general lack of space for civil society and partly because the types of services typically associated with the nonprofit sector were already provided by the state. With the breakdown in central authority, humanitarian need, and influx of international aid dollars that characterized the conflict, both local and transnational NGOs proliferated during the war and in the aftermath. These groups, often competing with one another for contracts from international organizations as "implementing partners," came to constitute a parallel layer of governance in postconflict Bosnia. They worked in all areas of postconflict reconstruction, including democracy and human rights advocacy, legal assistance, refugee returns, microcredit, trauma counseling, health, education, vocational training, and conflict resolution. During the war, some NGOs were organized according to ethnic constituencies; after the war, as grants from the international community increasingly set the NGO agenda in Bosnia, a consociational "civil society" discourse was reflected in most NGO mission statements. However, as Walsh points out, "it's not clear that all groups share the same understanding of the term," and organizations vary greatly in the extent of their actual commitment to inclusiveness and integration.[77]

My interviews focused on three sectors of civil society I expected to have expertise that might be brought to bear on the issue of children born of war. One likely group of organizations seemed to be those that dealt with children in the aftermath of conflict. According to the 2002 International Council on Voluntary Associations *Directory of Humanitarian and Development Organizations in Bosnia-Herzegovina*, organizations categorized as "children and youth" were the fourth most numerous sectoral group, after those identified with "education and training" and "civil society." Twenty-two percent of all organizations in the directory listed "children and youth" among their concerns.

NGO workers I interviewed often referred to the "cult of the child" in Bosnia, and this is reflected in the nominal attention many organizations give to child protection or children's health and education, at least in their mission statements. It also reflects a traditional interest among donors with funding activities targeting war-affected children. Orphanages I visited in Sarajevo seemed extremely well endowed, full of happy, energetic, well-fed children. Some of these were run under state auspices, but many, such as SOS Kinderdorf, were projects of international NGOs. Other "children and youth" NGOs worked in areas such as family counseling, psychological support through organized activities, and health. For example, the International Children's Institute "helps children who have experienced traumatic events to develop coping skills through a comprehensive community program."[78] Few organizations specifically include promotion of children's rights in their mandate. One example is Amici Dei Bambini, an Italian NGO based in Sarajevo.

Many women's NGOs also encompass children in their mandate in order to appeal to a gendered donor narrative that situates women as peacemakers and mothers.[79] Women's groups have proliferated since the end of the war, partly because of an influx of donor funding for projects to assist women and children and partly because, as in many conflict zones, the experience of war created a space for women's mobilization. Because women were largely marginalized from postwar formal political institutions and the market economy, women's activities gravitated toward the NGO sector, where they benefited from donor funding, skill sets conducive to employment with transnationals, and the ability to claim aloofness from politics in the pejorative sense.

Yet it would be superficial to speak of a women's NGO sector in Bosnia-Herzegovina. As Walsh points out, 39 percent of Bosnian NGOs in 1999 included "women" in the sectoral areas where they work, but only 19 percent mention women's issues in their mission statements. Women-headed organizations do not necessarily target women's needs exclusively.[80] And of the organizations consisting primarily of women and working primarily to meet women's needs, significant rifts exist. Some organizations are motivated by nationalist concerns, organizing primarily for Croat or Bosniak women; others adopt a more transformative feminist discourse, seeking to include members from all ethnic groups and striving for solidarity on the basis of a common experience of marginalization by men and masculine politics.[81] Such groups also work in different sectoral areas, some focused on increasing women's political empowerment, some focused on economic interdependence for women (microcredit schemes and vocational training), some focused on assisting female returnees through material and psychological support, others doing legal advocacy for women.

But groups operating in the same sectoral area are not necessarily allies. For example, a significant number of women's organizations are focused on violence against women. Having cropped up during the war to address the needs of rape survivors, they have turned to the issues of domestic violence, trafficking, and prostitution in the postwar period. But they may compete with one another for available grants and access to the projects of wealthier international organizations, and they may openly criticize one another's methods or resent one another's relative success in the NGO hierarchy.

Beyond organizations with a particular mandate toward children's or women's issues, there are also a variety of organizations working with torture victims or concentration camp survivors or generally for human rights in Bosnia. For example, the Center for Torture Victims, founded in 1997, provides direct psychotherapeutic help to those tortured during the war. The Association of Concentration Camp Survivors provides more general support and works to document the stories of those who were tortured specifically in camps. As rape has been recognized internationally and locally as a form of torture, and trauma therapists regularly work with both male and female rape survivors, such organizations might be expected to have some case experience dealing with pregnancy as a sequela to rape.

Given this diversity and activity, and the widespread acknowledgement that rape and forced pregnancy were prevalent during the war, I found a surprising lack of awareness about or programming for the children of rape survivors. Comments I heard about such children generally fell outside the respondent's firsthand case experience, and I was rarely told of a specific organizational approach to dealing with the issue:

> A doctor had such a case. Woman gave it up for adoption; but it couldn't easily be adopted. . . . Basically such women said they did not feel any wish to give birth to these children. Other women had very late abortions.

More often, respondents I spoke to in women's, children's, or war survivors' NGOs claimed to have simply never considered this issue before. These findings were replicated in the survey conducted by the UNICEF research team in 2004. Although the available case data collected by the team suggest that some of these children are still in Bosnia and facing particular vulnerabilities, 55 percent of civil society respondents surveyed in that study claimed to know little or nothing about them. Only three organizations beyond those on the advisory board to the UNICEF project turned out to have direct case experience with such children or their mothers; two organizations had heard of such cases; four respondents claimed to recall stories of such cases from during the war.

There was also a "let well enough alone" tendency among some respondents to that survey, who seemed to argue that the shroud of silence surrounding the

issue served as a form of protection: "Most mothers are living in other countries or have given their children up for adoption, and in any case they don't
want to be confronted by these horrors again. They are only trying to forget
and lead normal lives."

I heard similar comments repeatedly in interviews I conducted. Civil society activists told me, when asked, that most such children had left Bosnia
and that therefore this was not a social issue for Bosnian government or civil
society to deal with; that the children had been adopted "into the best Bosnian
families" and were therefore doing fine; or that, regardless of where they ended
up, they were surely facing no specific social difficulties because their origins
had been hidden. However, these comments were interspersed with narratives
that contradicted the view that such children faced no problems:

> We know that these children are much loved, and as far as you know they
> don't have any problems, except that this one, the whole family gave up on
> her. Everybody gave up on her, her father, mother, brothers.

Organizations that acknowledge the existence of the children and the significance of the problems they face disagree over what to do about it. I documented a number of distinctive approaches to the issue of rape and children
born of war among these organizations, which generate fierce debates over
whether and how to protect these children. This range of disagreement has
contributed to the lack of a unified approach by civil society vis à vis the government and international donors (Figure 7.3).

FIGURE 7.3
Approaches to Children Born of War Among Bosnia-Herzegovina Civil Society Organizations

One cleavage among civil society organizations in Bosnia separates the groups that are interested in data gathering for the sake of "justice"—that is, gathering facts for the international tribunal—and those whose work is restorative, aiming to help victims regain their dignity in postwar society. It may seem that these two goals operate in tandem because there is so much lip service in transnational society about the importance of bringing perpetrators to justice in order to help victims heal. However, these two approaches can often conflict with one another. War crime trials require detailed attention to forensic evidence; closure for victims' families means collecting and commemorating the bones of the dead.[82] Punitive justice relies on victim testimonies; many victims prefer to remain anonymous and move on. I have heard the desire to bury the past excoriated as cowardice by activists who privilege bringing truth to light.

Here is how the distinction can play out with respect to specific cases of rape survivors and their children. Activists at two separate women's organizations in Sarajevo told me the story of a family in informal conversations, with wildly differing perspectives on what should be done. The case involved a woman who was raped after her husband was killed, and she gave birth. She had convinced the government and her in-laws that the child was her husband's, in order to obtain family acceptance and, importantly, veterans' benefits on the child's behalf, for which the child would otherwise be ineligible. An organization focusing on victims' rehabilitation spoke of the woman's strength and cleverness and suggested that in cases such as this, lies can be in the best interest of the child, although it was admitted that there could be problems when the child began digging deeper because the birthdates were all wrong. However, a representative of an organization focusing on collecting rape testimonies for the tribunal argued that this woman was acting immorally. I was told that by hiding the truth in order to get social benefits, the woman did a disservice to all the other rape victims whose voices were silenced by the perpetuation of the taboos surrounding war rape. When I asked about the impact on the woman's child of being exposed as a war baby, I was told that the child was not the issue. Rather, justice needed to be served and truth established.

Among civil society activists who adopt a victim-centered approach, there is further disagreement about whether the point of departure in considerations of forced pregnancy should be the child or the mother. Compare the different narratives in the following quotations:

We must build the awareness in our society, that children must be equal to any other children, because it not their fault, nothing is their fault, and normal life must be secured for them to be treated in the family, be treated normally in schools and in the world generally. These are children like any other child in the world.

If I chose this subject myself I would take a broader perspective. The rape is the key phenomenon; these children are simply byproducts.

Interestingly, the organizations with the most information on these children were women's NGOs rather than NGOs emphasizing child rights or human rights more generally. For example, Medica Zenica with its pro-feminist and holistic approach to psychotherapeutic help, has kept one of the only sets of detailed records on pregnancy sequelae, complete with follow-up and psychological analysis of the children born to their clients who survived rape.[83] Vive Žene, a Tuzla-based women's psychotherapeutic organization, frequently speaks to the press about these children and their mothers and has been closely monitoring clients who are raising children of rape. This may be because approaching the issue necessitates a gender-sensitive lens that women's groups are more likely to possess. It may also be because these groups are more likely to have been in touch with and informed by rape survivors.

However, mothers (rather than children) are the point of reference for women's groups. This has implications for the scope of attention such organizations can give to these children.[84] For example, the children about whom the women's NGOs knew the most were those kept by their mothers; those adopted or institutionalized were typically not being monitored by women's groups.[85] Programming by women's groups to assist mothers has no doubt had a positive effect on specific children, but alone it may not be adequate to address the rights of children born of war in general.[86] Indeed, several women's organizations surveyed by UNICEF in 2004 acknowledged the children existed but claimed that their mandate to protect their female clients' psychosocial health precluded asking sensitive questions about a rape survivor's children:

> I don't know. It is not focus of my association. Because some of them would like to be protected about that, they don't want to mention it, and I understand things they suffered. Because of that, they are members of my association, and I don't want to mention it.

> [We] never had to deal with these children, just with the mothers. . . . We would not initiate any kind of conversation about the rape or about the children, because the initiative has to come from the mother.

Children sadly are not our problem, and except for these donations that I mentioned, we don't have any kind of projects for the children—mostly for women.

Among activists who genuinely see the problems faced by the children as distinct from women's issues, there is some disagreement as to how to best assist the children. I heard wildly conflicting opinions about whether it was productive to treat these children as a distinct group for lobbying purposes or for programming. Similarly, there are differences of opinion as to whether silence can constitute an appropriate protection mechanism for children born of war. The desire to keep information secret is embraced by a number of humanitarian actors, sometimes out of a desire to protect women's interests, but often couched in terms of the child's best interests as well. Psychologist Catherine Bonnet writes, "It must be remembered that the women are protecting the babies from a stigma that would mark them for life."[87]

Yet some activists I spoke to disagreed:

The silence helps the neglect, the conspiracy, like it never happened. We must make it an open subject so that everybody can see that there is a place for [these children] in the world.

I think it would be good. Talking is better. The children need to know the truth, the sooner the better. I think it's a horrible disappointment if he would find out in the school, for instance.

Many of those I spoke to described the "problematique" of balancing a targeted approach to assessing the needs of these children with the desire to protect them from further discrimination:

This problem of secrecy, it's a very sensitive subject because of the patriarchal community. Mothers themselves: How much do they participate in this? It's not such an exposed problem in public life, and the question is even if you should expose them; that would mean discrimination. At the same time we have to recognize them as researchers, so that's the problematique.

There is a question of the collective awareness of this issue. Nothing is defined so as to protect these children. Maybe this is the reason why many of these women are forced to hide. We have been thinking about this a great deal: In what way can we help? We do help as much as we can, but we are struggling over this problematique. And there are a lot of cases.

A Tale of Two Films

I want to illustrate the complexity of perspectives on speaking out about this issue in Bosnian civil society through reference to two films about children born of war that were released in Bosnia-Herzegovina during the period of this study. As critical theorists of international relations have explained, film reflects and constructs sociopolitical currents within society and can reshape the space in which to articulate issues of social policy.[88] Indeed, each of these films originated in its director's desire to play an agenda-setting role: to challenge the taboo around acknowledging children of war rape and to provoke the government to pay closer attention to the needs of these children and their families. Both films also aroused controversy by triggering the nationalist issue.

Yet *Boy from a War Movie* and *Grbavica* differed markedly in the way they framed the issue, how they interacted with actual children of war in the production process, and how they were received both by civil society during the production phase and by popular society after their release. These differences exemplify the state of the debate in Bosnia in the early 1990s and say something about the available space for articulating these children's needs and vulnerabilities. And the kind of controversies both films provoked say a great deal about the way in which children's rights are construed in Bosnia-Herzegovina by the government, international actors, and local civil society.

The story of the first film begins in 1992.[89] Semsudin Gegić was working in postproduction on a war film titled *Remembering Goražde* when he came into contact with and came to know a refugee who had given birth as a result of rape—and subsequently her birth son's adoptive family in Goražde. Although he lost touch with her, he kept himself apprised of developments with the child's family, which was a frequent subject of media attention between 1993 and 2001. According to Gegić,

> Unfortunately after the war the same journalists began focusing on the boy. . . . I knew that one day all this sensational dimension of this story was going to affect the boy, that he would eventually find out that he is an adopted child, and the facts behind his origins. After the child found out who he was [at age 10], I felt obligated morally and professionally to help him and assist him. And that the fair way and honest way was to help the boy answer to all the people who wrote about him.

Gegić approached the Muhić family in 2003 about a possible documentary. At the time, he had imagined using a different actor, but as he became friends with Alen it became obvious to him that the film would be most powerful if Alen were willing to star in it himself. According to Alen, when Gegić broached the subject with him, he was delighted to participate:

> He said to me, would you want to be the actor? I said yeah, and then he made a suggestion to make such a movie and for me to be an actor in it. Of course I liked the idea, though I didn't know the movie would get so big and hit the United States. I was very glad to do it. It was part of my greatness.

When I spoke with Gegić at Flash Productions in Sarajevo about the film, just before its release at the Sarajevo Film Festival in August 2004, he characterized it as a humanitarian project, a form of activism aimed at shattering taboos, highlighting the impact of the crime of war rape on the children, generating much-needed social change, and empowering Alen himself:

> As far as being an activist, I am a minor activist. But as an artist with the weapon that I used for fighting against these things, and that's the cinema, I decided to try to defend this boy, the starring character of my movie and the boy's movie. This boy who is the representative of the thousands of other children born as a product of the war crimes. This film had to be made, to open the topic. To use the video production to protect Alen so that these silent and quiet provocations stop that are present in everyday life of these people. After this film, Alen can say to those people, you don't have a reason to provoke anymore because I know who I am, I am exactly like you.

Some civil society actors felt strongly otherwise about the film, about Gegić's motivations, and in general about the possibility of exposing children by allowing them to identify with their origins. The UNICEF program officer in the country was completely skeptical about the utility of focusing on such empowerment initiatives for children as a project that could garner UNICEF support. "I wouldn't go there," he said. "I can't see creating a support group for twelve-year-olds. Maybe when they are eighteen." For Medica Zenica, it was "maybe when they are thirty."

When Gegić approached Medica for support and advice about the film, Medica refused to become involved. Medica staff originally cited confidentiality concerns with respect to information the organization had about Alen's mother, but I was later told that a predominant reason was that "we feared for the child's psychological health." In interviews I conducted with Medica in 2004, Gegić was sometimes used as an example of a journalist with the wrong approach when my informants talked to me of their standards with respect to media ethics. One informant told me, "We think that he did a major damage psychologically to the child. He can't take as a voluntary consent of a child that is 10 years old because the child then doesn't know." Others in the film industry were also skeptical of Gegić's project. A feminist film director I interviewed said, "I really thought only a man could do this film, awful, awful to expose this kid. I thought it was a criminal act to show this little boy like that. He really made a promotion of himself, showing this little boy."

But some civil society advocates were more encouraged by his project. A respondent from the Association of Concentration Camp Survivors spoke approvingly of Gegić's efforts. A year after the film was released, even a psychologist working with Medica modified her position somewhat in hindsight. "I think it was maybe a very brave idea, from the director and this boy. Maybe it helped to open other children to ask, and to understand."

The film itself draws strongly on nationalist imagery. The flyer advertising the film reads, "This documentary is about the tragedy of the Bosnian people; it shows how beautiful and how cruel the Bosnian people and the Bosnian nature can be." Gegić's own thinking about the issue combines a concern for children with nationalist outrage at the use of gender-based violence during the war:

> The children weren't born because they were wanted. The children were born to hurt and to harm the women. To hurt and harm the nation. To harm and hurt the religion. And they didn't even think in their smallest percentage of their minds, they didn't think about what was going to happen to these children.

The film emphasizes the relationship between the child and his family and the child and his country's history using an interplay of documentary images, archives, interviews, dramatizations, traditional songs, and poetry. In my conversations with him, both in 2004 and again when I returned to the country in 2006, Gegić emphasized film as a form of narrative for developing political consciousness, both that of civil society and of Alen himself. Gegić stressed Alen's right to participate in shaping that narrative and, emphasizing Alen's role as co-creator of the film, described himself as a facilitator of the boy's freedom of expression: "Such children should be helped in whatever way they can construct for themselves. Alen with all his heart wanted to make the movie. . . . Alen, like most kids, believes in the power of film even more than adults."

Yet aspects of the production process contradict the idea that the film was primarily a way to empower Alen and that the child was a genuine collaborator on the project. For example, Alen never had control over the process or the screenplay, and he was asked to sign a form committing himself to complete the project before filming could begin, which meant signing away his right to withdraw participation. His father complained about the film process and the fact that Alen was not paid for his participation as an adult actor would have been:[90] "It was very tiring. For me, my wife, daughters, Alen. They would pick us up and take us around and tape. He'd come back cold, frozen, hungry." Nor did Alen have the opportunity to view and comment on the film before it was released publicly, and the director retained the monetary rights to the film.[91]

Still, Alen's conclusion about the experience was positive, contradicting the claims of civil society organizations that the film was purely a form of exploitation. When I spoke with Alen in 2006, I asked him whether he had second thoughts now that the film had been released. He answered,

> I'm happy because of the shooting of the movie. I wanted to do it for that [boy who bullied me] so that he could see that I'm brave, that I could fight for the truth.

As an advocacy exercise designed to reshape discourse and understanding around the needs of children born of war in Bosnia, *Boy from a War Movie* stands in stark contrast to a different film released the next year, *Grbavica* (Figure 7.4). Whereas the former is a short documentary involving a war child directly, *Grbavica* is a feature film based loosely on an actual family, telling the story of the everyday life of a rape survivor and her daughter in postwar Bosnia-Herzegovina, through the eyes of the mother.

The story centers on a family living in Grbavica, a Sarajevo neighborhood that was held by the Bosnian Serb Army during the war. The film begins with Esma's search for a night job; her day work as a seamstress doesn't earn enough money to pay for her daughter's field trip with her schoolmates, so she takes a waitress job in a nightclub that turns out to be a focal point for sex and arms trafficking. The film portrays the day-to-day struggles of single mothers in Bosnia to maintain a sense of dignity in the face of hardship, of the class and gender tensions in the postwar Bosnian economy, and of the long-term psychosocial impacts of wartime trauma as a nation moves on.

Although the mother, Esma, is the lead character, *Grbavica* revolves, in many respects, around the character of the daughter. Growing up without a

FIGURE 7.4
Billboard for the Film *Grbavica* Outside a Women's Clinic, Zenica,
Bosnia-Herzegovina, 2004

father in postwar Bosnia, she has been told that she is the child of a *šehid*—that
her father was killed in the war. But the reason Esma must earn extra money
to pay for her daughter's school trip is that she has no papers to prove this
relationship and thus qualify for state benefits. That the child of a *šehid* would
need to pay for a trip arouses suspicion among her classmates and introduces
tension into the mother–daughter relationship, sparking demands to know the
truth about the past. The film concludes shortly after the girl learns the truth,
and the viewer is left wondering about how she will cope with the resulting
changes in her identity.

Psychotherapists I spoke with in Bosnia-Herzegovina who have worked
with families similar to the one in the film have spoken in positive terms about
this film as a means to raise awareness and to open communication channels in
these families. A representative of Vive Žene put it this way: "I really think this
movie will influence the opening of many subjects; many secrets, actually that
exist within the families . . . a trigger for the secrets that they keep inside. They
will connect that, and it could have therapeutic effects."

Yet popular reviews of the film have interpreted it not primarily as a story
about child rights (to identity, to information, to social benefits, to nondiscrimination) but as a nationalist or feminist narrative. Like *Boy from a War Movie*,
Grbavica focuses on a Bosniak rape survivor whose rapist was ethnic Serb. It
thus tied into the conventional postwar ethnic narrative about the victims and
perpetrators of war crimes in the conflict. Consequently the film both appealed

to Bosniak nationalists in the region and offended Serbian nationalists.[92] In fact, the film was eventually banned in the Republika Srpska.[93]

The outspoken director, Jasmila Žbanić, has routinely expressed satisfaction at having aroused such controversy. But she is critical of nationalists on both sides of the aisle. Speaking after a film screening at the 2007 meeting of the International Association of Genocide Scholars in Sarajevo, Žbanić commented on her decision to cast a Serb actress in the leading role of Esma: "I didn't cast her because she was Serb, but because she was the best actress, but I'm so glad I did, because it provoked so many nationalists. Serbs who said she's a Muslim whore. Muslims who say, how can you let a Serb represent our women?"

For Žbanić, the rationale for the film was not nationalist but feminist. When I interviewed her before the release of the film, she described her reaction as a woman during the war, living close to the front lines, fearing for her safety; and later, after giving birth, her consciousness as a mother of the paradox that must be faced by women who had made the decision to raise their children after enduring rape. She was also aware of the lack of state support for rape survivors and wanted to do something.

And Žbanić wanted to reflect the genuine standpoint of the women whose lives she was portraying. She researched her topic by using feminist organizations such as Medica Zenica as an access point. Medica agreed to allow Žbanić access to one of its clients who was raising a child of rape. Žbanić spent time with this woman to try to understand her everyday life. "Not interviewing like you are, asking questions, but just talking, having coffee, waiting to see if the topic comes out. If not, I never asked. We only talked about it how it was for her, you know, when daughter comes to do homework, how she goes to doctor, what is her blood pressure, because she has a lot of problems—only today's life. But through that I find out much more about it than if I was asking her."

However, although the daughter's character is central to the film, Žbanić insists she did not attempt to tell the story from a child rights perspective. "The child is not the point of departure, but rather than mother," she told me. The explicit subordination of child rights to the frame of mothers' rights is also evident in the strategies and the policy responses the film triggered. Although Žbanić made careful efforts to interview and befriend rape survivors to gather insights and perspective for Esma's character development, the teen children of these women were never interviewed for the film.

Grbavica was widely viewed in Bosnia and won a number of awards, including the Golden Bear.[94] Its popularity triggered legislative changes in Bosnia-Herzegovina with respect to civilian war victims. In fact, its release was timed to do just this: "Our strategy was to try to change this law. In every interview we gave we promoted that the law should be changed; after a few months women were recognized as a civilian war victims."[95] Representatives of Medica Zenica I met with in 2006 spoke with great excitement about the film as an advocacy tool. But these important changes did not address the human rights of children born of war, instead focusing on their mothers. In particular, it was in 2006 that the government finally revised its civilian war victim legislation, permitting rape survivors to apply for benefits from the state—a small but quite important step forward for Bosnia's women.

Medica representatives argued that to the extent that the legislation had a positive impact, it was an impact for the children as well. The assumption was that what is good for women is positive and sufficient for their children. Medica cited UNICEF's consensus that this was the case as justification for this position. The frame took as its starting point the assumption that the children would have remained with their mothers. The legislation did nothing to address the needs of children such as Alen or the mental health of adoptive mothers such as Alen's mother, Advija, who had clearly also suffered various forms of psychosocial stress from the war.

Yet *Grbavica's* greater success and salience in postwar Bosnian society than *Boy from a War Movie* bespoke its fit with the dominant frame about war rape: the frame that situates the child as a consequence rather than a secondary victim of the crime, the frame that focuses on the crime of the father rather than the environment around the child as he or she grows up, and the frame that views the appropriate target of assistance and empowerment to be the mother rather than the young person.

In the end, Jasmila Žbanić would deny that her film was aimed to be political at all: "I purposely choose not to talk politics in film but to talk about humans. Because when we start talking about politics human beings are lost."[96] This reflects Helms's observations about the construction of politics in Bosnia-Herzegovina as a masculinized place devoid of feminine attributes such as caring, altruism, and integrity. She suggests that activists in Bosnia-Herzegovina often downplay the political nature of their efforts to secure rights and social benefits for women as a strategy of moral influence. Such players, she writes, "use the fact that they are women, mostly mothers and only work with other women to emphasize the humanitarian, apolitical and therefore noble character of their work."[97]

But agitation against those who have power in society to protect the less powerful is always a form of practical politics. Those with power include ministers and legislators, but also anyone with more wealth, greater status, or greater authority, be they men in the household or older, stronger children on the play-ground. If the feminist dictum that the personal is political holds true any-where, it holds true in the politics of making meaning out of children's identi-ties that seem to occupy a liminal status vis-à-vis a postwar state and society; it holds true in the politics of allocating resources, opportunities, and acceptance on the basis of those identities.

These two films highlight the great cleavages in Bosnian civil society about whether and how to pursue that agenda. They suggest great contestation over what the term "best interests of the child" means. They suggest that the needs of children are easily subsumed into the needs of women and of nations, and that this can affect the space for articulating their rights in complicated ways.

CONCLUSION

In her monograph on gender violence, Sally Engle Merry sums up the various challenges of translating international human rights law into local justice as follows:

> Human rights law is committed to setting universal standards . . . yet this . . . impedes adapting those standards to the local context; . . . human rights ideas are more readily adopted if they are packaged in familiar terms, but they are more transformative if they challenge existing assumptions about power and relationships. To have local impact, human rights ideas need to be framed in terms of local values and images, but in order to receive fund-ing . . . and international legitimacy, they have to be framed in terms of trans-national principles; the human rights system challenges states' authority over their citizens at the same time as it reinforces states' power.[98]

The politics of constructing children of war through a human rights frame in Bosnia-Herzegovina illustrates the various conundrums Merry describes. The most transformative messages about child rights in Bosnia-Herzegovina are the least palatable to local civil society because of the way in which concep-tions of Bosnian identity are wrapped up in narratives about atrocities during the war. They also challenge the paternalism inherent in transnational con-structions of the "best interests" principle. And efforts to look to the state as the provider of rights may fall short unless the Bosnian state is reformed to ensure the capacity to implement these rights.

More crucially, important tensions exist in Bosnia-Herzegovina today between those who view children's human rights through the liberal logic of international law and a logic that views children as the property of others, particularly their mothers, and those who view child rights through what Brysk calls a "patrimony" frame. According to Brysk, "the logic of patrimony views children as bearers of a group identity for the family, ethnie, or nation." For proponents of this view, Brysk argues, group identity "trumps [children's] rights or needs as individuals."[99]

Even those who genuinely focus on children in their own right disagree over how to draw the line between protection and empowerment. On one hand, a long list of affirmative rights is enumerated in international law. On the other hand, some of those rights work against one another in practice. Does the right to know one's family mean that an older war child who has learned of his or her origins has the right to contact his or her birth mother, even if she wants to remain anonymous? Is the best interest of the child protected by silence and denial about his or her biological origins, as some advocates argue, or by finding a positive space for acknowledging this past and nonetheless integrating the children as equal members of society?

The general consensus is that some public dialogue is needed but that individual children should not be exposed as poster children for the issue: "It is risky to work with these children, because you could mark them. Any help is good, but it should come from the shadow," said one NGO activist. But instead, the need to protect both the mothers and the children from stigma has been invoked by ministers, social workers, and orphanages to justify the systematic repression of information about children born of war in the former Yugoslavia.[100]

There is indeed a tension between a child's right to know his or her identity and a rape survivor's right to anonymity. But whether the child's best interests are indeed protected by lack of information is unclear, and the complexity of the issue increases as the child becomes older. At any rate, these disputes have complicated the ability to speak for the needs of Bosnia's children of war through a rights-based frame at all.

Much depends on whether one adopts a broad or narrow view of rights. Is the role of the state to prevent and punish violations of human rights only at the hands of the state? Or is its role to ensure an environment that prevents violations of rights by social actors as well? Advocates of a broad set of rights for children of war want to see specific measures taken to ensure a decent standard of living, equal opportunity, and social inclusion for these children.[101] But Michael Goodhart argues that this is perhaps expecting too much of the state.[102]

For Gegić, child rights include the right to articulate one's own political iden-tity, and it is the responsibility of adults to assist marginalized children in this enterprise. But other actors take a more measured view of this position.

This debate ties into a more fundamental dynamic in postwar Bosnia-Herzegovina: The meaning of *human rights* in general remains very closely tied to memories of the war itself. Bosnians are readier to talk about *human wrongs*—human rights violations by their wartime enemies—than about their human rights treatment today, at the hands of their new government. And as I show in chapter 8, this blaming greatly limited the political will of human rights organizations to frame new rights claims on behalf of such children.

8.

"A VERY COMPLICATED ISSUE"

Agenda Setting and Agenda Vetting in Transnational Advocacy Networks

I would be quite happy with an acceptance on the part of an organization like UNICEF . . . that war children would at least be mentioned as a group potentially with particular needs, under certain circumstances. At least keep it in the backs of your mind please that something like this exists, and that when you're in the field you can think about it. All things begin like this.

—Elna Johnsen, war child activist, Cologne, Germany, December 2006

IN THIS CHAPTER I return to the question asked in chapter 3: Why did most of the key organizations central to the advocacy network around children and armed conflict largely ignore children of rape between 1991, when news of stigma against war babies broke, and 2007? My answer is that the discourses identified in the preceding four chapters helped constitute a political context in which transnational gatekeepers—the organizations most associated with an issue area and whose adoption or nonadoption of an issue facilitates or impedes its dissemination through a network[1]—came to consider children born of war too sensitive and complicated for direct advocacy. In short, my data suggest that the previous discourse about a policy problem affects the thinking of transnational advocates when they consider whether and how to construct a new issue or category of concern, through at least three causal pathways.

First, the way an issue is constructed early on can shape human rights practitioners' perceptions about the nature of the issue, about which local populations must buy in for a transnational issue to be viewed as legitimate, and therefore about the likelihood that advocacy will actually result in rights-based practices. Second, existing narratives about an issue can condition transnational advocates' thinking as to where an issue belongs within an advocacy network. Third, such constructions can cue network players as to whose rights may conflict with the new population of concern.

Although it is unclear how generalizable these patterns are to other cases of global agenda setting, these dynamics functioned in tandem to complicate the emergence of attention to children born of war as a vulnerable category within powerful organizations at the center of the network around children and armed conflict during the period of my study. Drawing on focus group data and interviews, I describe each of these factors in detail in this chapter and suggest questions that established human rights organizations ask themselves as they consider claims pressed by advocates on the margins of networks. I then illustrate these factors at work in my understanding of decision making by the United Nations Children's Emergency Fund (UNICEF) about children born of war between 2004 and 2007, where I engaged in participant–observation work as it gradually shifted roles from bystander, to gatekeeper, to champion.

RIGHTS-BASED NONADVOCACY: WHO IS VULNERABLE? SAYS WHO? WILL ADVOCACY HELP?

Human rights activists are first and foremost committed to human rights.[2] Practitioners' assessment of the human rights value of advocacy for a particular group is an important enabling or constraining factor. Yet practitioners' understanding of what that means is shaped both by their organizational culture and by their perceptions of the political and cultural context surrounding the issue. These perceptions were very much shaped by earlier, more sensationalist constructions of children born of war.

Consider debates over how to construct advocacy language about children born of war. Adult war child activists themselves use the term *war children* or *war babies* to avoid associating themselves or other children with a particular event surrounding their conception and emphasizing instead the way they are treated afterward and society's perception that they are associated with the conflict in which they were conceived.[3] This language was created to emphasize the children rather than their mothers, who may have survived violence, and was broad enough to include children of consensual relationships, who may also be stigmatized because of assumptions about their fathers' relationship to a conflict. Moreover, it was an identity that they saw as intergenerational, not limited to the period of time when a person was a child.[4]

Yet practitioners in the mainstream human rights movement perceived this terminology to be problematic. Whereas some of the considerations were practical[5] or conceptual,[6] a great deal of discussion over how to refer to the children in advocacy documents, if at all, hinged on the moral frame being communicated and the need to avoid contributing to stigma, specifically as an antidote to earlier media language perceived to have been stigmatizing. For example, one informant told me that from UNICEF's perspective, any label to describe this group had to begin with *children*, not with *war*, to emphasize "that the child is a child first," an effort to reframe and diffuse the stigma rather than name it directly.[7] In sum, human rights advocates who recognized the importance of this issue held differing opinions on how to conceptualize it and what language to use in the service of a rights-based approach.

There were also normative disagreements within the network about whose perspective on such issues is most legitimate. Adults in local organizations operating in recent conflict zones were viewed by practitioners as more authentic voices on the subject than were actual war children themselves who had grown up in the aftermath of older wars. Similarly, many of my respondents embedded in operational agencies perceived outsider champions (intellectuals, donors, journalists, nonoperational nongovernment organizations [NGOs]) to often sensationalize issues and lack a field practitioner's understanding of context. As one respondent explained, in reference to a workshop organized by an academic interested in children born of war,

> We as practitioners in child protection have had a particularly difficult history, going back ten years, with interfacing with the academic world, . . . academics that become interested in our issues, our work. . . . Some of the earliest tense interactions around that were around psychologists getting interested in the issue but wanting to come into a field situation, interview kids about traumatic experiences, and fly away. . . . Unintended things can happen if we come in and focus on this subcategory of children in need of a protection response, creating stigma instead of helping it.

Human rights concerns were also raised by those who argued against naming the issue altogether. For many practitioners to whom I spoke, language was irrelevant because their position was that the children's best interests would not be served by treating them as a separate category. These respondents admitted that the stories one hears are "horrifying" but argued that classifying the babies as a specific group could do more harm than good, drawing jealousy from other groups, increasing stigma, and perhaps forcing an identity on a child unnecessarily.[8]

> If humanitarian organizations come in and specifically target women who have been impregnated it may create jealousy and tensions with the rest of the population.

Is there a danger of creating this kind of category that is the same danger that you see in so-called AIDS orphans, which . . . creates a backlash in the communities, adds additional stigma, you know, puts into place things that aren't necessarily required in order to address these issues?

These concerns are valid and have many parallels in humanitarian programming broadly. Yet, where political will exists, they are not so hard to overcome. The consequences of targeted rights-based programming—creating jealousies or backlash from other recipient groups, identifying people as victims, exacerbating stigma—exist around programming for many vulnerable populations in conflict zones whose cause is very much on the international agenda, including HIV and AIDS victims, rape survivors, and demobilized child soldiers. In many of these cases, such fallout is managed creatively by practitioners in the field while the problem is discussed openly at the global level and in planning and resource allocation. A focus group participant articulated such an approach:

What we found [when we undertook a sexual violence study] is that women actually were surprisingly open about what had happened to them and the phrase we kept hearing was, "Tell people what you want, but just don't tell my neighbors. Tell the people in the larger global context, but don't tell the people I live with."

Where political will is absent, however, the "do no harm" perspective can function as a rights-based rhetorical justification for avoiding human rights advocacy. Such pressures constitute obstacles that must be overcome through savvy framing choices if an issue is to take off in an advocacy network.

ISSUES AND ADVOCACY TURF: WHO OWNS THE PROBLEM?

Why might such political will be absent? Transnational advocates do not make agenda-setting decisions for normative reasons alone. In addition to rights-based concerns, the most powerful organizations in advocacy networks also consider a variety of practical factors when weighing the merits of mobilizing around a new global problem. For example, depending on their funding sources, they may need to distance themselves from issues antithetical to the interests of powerful donors.[9] Some are concerned with their "market share" in transnational civil society, which can affect organizational survival.[10] In order to retain their niche, they may reject issues that they consider too far afield of their mandate for inclusion.[11] Therefore, they may block issue proponents whose ideas are inconsistent with their principled beliefs.[12] As one informant told me, "It's the politics of the issue, it's the players. In the UN much of it is very strategic in trying to name your issue in a way that fits the political landscape."

At the individual level, transnational advocates are concerned not only with their organizational survival and mandate but also with their personal career trajectories. Concerns over professional reputation may make people unlikely to publicly support emergent issues unpopular among colleagues.[13] Beyond this, the intellectual history and professional training of specific career civil servants may predispose them to consider or reject specific principled and causal claims by issue entrepreneurs.[14] Those with legal training think very differently from those trained in social work. Those I interviewed in the children and armed conflict network tended to vary in their approach to the issue of children born of war depending on whether they saw the problem through lenses of international law, criminal justice, social science, programming, or advocacy.

The most important tactical constraints I observed in following this issue as it percolated through the child rights network centered on the relationship between child rights advocates and other issue advocates in transnational civil society. Although the human rights network is often referred to as a single community of ideas and practice, it encompasses numerous smaller issue networks, each with specific agendas, interests, and influence but often highly interdependent in terms of staffing, resources, and division of labor.[15] As Ann Mische argues, "important problems (as well as opportunities) are posed by the overlap between multiple types of ties and affiliations, and the diverse projects and practices actors bring with them into cross-network interactions."[16] The dynamics between these multiple issue networks can impede issue adoption in particular in at least three ways.

First, the assumption by one network that another network for which the issue is salient may or should already be addressing it can create a disincentive to expend resources on advocacy. Interviews I have collected demonstrate a tendency toward issue-related buck-passing: Respondents expressed the expectation that the issue of children born of war was being or probably ought to be addressed by some other set of actors in an adjacent issue area but not by organizations with a mandate similar to those in which the respondent was embedded:

> I will tell you that we are not really considering specific projects on this, and
> if anything were to be done it would be done in conjunction with the pro-

tection of the mothers, with these women who have been raped. And in this case, our "Women and War" project is definitely is in a better position to know, what do we do to protect the woman and the newborn child?

There is no data on this that I know of. . . . I never tried to compile those numbers. But you should talk to UNICEF; child protection organizations must keep track of these things.

I think it's a child rights issue, not a women's rights issue. I think we would get in if there were particular ways in which girls—you know, the enslavement or the stigma or whatever was being played out in relation to gender issues.

In short, no one in the human rights network owned this issue. Child protection advocates conceptualized it as a gender-based violence (GBV) issue, which they tended to leave to groups with gender expertise. Those groups or professionals focus on the care of women and girls, not infants per se. This compartmentalization of ideational space within transnational advocacy networks may account for inattention to some issues as practitioner attention is funneled toward certain problems and away from others. For example, in one interview the respondent repeatedly segued away from children born of war, linking the discussion instead to children who themselves were sexually exploited. This may account for the many times I was told by advocates and humanitarian practitioners that it was obvious "now that you mention it," that this was an important issue, but they simply hadn't considered it before.

Second, the necessity of strategic social construction across networks complicates the possibility of advocacy on issues where a suitable cross-network advocacy frame may be difficult to negotiate.[17] The most successful issues on the international agenda are the ones on which several partner networks can agree. For example, the "conflict resources" frame has brought together environmentalists and human security advocates, and the anti-landmine campaign forged connections between disarmament advocates and those concerned with human rights. But because different subnetworks take different sets of victims as their frame of reference, issues that span network agendas but invite conflicting understandings of a problem may cause tension between otherwise allied networks.

Thus, as Sidney Tarrow points out, coalitions, often described as a key factor in the success of advocacy networks, can actually complicate the development of advocacy frames.[18] Advocates may avoid potentially conflicting issues partly out of deference to their coalition partners. Because many transnational advocates occupy professional positions or affiliations in several related networks over the course of their career, potential issue adopters' identities may be bound up in identifying issues that avoid normative conflicts between the multiple communities in which they are embedded.[19] One interview respondent described the complexity of addressing an issue such as this one because it entails taking two different and in some ways competing perspectives:

> I don't know; it's complicated. . . . I've been sitting on that fence for the past year as a gender-based-violence officer in a child protection unit. . . . Child protection maybe still has a little controversy to it, but sexual violence has a lot, senior managers get uncomfortable when you tell them a 13 year old is raped . . . so they're very much inter-linked, very much multi-sectoral. . . . The children born of this population as well; you can't separate it out.

CONFLICTS OVER RIGHTS: WHAT'S AT STAKE IN ISSUE ADOPTION?

The third way in which the construction of issues matters is that it can create the impression of rights conflicts. These in turn can generate concerns over political tradeoffs in adopting a new issue on an advocacy agenda. The human rights of marginalized groups such as children or women often conflict with other rights, such as the cultural rights of groups or the rights of states. Although in principle human rights theorists would argue that the concept of rights should come down on the side of the individual, in practice the effective promotion of human welfare often entails an approach that respects the cultural practices of communities. As a result, liberal-minded Western activists often tread lightly around what they consider to be culturally sensitive issues. They also look askance at issues that may pose tradeoffs with concerns currently on their agenda.

The civilized international order is an order of states; therefore the discourse of state sovereignty remains a powerful normative constraint on discussions of the human rights of vulnerable groups such as children. It can also be a means of sidelining them. A representative of the Rwandan government gave a plenary lecture at the 2003 Biennial Conference of the International Association of Genocide Scholars. When I asked him about the government's approach to protecting children born of rapes during the genocide, he reiterated what was generally known: that many children were born, that most were being raised

by their mothers, and that both the mothers and children were deeply stigmatized by their extended families. But in answer to the question about whether
their specific vulnerabilities were being addressed, he said simply, "This is a
very complicated issue, and we have no magic answers. Thank you." Possibly,
the anticipation of such responses colors human rights advocates' willingness
to broach the issue with states, not only because NGOs operate in host countries only with governments' blessings but also because state sovereignty can
be a goal in itself for agencies assisting formerly victimized groups in securing
stable postconflict governance structures.

Additionally, given the general respect for local cultural particularities
among transnational advocates, there is a strong norm against advancing
cookie-cutter solutions when a problem may be context-specific. At the Children and War Impact Conference organized by the University of Alberta in
April 2004, I had the chance to ask Olara Ottunu, then the special representative to the UN secretary-general for children and armed conflict, about the
absence of advocacy around children born of war. He responded, "We have not
treated this group of children as a separate category. Their conditions are very,
very particular and vary a bit from one country to the other. . . . I couldn't give
you a general answer."[20]

There is also a powerful norm within global civil society, especially among
organizations with an operational presence in many countries, to respect cultural rights and ensure that advocacy and programming are conducted in a
respectful, culturally appropriate way. Participants in focus groups repeatedly stressed the importance of dealing with an issue such as this in a way
that "builds local capacities," "engages the local community," and is "culturally
appropriate." Rights-based arguments may be seen as more legitimate if they
originate among claimants themselves rather than well-intentioned outsiders
such as journalists, academics, or third-party activists.[21] For example, many
respondents in my dataset argued that the lack of such initiative on the part
of activists in conflict-affected countries meant that outsiders could simply be
blowing the issue of stigma against war babies out of proportion:

> 500,000 babies sounds like a big number, but when you think about it, the
> more people in this situation, the less taboo it becomes; you get a kind of
> critical mass, something that if pervasive is less stigmatizing.

> In most cultures, these children are actually more okay than we assume
> them to be as Westerners imagining the horror of begetting a child of rape.

It's happened to everyone, so there's not the automatic stigmatization we're assuming.

Although it may seem like a paradox in this case that local adult authorities would be required to speak on behalf of children stigmatized in their very societies in order to legitimize rights claims, this sort of deference is designed to maintain relations of respect with local societies on which the success of transnational efforts depends.[22] Earlier global advocacy campaigns, such as the campaign against child labor in Bangladesh, had been known to fail without a strong and supportive constituency in the country on whose behalf claims were pressed at the global level.[23] Thus, the emphasis on participatory programming and planning suggests a norm to allow recipient populations to speak for their own needs rather than imposing classifications on them based on outside understandings; it is also a practical measure to increase the success of advocacy efforts.

In such cases, the critical variable is transnational activists' understanding of who the affected population is and therefore who has a right to speak on their behalf. If the frame of reference is children born of war themselves, as with activists at the War and Children Identity Project, a participatory kind of advocacy would include identifying older children or young adults who could speak about their own experiences. But if the children are seen as extensions of the trauma inflicted on their mothers, then involving mothers in determining how to meet their needs is important. If they are viewed as a harm inflicted on entire war-affected communities, it matters very much whether leaders of those communities acknowledge their rights as a political issue.

If rights claims can conflict with state sovereignty, and if they can conflict with cultural rights, with specific local understandings, they can also conflict with human rights claims being pressed against other vulnerable groups.[24] In the case of children born of war, who are perceived to be consequences of rights violations against others, championing their human rights can also be perceived to come into tension with the human rights of female rape survivors, or women more generally. One of the key concerns raised by both child protection and gender-based violence specialists about advocating for children of rape is the potential that such an agenda might detract attention from the already limited programming and advocacy for survivors of sexual violence themselves:

How do you do sexual violence work without jeopardizing our other programs: communications, health, education. There's that thing that we run up against all the time, that challenge; it's huge, how to do that. And then the next layer of children is even harder. And we're not even doing the first part, getting to rape survivors for all their needs.

> The issue of sexual violence itself was under the carpet for a long time. Certainly we should look at the children too, that's a good point. Much more information on this issue is required, . . . but right now we're still fighting to get recognition for rape survivors, let alone their babies.

In short, championing the human rights of children in such cases has sometimes been perceived to come into tension with another significant goal of many transnational advocacy organizations: gender empowerment. In addition to worrying that programming for children born of war would draw attention away from sexual violence response, some practitioners were concerned that the issue did not lend itself to finger pointing at a politically acceptable perpetrator because the babies generally suffered at the hands of women and local communities who were themselves victims of crimes.

A particularly obvious example is some practitioners' understanding of infanticide as a human rights problem. Heated disagreements broke out in several focus group settings about whether to conceptualize infanticide as a crime against an infant or against the mother herself, insofar as the situation "forced her" to kill her baby, or whether to consider it criminal at all because in some ways this constituted her best avenue to exercise self-determination over her circumstances. "It is absolutely vital," said one interview respondent, "that we not treat [rape survivors who kill their infants] as cold-blooded murderers"; a participant in a focus group argued that "in cases where the woman has no other options, I have to say that I don't think infanticide is an impermissible alternative." Such an understanding of the tradeoffs can be traced to earlier constructions of genocidal rape: As noted in chapter 2, one renowned author on forced pregnancy writing in 1996 also argued that infanticide against such babies by their mothers "might even be considered healthy."[25] According to another interviewee,

> With trafficking questions you can follow them, blame the evil traffickers; here, you're delving into a much more intimate and personal realm, and there are those fine lines, and no one knows what to do with them.

This is very similar to the sentiment I heard from civil society NGOs in Bosnia-Herzegovina that struggled with the question of how to draw attention to war babies' rights without pointing the finger implicitly at abusive mothers who themselves are victims:

There are cases where the mother kills her children. Shocked from the trauma, she feels this child is not a product of love but a product of hate. She fears raising a monster. Of course, this should also be punished by law; it is wrong. But this category of women is difficult to deal with because this is a crime after a crime.

As they gauge the political risks to existing rights claims, advocates' understandings are shaped greatly by their estimate of preexisting, collective understandings about victimhood and blame. These tensions with existing transnational norms and normative commitments, and the transaction costs associated with negotiating them, created barriers to issue adoption by advocacy organizations, encouraging activists to approach children born of war, if at all, as if their needs could be addressed without formal attention to them as a vulnerable population.

To sum up, my analysis suggests that these three factors—rights-based concerns, bureaucratic politics within networks, and conflicts over the rights of governments, minority groups, and women—affected the receptivity of central organizations in the child rights network to claims on behalf of children born of war and that all these factors were shaped by earlier constructions of the issue and the manner in which they remained salient in the discourses of issue entrepreneurs, established organizations, and conflict-affected societies themselves. In the final section of this chapter, I demonstrate how these factors played out in a specific child rights organization's evolving engagement with this issue.

CASE STUDY: THE POLITICS OF ISSUE CONSTRUCTION AT UNICEF

Of all international organizations that one might expect to have taken a serious interest in children born of war in the 1990s, UNICEF seems to be a good candidate. Originally established as an emergency relief and development organization, it has increasingly come to serve as a focal point in international society for the promotion of child rights.[26] The organization also has a history of identifying categories of children in exceptionally difficult circumstances, including child soldiers, refugee children, girls, disabled children, or minority children.[27] Moreover, UNICEF's particular focus on mothers and maternal health as a factor in securing a protective environment for children seems to predispose the organization to concerns such as these.[28]

Yet like other child protection organizations dealing with children and war, until very recently UNICEF paid little direct attention to babies born as a result of wartime sexual violence. When it began to consider its responsibility to do so in 2004 in the context of Bosnia, that country office initially backed off out of concerns over the political sensitivity of the issue. By 2008, however, UNICEF headquarters had gradually developed a consensus that allowed it to launch the first fact-finding study of children born of sexual violence. This illustrative case study tracks UNICEF's developing approach to this issue and demonstrates how the organization was constrained by the factors described earlier in this chapter and how its understanding of this issue was influenced by the political environment created by preexisting narratives about children born of war.

From the beginning of my project, I sought out insight from UNICEF officials, both in Bosnia-Herzegovina and at headquarters in New York, as to what the organization had done to meet the needs of children born to rape survivors and why. One of my earliest interviews on my first field trip to Bosnia was with Jens Matthes, the child protection officer at the Sarajevo-based UNICEF field office in the country. Matthes's position involved implementing various service delivery and advocacy projects aimed at strengthening the capacity of civil society and the government to provide "an environment of protection" for children; protection from trafficking, mine awareness education, and interactions with the juvenile justice system were some of the concrete initiatives he mentioned. When Matthes explained to me, like many other international officials I spoke to in Bosnia, that his organization "hasn't addressed these children [born of war] directly," I asked him to clarify this point. In response, he told me, "I'm trying hard not to say it's not part of UNICEF's mandate, because it *would* be. It's that it's not come up."

Matthes's comment highlights the divergence between what an international organization aims to do—its mandate—and what is operationally possible and therefore attempted.[29] As Matthes explained it, UNICEF is necessarily selective in the way it categorizes problems afflicting children. The organization is concerned not with specific children but with broad problems, such as children without parental care, and like other service organizations, it tends to reflect the concerns raised by the local societies in which it works: "When we did surveys trying to understand the dimensions of [children without parental care], no one raised the issue of this category of children to us, so we didn't address it directly." Did UNICEF ever ask specific questions about such babies in its surveys? "No." He described the research assumptions involved in just listening to how the local population presented issues and admitted that certain issues, such as sexual abuse of children in institutions, would not jump to the surface until there developed a critical mass of attention. "And that's never appeared to be the case with respect to babies born of rape," he stated.

Matthes explained to me the importance of local NGOs pushing for an issue first, both because of the value UNICEF places on local needs and because it delegates service provision through local NGO partners. A problem must be well defined and well researched in advance in order for it to draw attention from the UN, he argued. "If you came up with a report, for example, where you had thirty cases of such children with various problems, of course UNICEF would look at it very seriously," Matthes stated. For UNICEF, concern over an issue must be grounded in the local population; otherwise, it would not be politically palatable.

However, later the same week, while I was still in Sarajevo, Matthes surprised me by calling my cell phone. He had received an e-mail from Joana Daniel, the researcher who had visited from Vienna the previous year, also asking questions about Bosnia's children of war for her master's thesis. Daniel had completed her degree and was looking for summer internships with international organizations. Matthes told me he had found the discussions with both Daniel and me compelling. His idea was to hire her and put her to work doing a preliminary fact-finding study under UNICEF auspices. Because he had little time to focus on it himself, he hoped I would be willing to design the initial study, parallel to my book project, and work collaboratively with Daniel to supervise the project. In return, UNICEF would provide the funding and institutional backing for the project and allow me to use any data that resulted from the project.[30]

Guided by Matthes's entrepreneurship, the study was grounded in a child protection approach. At the first meeting of the research team in June 2004, he described his vision for the project: "I feel UNICEF as an organization needs to have an understanding of this issue. The mere fact that no one talks about it and you don't hear cases doesn't mean it doesn't exist. And I think we owe it to the human rights of the victims and the children to see if there is a need to advocate on their behalf."[31]

Over the summer of 2004, while I drafted the desk review back in Pittsburgh, Joana Daniel and my former interpreter, Jasna Balorda, collected thirty additional interviews with civil society organizations in the Federation and in the Republika Srpska. In return for funding from UNICEF, several local organizations also became involved as an advisory committee to the project, training the research team, filling out anonymous questionnaires regarding their clients who had given birth to children as a result of rape, and providing input on methodology and feedback on drafts. The draft report concluded that there was evidence that "such children have specific protection needs in violently divided societies due to social attitudes regarding their biological origins."[32]

However, well before the report was finalized, Jens Matthes left Bosnia-Herzegovina. His replacement, Kerry Neal, was initially also quite enthusiastic about the study, despite never being quite sure how it had materialized or how to justify it to the Bosnian authorities. Neal oversaw the data collection and over the following year worked to edit several drafts of the report, which he imagined would be published by UNICEF and disseminated to stakeholders in Bosnia-Herzegovina to begin a dialogue with authorities about how best to meet these children's needs. But by early autumn of 2005, Neal had concluded, under pressure from local NGOs and government ministries, that the report should not be released publicly.[33]

This anecdote illustrates the process by which children born of war remained invisible as a subject of human rights concern in their own right in Bosnia-Herzegovina and, by extension, the political difficulties associated with raising them as a population of concern at the global level. First of all, like the government officials cited in chapter 7, international civil servants ostensibly concerned with child protection had formerly occupied a bystander role; they had simply never thought about children born of war before being asked to justify their inattention to them. As I have argued, this is related to the way in which children's rights have been conceived and distinguished from gender issues in global civil society and to the fact that children born of sexual violence were originally constructed as a consequence of sexual violence rather than as children with specific protection needs.

But it was not simply a matter of someone "raising the issue," as both Matthes and the ombudsman originally suggested. Even when the issue was raised, the loaded nature of the national and transnational political context posed obstacles to addressing these children's particular vulnerabilities through conventional human rights mechanisms such as fact finding, advocacy, and service provision. This caused UNICEF to exercise what Clifford Bob would describe as a gatekeeping role for a period, unready to publicly take a position on the issue until it had overcome many of these obstacles. Only when it had carefully developed a consensus about a frame and identified a country context conducive to gathering objective data was UNICEF prepared to assume the role of an issue champion and openly publicize its position on children born of war.

"TOO CONTROVERSIAL": RESISTANCE BY ETHNIC VICTIMS IN BOSNIA-HERZEGOVINA

One of the key constraints UNICEF faced when considering its organizational approach to children of war was the reaction of the governments and civil society organizations in conflict-affected localities where the organization maintains field offices.[34] In Bosnia-Herzegovina, digging into the vulnerabilities of such children through a child rights lens meant walking through a minefield of competing agendas and constructions, both by nationalists and by women's groups.

Because UN agencies operate in postconflict zones only with the permission of the government, and because all human rights claims are ultimately claims against states, UNICEF relies on political leaders for access and legitimation and seeks negotiation and consensus with officials regarding human rights problems it addresses within a country. The approach of the organization is one of partnership and assistance, not confrontation.[35]

Yet in Bosnia-Herzegovina, as in many postconflict zones, government cooperation could not be counted on in this area, because an official policy of denial seemed to be in place with respect to children born of wartime rape. This pattern, demonstrated in chapter 7, was confirmed when UNICEF began its survey in summer of 2004. The field team for the project initially attempted to survey government officials across the Muslim-Croat Federation and in the Republika Srpska. They found them largely reluctant to discuss the issue and found no evidence that the government was addressing the children's vulnerabilities. At the same time, they found an attitude of complacency by government officials to compensate for their lack of monitoring: According to the research team's field notes, the ombudsman for children's rights in Mostar "guaranteed that there are no such children." Thirty percent of respondents at the government-run Centers for Social Work and orphanages were also generally reluctant to cooperate with the UNICEF research team: The field team reported such respondents acting "surprised" and "irritated." The research team's field notes contained uncomfortable instances of government ministers who literally threw them out of their offices. Ultimately, UNICEF dropped government officials from the survey sample because of the resistance the organization encountered.

Instead, the report relied on interview data from civil society organizations. But while the draft report was under review in 2005, the Sarajevo field office ran into additional resistance from the political leaders. Several government ministries objected resoundingly to the findings of the draft, which was leaked to the local media and later distributed to the government in the summer of 2005 while still under revision. The deputy minister for human rights and refugees went on the record opposing publication of any material critical of the government's inaction toward children born of war.[36]

In meetings with government leaders, Neal came under pressure to reframe the report's findings to suit different political perspectives, each filtered through a lens of ethnic grievances. Writing to me in 2005, he underscored how nationalist discourse played into the government's response to the report: Representatives of the Federation were concerned by mention that rapes occurred on all sides; the Representative from the Republika Srpska wanted to see this section elaborated further. According to Neal, neither side seemed that focused on the children.

Pressure to reframe the findings of the report to fit an ethnic narrative came from civil society organizations as well. As noted earlier, Jens Matthes had originally organized the study as a collaboration between UNICEF and several "implementing partners" in Bosnia-Herzegovina, to benefit from local expertise and also to promote ownership by civil society. The advisory committee for the project included Medica Zenica, the Association for Concentration Camp Survivors, and the Institute for Research on Crimes Against Humanity and International Law at University of Sarajevo. These groups, all from the Muslim-Croat Federation, were expected to meet twice with UNICEF, provide input at the start of the project, and comment on a draft of the report.

The assistance of organizations with dissimilar goals and mandates—a prisoners' organization, a women's organization, and a research institute—made the analytical process more balanced, careful, and beholden to local perspectives.[37] The advisory committee urged a variety of changes in the methods, informed consent procedures, and recommendations. But they also argued for changes in the framing of the document. As early as the first meeting, some members of the committee argued, among other things, that the goal of the report should be to further highlight the violations of human rights during the war, in the context of punishing war crimes.

When the draft report was disseminated to the committee for comment the next year, feedback on the methods, findings, and recommendations were generally positive. However, several members of the committee expressed great concern over the absence of ethnic finger pointing in the draft report. Representatives from Medica Zenica felt very strongly that, consistent with the findings of the international criminal tribunal, it should be emphasized that the Bosnian Serb Army had raped in a systematic way, whereas rapes (and impregnations) by the other armed groups had been incidental to the war—a question sidestepped by the draft in an effort to focus attention on the situation of the children *after* the conflict. In a follow-up interview after the end of the project, one of my contacts at Medica underscored this point, saying that she felt angry when she saw the background section of the document and that the ethnic character of the rapes—the perpetrators and the victims—must be emphasized in the report.

The Institute for Research on Crimes Against Humanity and International Law was even more forceful in its comments to this effect. In its feedback to Kerry Neal on the draft, the representative of the institute wrote,

> Rape is a crime. It should be the primary statement of this study. Rights and status of the children forcefully conceived derive from this issue. . . . Given the fact that the rapes were ethnically-motivated, there is a need to clearly state which nation in B&H was a victim of this type of crime. . . . The rapes were used as genocide against the Bosniaks.[38]

Neal considered a variety of options for dealing with such objections without watering down the child rights message of the report. These included editing of portions of the report and permitting members of the government in both entities to issue their own specific forewords as part of the document. But ultimately, under pressure from the government on one hand and civil society groups on the other, UNICEF Bosnia-Herzegovina decided the report should remain an internal document only. As Neal told me in a later interview, "It became clear to me that there would never be a report on this subject that would be politically acceptable on all sides."

"KEEPING BOTH MOTHER AND CHILD HUMAN": COUNTERFRAMING BY GBV RESPONSE ADVOCATES

Kerry Neal's decision not to launch the report reflected not only his understanding of the domestic political climate in Bosnia but also his evolving convictions about the nature of the issue itself. Over time, Neal's perspective on the value of the project as a child rights study had shifted: He had come to believe that the proper focus of advocacy attention with respect to this issue was female victims of rape, not their children: "I originally thought it was a child rights issue, but my position on that has changed completely. . . . If I could do this over again I would do it from a women's rights perspective."

This position resonated with colleagues at UNICEF headquarters in New York, including those who were simultaneously considering the organization's responsibility to children born of war at a global level. A November 2005 meeting to conceptualize UNICEF's response to the issue had been spearheaded collaboratively by UNICEF staffers in New York's Child Protection Division and at the Innocenti Center in Florence, some of whom had helped get language about children born of war into the original Machel review document and who had been gradually pushing from within the organization to generate greater attention to babies in the context of the UN's response to GBV and sexual exploitation.

UNICEF's interest in this issue during 2004 and 2005 was also influenced by two external events. First, headquarters began receiving calls from field offices in Sudan about best practices for protecting babies born of what was widely considered genocidal rape in Darfur. Second, questions were raised within the UN system during this period about UN responsibility to children born as a result of rape or sexual exploitation of local women by UN peacekeepers, particularly in West Africa and the Democratic Republic of Congo.[39]

The efforts in Bosnia and the lessons learned from the failed pilot study there also drew attention to the absence of accurate data needed for an informed, evidence-based response and to the challenges of collecting it. By mid-2005, the idea was being floated that UNICEF New York should spearhead the multicountry study called for in the Machel document, one that would overcome some of the strategic and methodological limitations of the Bosnia-Herzegovina report. Such a study, it was understood, would have to be undertaken by finding local partners to assist fully in specific country studies, negotiating the support of the local government in advance, interviewing families directly rather than relying on testimony from civil society organizations, and involving significant consensus and buy-in from other humanitarian organizations.

The 2005 meeting in New York was designed in particular to develop this type of consensus among colleagues throughout the child protection network. One point of discussion at the meeting was whether the focus of fact finding or programming should be on the entire population of such children or on assistance to those who were kept by their mothers. A consensus emerged by the end of the meeting that GBV programming for female victims was the appropriate starting point for a response to these babies. This was expressed in the outcome document from the meeting: "The most effective way to provide assistance and care to children born as a result of rape is by supporting their mothers—the girls and women targeted for violence—and supporting family and community-based recovery and healing."[40]

Such a frame was quite different from that sought by war children themselves, including those at the War and Children Identity Project and their collaborators in Cologne, Germany. Academics writing on the issue, too, were concerned about subsuming the child protection dimensions of this issue under GBV response rather than mainstreaming them into child protection more broadly, a move that would have focused not on the circumstances of their conception but on their treatment in the aftermath of conflict and involved linking their particular vulnerabilities to those of other categories of children experiencing social exclusion, stigma, discrimination, neglect, or health risks.[41] Of course, it was recognized that effective responses to survivors of wartime sexual violence would do much to reduce the incidence of attachment difficulties these children might face with their birth mothers, the incidence of stigma from the women's families, and socioeconomic deprivation; and for activists such as those at the War and Children Identity Project, initiatives to assist birth mothers were seen as vital in their own right. However, programming aimed at birth mothers, though an important step, would not by itself address the range of rights violations experienced by the children, such as the right of older war children to information about their identities. Nor would a trickle-down approach to meeting mothers' needs be likely to reach abandoned, adopted, or institutionalized children. Moreover, it was feared, a mother-centered approach to protecting these babies' rights might forestall an effective response in cases where it was the traumatized mother who perpetrated abuse, neglect, or infanticide against the child or contributed to the stigma against the child through such actions as discriminatory naming.[42]

Why did UNICEF, an organization devoted to child rights, choose to emphasize the mother–child relationship in their programming for a category of child for whom that very relationship was in many cases problematic? Part of this was driven by UNICEF's organizational culture. The perception that one can adequately protect babies by meeting mothers' needs stems in part from the particular configuration of gender discourse prevalent at UNICEF. In Maggie Black's words, "From the moment of its birth, UNICEF accepted as a matter of course that the well-being of children was inseparable from the well-being of those in whose wombs they were conceived."[43] UNICEF staffers often expressed this association of children's needs with the needs of mothers when asked to consider the rights of children born of war independently from the victimization that had befallen their mothers:[44]

> These two perspectives have to be complementary. . . . There's no way you can take child and mother and separate them out, it has to be comprehensive.

UNICEF is quite sensitive about these things . . . to give emphasis, presence to the woman, the mother and child, and find some kind of terminology that keeps both of them human. . . . We'll tie ourselves in knots sometimes trying to find the right terminology.

Moreover, UNICEF officials sympathetic to the idea of addressing children born of war as a specific group were critically aware of the importance of framing the issue in such a way as to build consensus between those working on infant health and those dealing with GBV. "We need to find language that brings the NGOs and UN agencies together or we won't be successful," one staffer told me at an early stage of the process. Although at UNICEF sexual violence is treated as a component of child protection, within the broader humanitarian network these tend to be seen as two distinct issue clusters, and children born of rape tend to be conceptualized as falling in the GBV cluster. For example, focus groups with humanitarian practitioners in 2004 and 2005 found that far more participants connected these babies' needs with the umbrella issue of sexual violence than with the umbrella issue of child protection.[45] The position that these issues were distinct and that children of rape definitely fit one better than the other was articulated often by those to whom I spoke during my research. For example, commenting on the original idea of a *Where Are the Babies?* study in the Machel review document, one practitioner said,

The language was part of the chapter on sexual violence, not on child protection. It was always about women and girls. . . . Let's not forget the whole issue arose out of the violation to women's rights that is caused by sexual violence and exploitation.

Incorporating a concern for the sequelae of rape-related pregnancy into existing programming for survivors of wartime sexual violence, rather than thinking about children born of war as a broad category with needs distinct from those of sexual violence survivors, was more conducive to coalition building for two additional reasons. First, it resolved the concerns that women's programming would be obfuscated by a focus only on their babies. By situating children born of war as a consequence and subset of the problem of GBV, advocacy on their behalf stood to strengthen and mainstream, rather than isolate, GBV programming within the child rights sector. As one official at headquarters argued,

We shouldn't subsume gender-based violence under child protection because you know what happens when you gender-mainstream; gender gets completely watered down. UNICEF has an opportunity to rise to this in the context of gender-based violence, by emphasizing the maternal–child implications of gender-based violence.

Additionally, linking the issue to work with survivors helped overcome some practitioners' hesitancy to advocate directly for the children. Although many practitioners continued to argue that silence might be the most effective protection mechanism for small children, few would make this argument with respect to survivors of sexual violence themselves. By linking the issue to GBV response, UNICEF could engage in fact finding that was both ethical and participatory by including data from interviews with survivors raising their children. It was perceived that the same would not have been possible if the frame of reference were the entire population of children in a particular country, many of whom would be young and difficult to trace if they were no longer in the custody of their mothers.

But this frame was principled as well as tactical. For some issue entrepreneurs at UNICEF, this move was less about subsuming children born of war under sexual violence work than about promoting a frame in which the needs of both groups were reconstituted as complementary. Thus, one way to interpret this frame was a process of strategic social construction by people in a brokerage role at the interstices of both child protection and GBV response communities. One staffer explained it this way:

> We need to do it in the context of both gender-based violence and child protection. I'm glad to see there is political momentum to do more for gender-based violence in general as well for children born as a result.

Although the resulting framework may have been narrower than that sought by adult war children themselves, this strategy enabled UNICEF to move forward with fact finding while remaining within its mandate and obtaining the support of local actors in the country context where it began work. A study on children born of sexual violence and their mothers in the Democratic Republic of the Congo was eventually launched as a result of the 2005 meeting, one that used mothers' testimonies about their children as a primary source of data and involved collaboration with a local partner, the Pole Institute. In this way, UNICEF continues to pursue a strategy to balance the desire to bring some attention to the issue of the children with its organizational need to situate such work in the context of assistance to sexual violence survivors and acknowledgment of their needs.

Although it represents a first step rather than a comprehensive approach, UNICEF is making a genuine effort to articulate stigma as a child protection issue without compromising organizational priorities, to gather and present data so as to both achieve buy-in from local societies where they have a field presence and respond to the counterargument that such concerns are overblown, and to frame the issue so as to promote attention to children of rape without compromising the rights of survivors. However, it is an effort shaped by the politics of transnational coalition building and agenda setting, in a context where earlier narratives created preconceptions about the issue and the children's needs; and it is an effort that, because of these very constraints, was not previously considered politically possible or wise.

Even recently, it has been a slow, tenuous, and politically difficult task. It has taken nearly four years since the original 2005 meeting for a report on a single country to be funded, carried out, and drafted; at the time of this writing, it has not yet been released. It remains to be seen whether UNICEF's report on the Democratic Republic of the Congo, when released publicly, will produce a fundamental shift in UNICEF's programming and advocacy priorities for children and armed conflict and, more importantly, whether its release will increase awareness in the network on war-affected children.

CONCLUSIONS

My interactions with the transnational child rights network over the past five years and my observations of how this issue percolated haltingly through UNICEF's organizational culture led me to three initial conclusions. First, not all human rights problems are easily viewed by human rights gatekeepers as being best solvable through a rights-based approach. Some advocates genuinely worry that the best interests of these children cannot be served by global advocacy. Others worry that pursuing one rights claim will entail undesirable tradeoffs with other agendas.

Second, when people in leading human rights organizations have these concerns (or have other reasons for wanting to avoid taking a public stance on an issue), human rights claims are particularly easy to dismiss if the issue is promoted by "champions" rather than rights claimants themselves. This dynamic leaves marginalized groups such as children particularly disadvantaged when it comes to having their needs represented in the language of human rights in transnational civil society. Yet understandings of the relevant claimants are also constructed by existing narratives about who is the victim. The emphasis in the early 1990s on forced pregnancy as a crime against ethnic groups and women, documented earlier in this book, determined the frame through which transnational actors viewed the legitimacy of particular rights claims on behalf of the babies and made it easy to dismiss adult war child activists, whose frame and goals as a global population of claimants were much broader. For this reason, deference to the sovereignty of local communities impeded decisive advocacy on behalf of children born of war.

Third, relationships between issues and issue networks matter. Obstacles to constructing children born of war as a global issue stemmed in part from coalitional politics between the issue network around children and armed conflict and the issue network around women and armed conflict. Child protection specialists paid little attention to babies born of rape in the 1990s because those advocates thought of this issue as a subset not of child protection but of sexual violence, an area in which the women and armed conflict network was assumed to have primacy. At the same time, activists focusing on women were more likely to view the issue through the lens of the rape survivor's needs than those of her child and to oppose advocacy discourse that might situate rape survivors or their persecuted communities as perpetrators of child abuse. From this perspective, the emphasis tended to be on preventing rape and rape-related pregnancy in the first place rather than responding to the needs of the child as a human rights subject afterward. Although this dynamic is a result in part of the political opportunity structures within and between networks, interpretations of political problems are the result of preexisting narratives about who was wronged during the war.

In short, because of the organizational, tactical, and political constraints within which advocacy organizations operate in international society, the way in which a particular problem is constructed early on and linked to other human rights problems can exert a powerful effect on the decisions of leading advocacy organizations as to whether to publicly discuss the issue. If the issue is framed in a particular way, this can exert an inhibiting effect or shape the way in which an issue will be addressed. In such cases, issue entrepreneurs pitching a new problem or a new frame to a powerful hub in a network predisposed to view the problem differently are unlikely to be successful.[46] Courage, ideational savvy, and strong leadership from within an organization are the likeliest routes to policy change.[47] Even then, champions of a new issue within an international organization must navigate opposition among colleagues and partners within an organization through a careful process of coalition building.

Finally, there are serious limitations to the way in which leading players in the transnational child rights network view the very concept of children's human rights. In part, children born of war have escaped attention because the concept of the war-affected child has been constructed according to a certain paradigmatic notion of what being affected by war entails.[48] This paradigm posits a notion of a normalized childhood disrupted by the onset and continuation of war. For instance, the Graça Machel report *Impact of Armed Conflict on Children* describes war's impact on children with the following examples: "Children are slaughtered, raped, and maimed, . . . exploited as soldiers, . . . starved and exposed to extreme brutality."[49] Implicitly, this frame privileges and renders salient the harms faced by older children already living at the outbreak of armed conflict: loss of family members, disruption of normality, mutilation, recruitment, sexual abuse, deprivation, displacement, and the psychosocial effects of witnessing violence. Few of the issues that have become salient on the international agenda to date emphasize the ways in which infants experience armed conflict or the consequences for normal development of those born into a war zone in which their prospects for acquiring an initial sense of normality and identity or even being accepted into a family are diminished from the start.[50]

In addition, for most advocacy organizations, *children* means people under the age of eighteen. They direct their initiatives to issues affecting people who currently fall into that category. But adults who suffered stigma as war children conceptualize their own experiences throughout their lives as a legitimate concern for the child rights regime. Such activists tap into the intergenerational effects of their childhood experiences on their adult lives, invoking their identities as war babies or children of war as lifelong signifiers of a particular social status, a way of being and being perceived in the world in relation to states and nations. This approach has been a tough sell in UN circles and among mainstream NGOs that must work in the context of UN discourse, a discourse that posits an inherent distinction between "people called children" and "people called adults"; it has encouraged a bystanding approach by many entities in this network.

Even if one concedes that the key focus is the treatment of war children who are now, as children, the most vulnerable, there are other conceptual obstacles to thinking comprehensively about their needs using a rights frame. Global civil society's current focus on survival and protection rights often sidelines empowerment and identity rights. And some people in the child rights network believe that rights make sense only when secured against the state. Such global civil servants are likely to dismiss advocacy around issues where the state is not itself clearly to blame. If they are in a position to play gatekeeper, they can block attention to new issues that rely on a more expansive notion of human rights.

Although the tentative steps by a few players in the child rights network are small compared with those of entrepreneurs who hoped for a broad articulation of the human rights of children born as a result of war, Elna Johnsen's plea in the epigraph of this chapter, for mere acknowledgment that such issues exist, is in some ways being answered for the first time. Yet the social construction of such issues itself is a result not only of principled action but of politics, a politics to which scholars of the human rights movement must pay closer attention.

9.
THE SOCIAL CONSTRUCTION OF CHILDREN'S HUMAN RIGHTS

IN 2007, as I was nearing the end of fieldwork for this project, I wrapped up a week in The Hague, Netherlands by visiting the International Court of Justice. The court is housed in the Peace Palace, an ornate building dedicated to the principle of peaceful conflict resolution. The palace was founded by the last czar of Russia, funded by Andrew Carnegie, and lavished with paintings, woodwork, and statuary that represent the support of all nations for this dream.

In the Great Hall of Justice, where the court meets, a grand painting hangs to the side of the room (figure 9.1). The English translation of the painting's title is *Peace Through Justice*; it was painted by nineteenth-century painter Albert Besnard and donated by the French Republic. A triumphant, bare-breasted woman holds a child in the foreground. Men with spears on horseback are in retreat behind her. Above, presiding over both from high on rocks, stand robed male figures, representing science, philosophy, and art.

The meaning of the painting is fairly obvious: According to the tour guide, the painting depicts Lady Justice cradling an innocent child and holding the masculine forces of war at bay. Similar imagery appears in paintings and statutes throughout the Peace Palace, suggesting how deeply the idea of women as simultaneously protectors of children and symbols of justice are enshrined in conceptions of international order. The image of children as weapons of war against women's bodies or women as perpetrators of crimes against children

FIGURE 9.1
La Paix par la Justice, Alfred Besnard, 1926, Great Hall of Justice,
Peace Palace, The Hague

sits uneasily with this gendered narrative.[1] These images through which we think about war and peace are certainly as much to blame for rendering children invisible as the savvy framing strategies by which human rights advocates have maneuvered in the context of these older constraints.

Outside the palace gate stands a shrine to international peace, the Peace Flame. In July 1999, flames from each of five continents were flown on military jets and joined together to create a single flame that has been continuously burning ever since in a shrine that symbolizes humanity's common commitment to peace. One hundred ninety-seven countries and regions have contributed to the shrine, with stones from each territory placed in a circle surrounding the flame.

Using the language of human rights, the ambassador's statement for peace on the plaque by the shrine affirms "that every single human being has the right to peace and justice." In the oncoming rain, I noted each stone: some ornate marble or obsidian, some simple quartz or granite, with many twigs and bits of shell in between. It is a shrine of nations, not of people—suitable, perhaps, if it is nations that make war. But my thoughts were drawn to the orphans of nations, the many individuals who exist uneasily on the margins and in the spaces between the boundaries of the stones. I thought about what peace and what justice means for them.

If there is one thing that the case examined in this book teaches scholars of international relations theory, it is the substantive importance of taking seriously childhood as a site for theorizing international politics. As Brocklehurst demonstrates, political practices "construct children as politicized bodies. . . . Children's everyday activities can be politicized and harnessed to assist nationalization and militarization."[2] I would go farther to argue not only that children's activities may be harnessed in this way but that their very physical presence, their very bodies, may be imagined to signify and demarcate political community. For children viewed as out of place in the ethno-territorial imaginary of political communities overcoming violent conflict, this can impede efforts to secure the sorts of rights outlined by governments in treaty law, rights that are imagined to inhere in biological families as the natural units of society.

Because of this, because a primary function of children is to reproduce group identities, the global politics of child rights is inseparable from understandings of political community, security, and global order. Brysk observes that "citizenship is the primary vehicle for individuals' realization of their rights in the contemporary world, and the state is the default addressee for rights claims . . . yet children are systematically disadvantaged in access to citizenship—and children across borders are especially at risk."[3] The borders she is examining in her study of migrant and trafficked children are the territorial borders of states, but *bordering* in the broader sense refers to the everyday politics of politicizing identity and constructing difference.[4] The rights of children born of war are complicated because their existence complicates not only contemporary notions of nationality but also the imagined boundary between public spaces and activities, of which wars are perhaps the most extreme example, and the private realm of family, imagined to shelter and nurture the innocence of children and childhood.

The chapters in this book buttress social constructivist arguments that the constitution of meaning must continue to be a vital object of study within international relations, precisely because of its concrete political impacts on individual human security. Why did the world forget children born of war in a high-profile conflict such as Bosnia-Herzegovina, to say nothing of those scattered across conflict zones worldwide? I have shown that the children weren't entirely forgotten, but the manner in which they were imagined by key players in the human rights regime mitigated against taking their rights and particular needs seriously. In other words, it is only through references to the social construction of meaning that the situation of these individuals can stand in such contrast to the lofty standards enshrined in international human rights law and promoted by child rights advocates in conflict zones.

War reporters noticed children born of war. But media coverage failed to trigger a rights-based response because it fed into and reinforced three dominant representations of Bosnia's war babies, none of which were conducive to a child rights interpretation of the issue. I argue that stories about the children invoked the children as signifiers of atrocity against nations, women, and civilized international order rather than subjects of human rights concern.

This influenced the space available to humanitarian agencies to protect these children as a specific group and encouraged them to fold the babies into broader humanitarian programming for war-affected children. However, this broader programming is insufficient to provide a culture of protection for children born of war because it is predicated on supporting families who genuinely want to keep their children alive in conflict zones, which can turn out to be a faulty assumption in the case of these babies. It also hinges on a denial that the children have particular vulnerabilities; on a sometimes misplaced hope that absent specific attention to them, they will be able to hide or blend into their communities without trouble; and on an obliviousness to how their needs will change over their lifetimes.

One thing is certain: The secondary harms suffered by these children at the hands of the communities into which they are born are unlikely to be addressed by international institutions concerned with punishing war crimes. Rather than placing the long-term harms they face front and center alongside those of their mothers, international criminal law has served as a site for perpetuating the worst view of these children, the view least consistent with promotion of their rights. They have been constructed as tools of genocide, weapons of biological warfare, members of the perpetrating group, and signifiers of their mothers' trauma. Thus the suggestion that babies born of rape might themselves deserve restitution makes little sense to career civil servants working in the tribunals, and punitive justice mechanisms of this type, unless substantially reformed, will be of limited use to these babies and their mothers.

Many international agencies stayed after the war to do postconflict reconstruction work and disseminate a human rights culture in post-Dayton Bosnia-Herzegovina. But disincentives to even consider children born of war influenced government and civil society actors. Those who did consider them ran up against discursive, economic, political, and organizational obstacles. Although some space is opening up for a dialogue about the "problematique" of children born of war in Bosnia-Herzegovina now that they are young adults, it is far from clear whether this will translate into concrete programs to resolve the social, economic, and psychological issues faced by these young people and their families or whether the policy response will remain directed at women who survived rape.

In part, children born of war fall through the cracks because there is no global movement to ensure that they do not. It is a genuine puzzle why the issue agenda for the network around children and armed conflict has come to include so many other populations of concern but makes so little mention of children born of war as a vulnerable group. My analysis demonstrates that transnational networks, while setting the global agenda, may have interests in keeping certain issues *off* the agenda. These interests are driven by a combination of parochial, economic, and normative concerns, and these decisions feed into the ability of local human rights advocates to press new claims against states—a type of reverse boomerang effect. In fact, the discourse of human rights itself can be used to preclude attention to specific issues or populations.

One point of scholarly debate among those who have studied children's human rights is whether the discourse of rights imposed by outsiders—adults speaking on behalf of children, and increasingly Northerners speaking on behalf of children in developing countries—empowers or disempowers children.[5] On one hand, child rights advocates such as Michael Freeman see great value in the global norm-building process, arguing that the Convention on the Rights of the Child is a significant achievement whose primary weaknesses are lack of teeth and limited scope.[6] However, Vanessa Pupavac argues that the children's rights regime pathologizes the global south, imposing a Western construction of childhood on other cultures and reflecting a disenchantment with adult humanity through its desire to impose a constructed innocence on children everywhere.[7]

The analysis here presents a counterpoint to both the naïve view of child rights advocacy that sees the politics of child rights as an emancipatory and norm-driven (rather than primarily political) enterprise and a cynical view that sees the international discourse of child rights as inherently imperialistic. Between these extremes lies a discourse of much utility to real people. By exposing the challenges of translating multilateral human rights standards into effective transnational practices, I have aimed to illuminate new spaces in human rights thinking and demonstrate the pragmatic obstacles savvy activists for marginalized groups must consider as they forge ahead. By studying the nonemergence of a human rights concern rather than process tracing a successful issue familiar to the reader, I have offered a view of the international human rights regime that provides new insights into the politics of human rights issue construction.

What would a world look like in which the human rights of children born of war were secured? It would be a world in which governments made decisions about the placement and care of these children on the basis of the child's best interests rather than the interests of demographic or nationalist policies, one in which they took proactive steps to ensure a culture of protection around such children and monitored the effectiveness of such programs. It would be a world in which older war children seeking their fathers would be permitted to access identity records by relevant states.

It would be a world in which aid workers incorporated questions about children of war into research tools for assessing the consequences of gender-based violence in conflict and postconflict settings, where they took concrete steps to protect children not only from deprivation and attack by outsiders but also from crimes perpetrated by their own families, where their assistance programming in conflict and postconflict areas included relevant psychosocial and economic support for these children and the availability of alternatives for mothers who choose not to raise their children.

It would be a world in which international organizations and troop-contributing governments would recognize the children conceived by their multilateral staff in conflict zones as citizens, with the right to child support and the right to emigrate with their mothers rather than stay in conflict zones. It would be a world in which the media reported concretely and consistently on the practical situation faced by the children rather than belaboring the circumstances of their conception. It would be a world in which a space would be available for these children to articulate their own political identities and feel comfortable in their skins.

Some have argued that the problem is too big, too complex, too multifaceted. Some have asked, "What, in practical terms, could be done for such people?" But adult children of war and those working closely with families in this category have many concrete ideas. Michael Goodhart argues that international tribunals should prosecute "wrongful procreation" alongside forced pregnancy and rape, to reflect the harm intentionally inflicted on a child by a rapist who intends that he or she experience stigma after birth.[8] He argues that if this occurs, the stigma will move away from the child and onto the perpetrator. Susan Harris Rimmer believes that mothers and their children should be eligible for veterans' benefits and status in postconflict societies such as East Timor, assisting families economically and removing the taboos around children of war.[9] The War and Children Identity Project argues for global standardization of birth registries and privacy laws, to facilitate individuals' discovery of their roots when they are old enough to wonder.[10] A representative from Uganda suggested to me at a workshop in Oslo that citizenship rights must be standardized through treaty laws to reflect a new norm of dual citizenship and dual responsibility for such cases as children born in captivity to Ugandan rebels camped on Sudanese territory.[11]

But none of these solutions will materialize as long as the silence regarding children born of war is perpetuated.[12] Many of those to whom I spoke in this study identified the taboo nature of the subject as the main obstacle to positive change. Children born of war themselves speak most clearly on this point:

> I think the only way is to speak in an open room about the subject, to prepare the society for the moment when the child asks. It's worse not to know than to know something terrible.[13]

> I really want the issue to be talked about. I want it not to be hidden . . . and all of a sudden you have this lobby, this strength, and people following behind it, and the government decides to do something . . . towards making it something that's not embarrassing, making it something that's accepted as part of history.[14]

> I'm happy that the whole world found out about my movie, found out about the truth.[15]

This book has investigated the obstacles to such issue advocacy in the global human rights regime. Aside from the taboos around the topic, the absence of children born of war on the global agenda results from the low priority given to children and women by postconflict governments, the parochial concerns of human rights and humanitarian organizations, and international laws and nationalist narratives based on assumptions about how political community is inscribed on the bodies of children.

But mostly, it results from lack of political imagination and political will. These are the factors that make the difference between issues that get noticed—that get named, defined, and discussed in the halls of nations, that draw donor money and programmatic responses—and issues that stagnate, fizzle, and die or never receive lip service. At the turn of this century, children born of war constituted one such issue. A broader research agenda awaits those who would explore the similarities between this and a wider range of cases in global agenda denial.

In the meantime, scattered around the globe, children born to rape victims struggle for food security in the refugee camps of Darfur and Chad, yearn for family in East Timorese orphanages, worry whether their mothers will abandon them in low-income households and collective centers around Bosnia-Herzegovina and Rwanda, search for their birth mothers or fathers across oceans, or long for a day when the subject can be addressed in the councils of nations. And Alen Muhić plays soccer in Goražde, ignores the children at school who bully him, worries about his aging parents, and dreams of becoming a doctor.

NOTES

PREFACE

1. Personal interview, Alen Muhić, Goražde, 2006.

1. THEORIZING CHILD RIGHTS IN INTERNATIONAL RELATIONS

1. Estimates of the numbers vary. They range as high as 4,000. See the War and Children Identity Project, "Who Are They." Relief workers and doctors involved in deliveries during the war were consistently quoted as estimating between 400 and 600. See Williams, "Bosnia's Orphans of Rape," 1; Horvath, "Children of the Rapes," 11.
2. Jordan, "Born of Rape."
3. "I will strangle it with my own hands," a woman is quoted in Drakulić, "Women Hide Behind a Wall of Silence," 270. "We had to put blindfolds on the women for the deliveries," said Dr. Asim Kurjak at Zagreb's Holy Spirit Hospital, quoted in Williams, "Bosnia's Orphans of Rape," 1. See Niarchos, "Women, War and Rape"; Stiglmayer, *Mass Rape*; Horvath, "Children of the Rapes."
4. Keck and Sikkink, *Activists Beyond Borders*.
5. Price, "Reversing the Gun Sights."
6. Cooley and Ron, "The NGO Scramble"; Ramos, *Setting the Human Security Agenda*.
7. Finnemore, *National Interests in International Society*.
8. In this book, I use the terms "children born of war," "war children," and "war babies" interchangeably to denote children born of sexual violence or exploitative relationships in war zones, where the child's father is perceived to be a member of a foreign or enemy community. But as discussed in chapter 9, the terminology itself is laden

with political meaning and contested. See also Carpenter, *Born of War*. Some children born of war themselves have identified with these various terms, however, so I have chosen to honor them at various places in this manuscript.

9. Grieg, *The War Children of the World*.
10. Wax, "Rwandans Struggle to Love Children of Hate"; Evans, "Legacy of War"; Smith, "Rape Victims' Babies Pay the Price of War"; Powell, "East Timor's Children of the Enemy"; Raghavan, "Rape Victims, Babies Face Future Labeled as Outcasts"; Sullivan, "Born Under a Bad Sign."
11. McKelvey, *The Dust of Life*; Rains et al., *Voices of the Left Behind*.
12. My concept of "regime" draws on Krasner's famous definition of "implicit or explicit principles, norms, rules and decision-making procedures around which actors' expectations converge in a given area of international relations." See Krasner, *International Regimes*, 2. For a broader discussion of the children's rights regime, see Pupavac, "Misanthropy Without Borders."
13. Keck and Sikkink, *Activists Beyond Borders*; Risse et al., *The Power of Human Rights*; Hawkins, "Human Rights Norms and Networks in Authoritarian Chile"; Thomas, "Boomerangs and Superpower"; Joachim, "Framing Issues and Seizing Opportunities."
14. See the Web site for the Office of the Special Representative of the Secretary-General for Children and Armed Conflict at http://www.un.org/special-rep/children-armed-conflict/ (accessed June 17, 2009).
15. Raghavan, "Rape Victims, Babies Face Future Labeled as Outcasts"; Matheson, "Darfur War Breeds 'Dirty Babies.'"
16. However, as Donnelly points out in *Universal Human Rights in Theory and Practice*, enjoyment of most rights involves both positive and negative action; even the right not to be tortured can be enjoyed only if the state puts positive resources toward training the police in human rights standards.
17. D'Costa, "Marginalized Identity."
18. Brysk, "Children Across Borders."
19. Barnett and Duvall, "Power and Global Governance"; Finnemore and Sikkink, "Taking Stock"; Fearon and Wendt, "Rationalism v. Constructivism."
20. Checkel, "The Constructivist Turn in IR Theory"; Wendt, "What Is IR For"; Kratochwil, "Politics, Norms, and Peaceful Change"; Hopf, "The Promise of Constructivism in International Relations Theory."
21. Finnemore and Sikkink, "International Norm Dynamics and Political Change"; Khagram et al., *Restructuring World Politics*; Lumsdaine, *Moral Vision in World Politics*.
22. Barnett and Finnemore, *Rules for the World*.
23. Finnemore, *National Interests in International Society*; Price, *The Chemical Weapons Taboo*; Klotz, *Norms in International Relations*; Katzenstein, *The Culture of National Security*.
24. Keck and Sikkink, *Activists Beyond Borders*; Gaer, "Reality Check"; Busby, *Listen!*
25. Price, "Reversing the Gun Sights."
26. Joachim, "Shaping the Human Rights Agenda."
27. Goldberg and Hubert, "Case Study."
28. Risse, Ropp, and Sikkink, eds., *The Power of Human Rights*.

29. Busby, *Listen!*

30. Kowert and Legro, "Norms, Identity and Their Limits."

31. See Finnemore and Sikkink, "International Norm Dynamics and Political Change"; Khagram et al., *Restructuring World Politics*; Bob, *The Marketing of Rebellion*; Carpenter, "Setting the Advocacy Agenda"; Checkel, "The Constructivist Turn in IR Theory."

32. Cox, *Production, Power, and World Order.*

33. D'Costa, "Marginalized Identity."

34. Brysk, "Children Across Borders"; Brocklehurst, *Who's Afraid of Children?*; Watson, "Children and International Relations."

35. Watson, "Children and International Relations."

36. Scheper-Hughes and Sargent, *Small Wars*; Stephens, *Children and the Politics of Culture*; James and Prout, *Constructing Reconstructing Childhood*; Mills and Mills, *Childhood Studies.*

37. Brocklehurst, *Who's Afraid of Children?*

38. McEvoy-Levy, "Human Rights Culture and Children Born of Wartime Rape," 149.

39. D'Costa, "Marginalized Identity," 129.

40. Enloe, *Maneuvers*; Mertus, *War's Offensive on Women*; Hansen, "Gender, Nation, Rape"; Skjelsbæk, "Sexual Violence in the Conflicts in Ex-Yugoslavia."

41. Enloe, *Maneuvers*; Tickner, *Gendering World Politics*; Zalewski and Parpart, *The Man Question in International Relations*; Steans, *International Relations.*

42. Indeed, it is important not to fall prey to what Nancy Scheper-Hughes calls, referencing Jill Korbin's analysis of fatal child maltreatment in the United States, a "misguided political correctness" that draws attention away from the responsibility of parents, particularly if they are perceived themselves as victims, for violence against their children. See Korbin, "'Good Mothers,' 'Babykillers,' and Fatal Child Maltreatment"; Scheper-Hughes and Sargent, *Small Wars*, 22; Carver, "Gender and International Relations."

43. Provencher, *War Babies.*

44. The number of abortions performed in major hospitals in Sarajevo and Zagreb increased in 1992, when the largest number of rapes was reported. See Mazowiecki, "Situation of Human Rights in the Territory of the Former Yugoslavia." For example, in 1992 Petrova hospital performed 730 more abortions than in 1991. Still, although both rape and rape-related pregnancy estimates vary, it is likely that at least several hundred children were brought to term as a result of this violence.

45. For example, factors said to exacerbate stigma against Bosnia's war babies relative to other country cases include the ethnic nature of the conflict and the explicit and documented intent to impregnate. Mitigating factors include the history of interethnic marriage and childbearing and the lack of visible racial traits that could be used to identify specific children.

46. This act, later codified as a crime in the Rome Statute for the International Criminal Court, involved systematically abducting and detaining women and girls of childbearing age, subjecting them to repeated rapes until pregnant, and releasing them only after it was too late for abortion. See Allen, *Rape Warfare.*

47. Minear et al., *Humanitarian Action in the Former Yugoslavia*; Wilmer, *The Social Construction of Man, the State and War.*

48. Bunch and Reilly, *Demanding Accountability*; Joachim, "Shaping the Human Rights Agenda."

49. Hansen, "Gender, Nation, Rape."

50. The failure of social science to systematically collect data on negative evidence, or "the significance of a thing's absence," is documented in Lewis and Lewis, "The Dog in the Night-Time."

51. Ethical issues attend the collection of data on sensitive subjects and hidden populations, particularly in war-affected areas. The study of taboo subjects not only may present methodological difficulties but also will affect the social climate with respect to the issue being studied in ways beyond the researcher's control. Regarding war rape in particular, it is sometimes said that the process of research itself may retraumatize trauma survivors, often with no direct benefits to them. See Bell, "The Ethics of Conducting Psychiatric Research in War-Torn Contexts." Survivors and their children are sometimes protected by silence about their experiences, so seeking to identify the parameters of such a population not only can be methodologically difficult but also can present risks of exposing individuals to their own communities. See Andrić-Ružičić, "War Rape and the Political Manipulation of Survivors." At the same time, participatory research ethics suggest that direct participation in the design and implementation of the research by the subject population is a virtue; failing to do so can reinforce power hierarchies within a community by allowing others to represent the voices of survivors. See Reinharz, *Feminist Methods in Social Research*.

52. Andrić-Ružičić, "War Rape and the Political Manipulation of Survivors."

53. Armakolas, "Identity and Conflict in Globalizing Times."

54. On a project such as this, one finds that the role of analyst is never so distinct from that of participant–advocate, both because civil society actors often hope and expect that research will contribute in some way to positive action and because a researcher's very presence asking questions about an underserved population can spearhead initiatives that did not previously exist.

55. The boy I did get to know was a particular case in that he had already identified himself publicly as a child born of wartime rape, signaling his willingness to speak about the issue.

56. Weitsman, *The Discourse of Rape in Wartime*; McKelvey, *The Dust of Life*; Daniel, *No Man's Child*; Carpenter, *Born of War*.

57. Rieff, *A Bed for the Night*.

58. Allen, *Rape Warfare*; Fisher, "Occupation of the Womb"; Wing and Merchan, "Rape, Ethnicity and Culture."

59. Helms, "Women as Agents of Ethnic Reconciliation?"; Zarkov, "War Rapes in Bosnia."

2. "PARTICULARLY VULNERABLE": CHILDREN BORN OF SEXUAL VIOLENCE IN CONFLICT AND POSTCONFLICT ZONES

1. Grieg, *The War Children of the World*. The production of war babies is far from a contemporary phenomenon, however. Older examples include children born of wartime rape in Bangladesh in 1971 and 1972, children born to Korean sex slaves during World

War II, and French children left behind by German soldiers at the end of World War I. See Provencher, *War Babies*; Rozario, "Disasters and Bangladeshi Women"; Harris, "The Child of the Barbarian"; Grieg, *The War Children of the World*.

2. Nowrojee, *Shattered Lives*.
3. Wax, "Rwandans Struggle to Love Children of Hate."
4. Bennett, *The Reintegration of Child Ex-Combatants in Sierra Leone*.
5. United Nations Secretary-General, *Women, Peace and Security*.
6. "Kuwait's Adoptions Rise as Iraqis' Children Born."
7. Rehn and Sirleaf, *Women, War and Peace*.
8. Human Rights Watch, *The War Within the War*.
9. Powell, "East Timor's Children of the Enemy."
10. Provencher, *War Babies*.
11. Salzman, "Rape Camps as a Means of Ethnic Cleansing."
12. Rehn and Sirleaf, *Women, War and Peace*, 18.
13. LeBlanc, *The Convention on the Rights of the Child*.
14. United Nations, *Universal Declaration of Human Rights*, Article 25 (2).
15. LeBlanc, *The Convention on the Rights of the Child*.
16. As Simon argues, for these rights to be realized, the state must both provide resources and protect children against those who would deny them their rights. The right to survive, for example, entails not just the provision of adequate food, shelter, and medical care but the active protection by states from those who would harm, abuse, or kill a child. Protection rights therefore require the state to actively ensure that a child's rights to survival and healthy development are not impeded through the discrimination or ill actions of others. See Simon, "United Nations Convention on the Wrongs to the Child"; LeBlanc, *The Convention on the Rights of the Child*, 123.
17. Donnelly and Howard, "Assessing National Human Rights Performance."
18. LeBlanc, *The Convention on the Rights of the Child*, 15.
19. Plattner, "Protection of Children in International Humanitarian Law."
20. UNHCR, *Protecting Refugees*.
21. The global covenants (the Universal Declaration of Human Rights and the International Covenants on Civil and Political Rights and Economic and Social Rights) specify a number of particular bases on which discrimination is prohibited, such as "race, colour, sex, language, religion, political or other opinion, national or social origins, property, birth or other status." Regional instruments have added to this list "association with a national minority, ethnic groups, fortune, birth or any other social condition." See Cohen, "The United Nations Convention on the Rights of the Child."
22. The Universal Declaration itself in Article 25(2) specifically protects children born of nonmarital unions, a form of protection particularly relevant to children of wartime rape: "All children whether born in or out of wedlock shall enjoy the same social protection." Article 10(3) of the International Covenant on Economic, Social and Cultural Rights specifies, "Special measures of protection and assistance should be taken on behalf of all children and young persons without any discrimination for reasons of parentage or other conditions."

23. Allen, *Rape Warfare*; Nikolić-Ristanović, *Women, Violence and War*.
24. Brownmiller, "Making Female Bodies the Battlefield," 180.
25. Allen, *Rape Warfare*, 91.
26. Brownmiller, *Against Our Will*.
27. Grieg, *The War Children of the World*.
28. Evans, "Legacy of War."
29. Powell, "East Timor's Children of the Enemy."
30. Human Rights Watch, *Shattered Lives*.
31. Harding, "The Other Prisoners."
32. Amnesty International, *Darfur*; Raghavan, "Rape Victims, Babies Face Future Labeled as Outcasts."
33. Wood, "Variation in Sexual Violence During War."
34. Askin, *War Crimes Against Women*, 289.
35. Seifert, "War and Rape."
36. Stiglmayer, *Mass Rape*.
37. Sideris, "Rape in War and Peace."
38. Enloe, *Maneuvers*.
39. Allen, *Rape Warfare*.
40. Goldstein, *Recognizing Forced Impregnation as a War Crime*.
41. Brownmiller, *Against Our Will*, 84.
42. Wax, "Rwandans Struggle to Love Children of Hate"; D'Costa, "War Babies."
43. Forced pregnancy has been used historically for nongenocidal purposes as well: for example, against German women under National Socialism or against blacks in the American South during the pre–Civil War era. See Koonz, *Mothers in the Fatherland*; Wing and Merchan, "Rape, Ethnicity and Culture"; Aafjes and Goldstein, *Gender Violence*; Baines, "Body Politics and the Rwandan Crisis"; Copelon, "Surfacing Gender."
44. Stiglmayer, *Mass Rape*.
45. Askin, *War Crimes Against Women*, 273–277.
46. Such camps are perhaps more properly called concentration camps. See Stiglmayer, *Mass Rape*; Allen, *Rape Warfare*.
47. United Nations Security Council, *Final Report of the Commission of Experts*.
48. Some of these testimonies are printed in Ajanović, *I Begged Them to Kill Me*; see also Stiglmayer, *Mass Rape*; Vranic, *Breaking the Wall of Silence*; Amnesty International, *Bosnia-Herzegovina*; Helsinki Watch, *War Crimes in Bosnia-Herzegovina*.
49. Askin documents cases of castration or execution of soldiers who refused orders to rape. See Askin, *War Crimes Against Women*, 271.
50. Stiglmayer, *Mass Rape*, 131–137.
51. Niarchos, "Women, War and Rape," 657.
52. The number of abortions performed in major hospitals in Sarajevo and Zagreb increased in 1992, when the largest number of rapes was reported. See Mazowiecki, *Situation of Human Rights in the Territory of the Former Yugoslavia*. For example, in 1992 Petrova hospital performed 730 more abortions than in 1991. According to a 1994 report from the Center for Reproductive Law and Policy in New York, in 1992

Croatian hospitals recorded thirty-eight rape-related pregnancies of refugee women. All of the early pregnancies and two of the advanced pregnancies were terminated; only seven pregnancies were ongoing or had been carried to term. See Pine and Mertus, *Meeting the Health Needs of Victims of Sexual Violence in the Balkans*, C1. A similar high rate of abortion for rape victims was noted by the 1993 Mazowiecki report: Of 119 verifiable rape-related pregnancies, all but 34 had been terminated. As Stiglmayer writes, "These statistics show that women generally do not want to accept children who are the result of a rape." See Stiglmayer, *Mass Rape*, 135. Indeed, numerous testimonies of forced pregnancy survivors indicate that rape victims often were loath to deliver such babies: "Thank God for the abortion," one survivor is quoted in a recent documentary film; "If I had given birth I would have killed it; then I would have killed myself." See Provencher, *War Babies*.

53. Mertus, *War's Offensive on Women*.
54. Bonnet, "The Silence of Croatia's Children."
55. Stiglmayer, *Mass Rape*.
56. However, some respondents reported cases of women aborting in "high pregnancy" where services were available. See also Granjon and Deloche, "Rape as a Weapon of War." At the same time, some women carried their children to term by choice. For example, in one concentration camp, women were forcibly aborted, and some women chose to hide their pregnancies, determined to carry them to term as a form of rebellion against their captors. See Ajanovic, *I Begged Them to Kill Me*. The case histories collected by UNICEF in 2004 also included a child who was reportedly carried to term intentionally by his mother, who also chose to return to the town where she had been detained and raped to raise him.
57. Although the European Community issued a controversial estimate of 20,000 women raped in 1993, subsequent UN reports cast doubt on this number, being "unable to discern a reliable method for the calculation of these figures." See Mazowiecki, *Situation of Human Rights in the Territory of the Former Yugoslavia*, Annex II. Gathering data on such numbers is complicated by the tendency of survivors to underreport rape because of the social stigma attached and the tendency of governments, conversely, to overestimate the numbers for propaganda purposes.
58. Estimates of the numbers of pregnancies vary widely and are largely unverifiable. The Bosnian government's estimate of 35,000 pregnancies was reported in *The Nation* in March 1993. Only a percentage of pregnancies would have resulted in live births, given victims' preference for abortion where available. See Stiglmayer, *Mass Rape*, 135. Studies conducted on rape survivors' mental and physical health outcomes by Medica Zenica in Bosnia and the Zagreb Obstetrics and Gynecology Clinic in Croatia reported conception rates of 26 percent and 56 percent among samples of fifty and twenty-five women, respectively. Of these pregnancies, 84 percent of the Medica sample and 35 percent in the Zagreb sample were carried to term. See Pojskić, *Research*. A postwar population-based, nationally representative survey of more than 5,000 family units in Bosnia-Herzegovina found that "among displaced women, 11% aged 16 to 49 said that they personally knew of a woman who had been sexually tortured/abused/raped during the war; they reported that 34% of the victims became

pregnant as a result; of the women reported pregnant, 31% were known to have interrupted their pregnancies and 9% were known to have taken them to term." See Reproductive Health Response in Conflict Consortium, *Conference Proceedings*.

59. An official at the Vojo Peric orphanage in Tuzla told a reporter, "In 1993 alone we admitted 700 children; it is possible that many of those were the babies of raped women, but there was chaos at the time and we had more important tasks than keeping detailed records." See Bećirbašić and Secic, *Invisible Casualties of War*.

60. As Julie Mertus has documented, the humanitarian sector was caught off guard by the extent of and publicity around sexual violence in Bosnia, and resources in place to respond to survivors were very limited during the war. See Mertus, *War's Offensive on Women*. It was only at the close of the Bosnian war in 1995 that the United Nations High Commissioner for Refugees issued comprehensive programming guidelines for treating and documenting sexual violence.

61. Jordan, "Born of Rape."

62. Mazowiecki, *Situation of Human Rights in the Territory of the Former Yugoslavia*.

63. Scientific studies conflict over the likelihood of rape resulting in a pregnancy, with estimates ranging between 4 and 10 percent. See Lathrop, "Pregnancy Resulting from Rape," 25. One recent study suggests rape is more likely than consensual sex to result in pregnancy, although scientists do not understand why. See Walker, "Insult to Injury." Recent U.S. data on "peacetime rape" suggest that 5 percent of raped women conceive a child as a result of a single-incident assault. See Holmes et al., "Rape Related Pregnancy." In wartime, women are often raped repeatedly; prevalence data from Sierra Leone suggest a 9 percent pregnancy rate due to gang-rape or repeated rape in captivity. However, the percentage of these pregnancies carried to term depends on various factors.

64. For example, in Rwanda the estimated rape-related births were in the thousands; in Bangladesh, some 25,000 infants were said to have been produced by genocidal rape in 1971.

65. Rodgers et al., "Sexual Trauma and Pregnancy."

66. Daniel, *No Man's Child*.

67. Hess, *Babies of Girl Soldiers*.

68. Nowrojee, *Shattered Lives*.

69. World Health Organization, *Reproductive Health During Conflict and Displacement*.

70. Hess, *Babies of Girl Soldiers*.

71. Shanks and Schull, "Rape in War," 163.

72. Center for Reproductive Law and Policy, *Meeting the Health Needs of Sexual Violence Survivors in the Balkans*.

73. Bonnet, "Le Viol des Femmes Survivantes du Génocide au Rwanda."

74. Drakulić, "Women Hide Behind a Wall of Silence."

75. Benhadj, *Mirka*.

76. D'Costa, "War Babies."

77. Nowrojee, *Shattered Lives*, 80.

78. Smith, "Rape Victims' Babies Pay the Price of War."

79. UNHCR, *Sexual Violence Against Refugees*; World Health Organization, *Reproductive Health During Conflict and Displacement*.

80. Salzman, "Rape Camps as a Means of Ethnic Cleansing."

81. One forced pregnancy survivor who aborted but later gave birth to a son by her husband stated, "Now I hate all men on this earth," and recounted that she abused her young son, "sometimes . . . beat[ing] him so hard that he bleeds." See Provencher, *War Babies*. Another survivor, who kept her daughter born of rape, admitted that "had her child been male, she would not have chosen to keep him." See Toomey, "Cradle of Inhumanity."

82. Horvath, "Children of the Rapes," 12.

83. Bećirbašić and Secic, *Invisible Casualties of War*.

84. Pojskić, "Research."

85. Canadian International Development Agency, *From Words to Action*.

86. Of the case histories collected as part of the UNICEF study, two ended in infanticide or attempted infanticide: One mother threw her baby into the river, and another "tried to poison herself and the baby." In three other cases, the mother reportedly considered infanticide as a solution. See Carpenter, *Children Born of Wartime Rape in Bosnia-Herzegovina*.

87. See International Planned Parenthood Foundation, "Country Profiles." Admittedly, these data are not representative, and the number of case histories is too small to be accurately compared with these country-level statistics. However, if anything the actual rate of infanticide for children born of rape may be higher than suggested in this sample, because the cases in the sample were identified by organizations that had provided psychosocial assistance to the mothers, whose children might therefore be at least risk of neglect or death.

88. Smith, "Rape Victims' Babies Pay the Price of War."

89. Allen, *Rape Warfare*, 99.

90. Provencher, *War Babies*.

91. Nowrojee, *Shattered Lives*.

92. World Health Organization, *Reproductive Health During Conflict and Displacement*.

93. Lathrop, "Pregnancy Resulting from Rape."

94. Swiss and Giller, "Rape as a Crime of War": Foeken, "Confusing Realities and Lessons Learned in Wartime."

95. Wax, "Rwandans Struggle to Love Children of Hate."

96. Toomey, "Cradle of Inhumanity."

97. Ibid.

98. Nowrojee, *Shattered Lives*, 82.

99. However, over time many of these family members came around; and in many of the cases the lack of support from one family member was weighed against the support from another.

100. Mazowiecki, *Situation of Human Rights in the Territory of the Former Yugoslavia*; World Council of Churches, *Rape of Women in War*.

101. Horvath, "Children of the Rapes."

102. Mazurana and Carlson, "War Slavery."

103. Salzman, "Rape Camps as a Means of Ethnic Cleansing"; Brownmiller, *Against Our Will*; Stiglmayer, *Mass Rape*.

104. Shanks and Schull, "Rape in War," 1153.

105. Mazurana and McKay, *Girls in Fighting Forces in Northern Uganda, Sierra Leone and Mozambique*; Baldi and MacKenzie, "Silent Identities."
106. Poverty can lead to desperate acts in order to survive. In interviews conducted in 2003, human rights workers suggested to me that because of a combination of caregiver ambivalence and extreme poverty, children born of rape victims or prostitutes in conflict areas are more likely to be trafficked or recruited or to become street children.
107. Daniel, *No Man's Child.*
108. McKinley, "Legacy of Rwanda Violence."
109. Powell, "East Timor's Children of the Enemy."
110. Williams and Lamont, "Rape Used Over and Over as a Systematic Torture."
111. D'Costa, "War Babies."
112. Wax, "Rwandans Struggle to Love Children of Hate."
113. Bećirbašić and Secic, *Invisible Casualties of War.*
114. One interview respondent emphasized that "statistics showed" that children born during war have a higher rate of disability. See Toomey, "Cradle of Inhumanity"; Daniel, *No Man's Child.*
115. Bećirbašić and Secic, *Invisible Casualties of War.*
116. Sullivan, "Born Under a Bad Sign."
117. Stanley, "Reporting of Mass Rape in the Balkans"; Pine and Mertus, *Meeting the Health Needs of Victims of Sexual Violence in the Balkans.*
118. Brownmiller, *Against Our Will*; D'Costa, "War Babies."
119. Mookherjee, "Ethical Issues Concerning Representation of Narratives of Sexual Violence of 1971."
120. Williams, "Bosnia's Orphans of Rape."
121. Gledhill, "Muslims Give Adoption Warning."
122. Weitsman, "Children Born of War and the Politics of Identity."
123. Lorch, "Rwanda."
124. Stanley, "Reporting of Mass Rape in the Balkans."
125. Chowdry, "War Babies."
126. Grieg, *The War Children of the World.*
127. Toomey, "Cradle of Inhumanity."
128. Grieg, *The War Children of the World.*
129. Weitsman, "Children Born of War and the Politics of Identity."
130. Daniel documents the fate of a number of physically handicapped children born in Croatia who were never claimed by the Bosnian government during repatriation processes. See Daniel, *No Man's Child.*
131. Pine and Mertus, *Meeting the Health Needs of Victims of Sexual Violence in the Balkans*, 29.
132. Jordan, "Born of Rape."
133. David et al. conducted a longitudinal study on Czech children whose mothers had twice tried to terminate their pregnancies and found a consistent relationship between being born unwanted and experiencing various forms of psychosocial difficulty across the first thirty-five years of life. See David et al., "Born Unwanted." See also Joyce et al., "The Effect of Pregnancy Intention on Child Development."
134. World Health Organization, *Reproductive Health During Conflict and Displacement.*

135. Wax, "Rwandans Struggle to Love Children of Hate."
136. Powell, "East Timor's Children of the Enemy"; Provencher, *War Babies.*
137. Bećirbašić and Secic, *Invisible Casualties of War.*
138. Pojskić, *Research.*
139. Machel, "The Impact of Armed Conflict on Children," 24.
140. McKelvey, *The Dust of Life.*
141. Grieg, *The War Children of the World,* 31.
142. Sullivan, "Born Under a Bad Sign."
143. Bećirbašić and Secic, *Invisible Casualties of War.*
144. Provencher, *War Babies.*
145. Toomey, "Cradle of Inhumanity."
146. Grieg, *The War Children of the World,* 31.
147. "Kuwait's Adoptions Rise as Iraqis' Children Born."
148. Williamson, *Bosnian Children of War;* Aaldrich and Baarda, *Final Report of the Conference on the Rights of Children in Armed Conflict.*
149. Rains et al., *Voices of the Left Behind.*
150. Provencher, *War Babies.*
151. On adoption reunions, see Trinder et al., *The Adoption Reunion Handbook.*
152. Jarratt, "By Virtue of His Service."
153. Toomey, "Cradle of Inhumanity."
154. This policy alone did not solve all their problems, and there are many lessons to be learned from this social experiment. However, this recognition for a time fulfilled an important psychosocial need for these young people.
155. Provencher, *War Babies.*
156. Carpenter, "Setting the Advocacy Agenda."
157. These included representatives of the United Nations High Commissioner for Refugees, UNICEF, Save the Children, Defense for Children International, International Rescue Committee, the International Committee of the Red Cross Child Protection Division, and the Office of the Special Representative of the Secretary-General for Children and Armed Conflict.
158. Personal interview, April 2004.
159. Raghavan, "Rape Victims, Babies Face Future Labeled as Outcasts"; Matheson, "Darfur War Breeds 'Dirty Babies.'"

3. "DIFFERENT THINGS BECOME SEXY ISSUES": THE POLITICS OF ISSUE CONSTRUCTION IN TRANSNATIONAL SPACE

1. A concern for children as the innocent victims of armed conflict dates back centuries, and major humanitarian and development organizations such as Save the Children and UNICEF emerged out of early twentieth-century efforts to protect child victims of war. See Beigbeder, *New Challenges for UNICEF.* However, only in the early 1990s did the broader human rights network and UN machinery begin talking about children and armed conflict as a specific human security issue area. See Oestreich, "UNICEF and the Implementation of the Convention on the Rights of the Child."

2. See Web site for the Office of the Special Representative of the Secretary-General for Children and Armed Conflict at http://www.un.org/children/conflict/english/issues.html (accessed September 15, 2009).

3. Machel, *Impact of Armed Conflict on Children*, 1.

4. United Nations Security Council, *Cross-Cutting Report on Children and Armed Conflict*.

5. International Criminal Court, "Child Soldier Charges in the First International Criminal Court Case."

6. For an example of the former, see the Center for Defense Information at http://www.cdi.org/ (accessed September 15, 2009). For examples of the latter, see Carpenter, "Setting the Advocacy Agenda."

7. Pan, *Liberia*; Robertson and McCauly, "The Return and Reintegration of Child Soldiers in the Sudan."

8. Beah, *A Long Way Gone*.

9. Mazurana and McKay, *Where Are the Girls?*

10. Wessels, *Child Soldiers*.

11. See, for example, the Office for the Special Representative of the Secretary-General for Children in Armed Conflict, UNICEF, Save the Children Alliance, the Children and Armed Conflict Unit at the University of Essex, Human Rights Watch's Children's Unit, and the Child Rights Information Network.

12. By contrast, 76 percent of Web sites mentioned child soldiers, 70 percent mentioned separated children or orphans, 60 percent mentioned displaced children, and 36 percent mentioned girls as a particular category of concern. The thirty-three organizations were identified using a manual hyperlink analysis, beginning with the Watchlist on Children and Armed Conflict Web site and including every linked organization within three degrees of separation whose site contained a Web page specifically focused on children and armed conflict as a multi-issue policy arena. For the complete results of this study, see Carpenter, "Setting the Advocacy Agenda."

13. See UNICEF, *Filling Knowledge Gaps*.

14. Almost all practitioners I've spoken to report that programming directed at children born of war is nonexistent. However, many claim that this does not necessarily mean they are underserved. Without any assessments, however, it is impossible to tell whether this is the case.

15. Carpenter, "Surfacing Children"; Daniel, *No Man's Child*; Weitsman, *The Discourse of Rape in Wartime*.

16. World Health Organization, *Reproductive Health During Conflict and Displacement*; Machel, *The Impact of Armed Conflict on Children*; Rehn and Sirleaf, *Women, War and Peace*; Lindsey, *Women Facing War*; United Nations Secretary-General, *Women, Peace and Security*.

17. Carpenter, "Setting the Advocacy Agenda."

18. Keck and Sikkink, *Activists Beyond Borders*, 27.

19. Jenson, "Changing Discourse, Changing Agendas," 65.

20. Joachim, *Agenda-Setting, the UN and NGOs*, 25.

21. For example, my earlier work on civilians demonstrated how the discourse of "innocent women and children" made it easy for humanitarians to overlook the presence

of vulnerable men in the civilian population. See Carpenter, *Innocent Women and Children.*

22. Bouris, *Complex Political Victims*, 39.

23. Machel, *The Impact of Armed Conflict on Children.*

24. Chairs of the Experts Meeting, *Caught in the Crossfire No More.*

25. Keck and Sikkink, *Activists Beyond Borders*, 8.

26. Bob, *The Marketing of Rebellion.*

27. Finnemore, *National Interests in International Society*; Finnemore and Sikkink, "International Norm Dynamics and Political Change."

28. Lake and Wong, *The Politics of Networks.*

29. Carpenter, "Gatekeepers and Global Governance."

30. WCIP Web site, "Our Goals," at http://www.warandchildren.org.

31. Indeed, as Clifford Bob and his contributors document in the book *The International Struggle for New Human Rights*, campaigns often take off precisely when leading authorities in an issue network adopt them as organizational priorities.

32. Meeting notes, Cologne, Germany, December 2006.

33. Keck and Sikkink, *Activists Beyond Borders*, 27.

34. On child soldiers more generally, see Wessels, *Child Soldiers.*

35. Keck and Sikkink, *Activists Beyond Borders*, 27.

36. Bob, *The Marketing of Rebellion.*

37. This perspective, associated in the particular with Richard Price's work on weapon taboos, suggests that the promotion of new moral standards is most likely to succeed if they can be grafted onto preexisting taboos. For example, the chemical weapon taboo was popularized partly because it built on an earlier prohibition on the use of poisons in warfare, and advocates of the Ottawa Convention banning antipersonnel landmines sought to move debate over landmines away from arms control discourse and graft it onto the robust norm of civilian immunity by emphasizing landmines' indiscriminate effects. See Price and Tannenwald, "Norms and Deterrence."

38. Dale, *McLuhan's Children.*

39. Ramos, "Setting the Human Security Agenda."

40. Carpenter, *Children Born of Wartime Rape.* However, advocacy networks also use the media to set their own agendas. See Ron et al., "Transnational Information Politics." It is not always so clear whether the media drive issue emergence, with advocates responding to it strategically, or reflects advocacy frames given other necessary conditions.

41. Cooley and Ron, "The NGO Scramble."

42. Bob, *The Marketing of Rebellion*, 29.

43. A women's rights activist told me wryly, "A certain Hollywood figure, I won't say who, during the Bosnian conflict was all the time asking women's organizations how to help the rape babies. The emphasis in particular was on making sure that American couples could adopt them."

44. In 1993, Tim Yeo, then the junior health minister for the British government, introduced controversial legislation in Parliament to streamline red tape for international adoptions of war rape orphans from Bosnia. See Stanley, "Reporting of Mass Rape in the Balkans." The effort was heralded by some as a "humanitarian effort" but criti-

cized by the Bosnian government as a form of imperialism, and some pointed out that Britain might have also extended asylum preference to rape victims in order to keep the mothers and babies together rather than focus on importing the children for adoption by British couples.

45. Indeed, several key human rights organizations involved in collecting data on the needs of war-affected children and women attempted to dampen enthusiasm to treat war babies as a programmatic concern in themselves, emphasizing the importance of allowing the Bosnian government to deal with the issue and provide generic support to local humanitarian initiatives. See Williamson, *Bosnian Children of War*; Center for Reproductive Law and Policy, *Meeting the Health Needs of Sexual Violence Survivors in the Balkans.*

46. Oestreich, *Power and Principle.*

4. "A Fresh Crop of Human Misery": Representations of War Babies in and Around Bosnia-Herzegovina, 1991–2005

1. Despite the fact that "Emina," the child in the article, had been adopted by a Croatian couple by the time the piece went to press, the baby is described as "anonymous, unloved," "forsaken," and defined in terms of her biological origins, as "born of horror," "born of inhumanity." The possibility of securing a future for such children in Bosnia is discounted, their "only hope" to be "airlifted to safety. . . . [This] policy is the only sure chance these children have of survival."

2. McCombs and Shaw, "The Agenda-Setting Function of Mass Media"; Dearing and Rogers, *Agenda-Setting.*

3. Cohen, *The Press and Foreign Policy*, 13.

4. Minear et al., quoting Sylvana Foa, Boutrous-Ghali's spokesperson. See *The News Media, Civil War and Humanitarian Action.*

5. Nisbet, "Evaluating the Impact of *The Day After Tomorrow.*"

6. Grant, "Anyone Here Been Raped and Speak English?"

7. For example, see "World's Untold Stories: Children of War," whose author comments, "Not only were the women immensely hurt—but also these poor kids! They are the result of a horrible crime—not a wonderful start for anyone!"; also see "Tales of Rape in DR Congo," whose author writes, "The plight of the babies born of rapes is another serious concern yet to be addressed."

8. Stanley, "Reporting of Mass Rape in the Balkans," 76; Hansen, "Gender, Nation, Rape," 55; Skjelsbæk, "Victim and Survivor," 374.

9. Costello, "Girl Tells of Mass Rapes in Bosnia."

10. This is by no means an exhaustive sample. Many articles I discovered through other means do not appear in this sample; however, the analysis here is based on these reports in the interests of replicability.

11. Keck and Sikkink, *Activists Beyond Borders.*

12. Even today, international journalists are widely seen as voyeurs in postconflict Bosnia. Interview respondents relaxed visibly when they discovered I was a university professor, not a news reporter. One said, "I'm only willing to talk with you because you're a serious researcher, which means you have some standards." However, in-

ternational researchers are also viewed with some hostility in postconflict zones, because we too are seen to profit from collecting stories, often without returning anything of value to the community.

13. Lindsey, "From Atrocity to Data," 60. For example, although the number of rape victims remains in dispute, news reporting of what came to be described as "systematic rape" largely regurgitated the estimates put forth by the Bosnian government and later international sources. These led to widely inflated estimates of the number of rape-related pregnancies and births and to a media narrative suggesting that thousands of Bosnian babies would soon be available for international adoption. See Stanley, "Reporting of Mass Rape in the Balkans."

14. Weitsman, *The Discourse of Rape in Wartime*; Stanley, "Reporting of Mass Rape in the Balkans"; Hansen, "Gender, Nation, Rape"; Pettman, *Worlding Women*.

15. See Andrić-Ružičić, "War Rape and the Political Manipulation of Survivors," 108.

16. Ibid., 108. To deal with the many requests for access to their clients and to address the general lack of professional standards among war reporters, some local women's organizations developed strict guidelines to govern their role as gatekeepers between the media and women under their care. According to a representative of Medica Zenica, a German-funded organization founded to provide emergency reproductive health care during the war, the first thing their organization does when receiving a request from a journalist is to search the Internet and attempt to establish whether the journalist has expertise in the area of gender-based violence. When Medica Zenica agrees to facilitate an interview, its staff requires reporters to sign a written contract "so that we can sue them if they violate anonymity; we want to prevent bad experiences."

17. Ibid., 108.

18. Grant, "Anyone Here Been Raped and Speak English?" 1.

19. Sullivan, "Born Under a Bad Sign."

20. Quoted in Kent, *Framing War and Genocide*, 374.

21. Stanley, "Reporting of Mass Rape in the Balkans," 75.

22. Ibid., 92.

23. Tamayo, "Abandoned Babies Conceived by Rape Are War's New Casualty."

24. Sadkovich, *The US Media and Yugoslavia 1991–1995*, 122; Kent, *Framing War and Genocide*; Auerbach and Bloch-Elkon, "Media Framing and Foreign Policy."

25. Whitney, "Peacemaking's Limit."

26. Quoted in Allen et al., "War, Ethnicity and the Media," 49.

27. Hansen, "Gender, Nation, Rape," 61.

28. As is detailed elsewhere in this volume, there is truth behind these dynamics, but the media exaggerated and distorted these truths. Many men supported female family members; many male community leaders, including religious authorities, took steps to protect rape survivors and the babies; and female family members were also complicit in stigmatizing or ostracizing survivors and their children where this occurred.

29. "The Babies of Bosnia."

30. Barton, "The Bosnia Rape Baby Who Puts the World to Shame," 16.

31. Banks and Murray, "Ethnicity and Reports of the 1992–1995 Bosnian Conflict," 154.

32. Allen, *Rape Warfare*, 89.
33. Zarkov, *The Body of War*, 146.
34. Robinson, "Putting Bosnia in Its Place," 379.
35. Willsher, "The Outcast."
36. Willsher, "The Baby Born of Inhumanity."
37. For example, Stacy Sullivan followed up in 1996 and discovered nine orphans conceived through rape in one orphanage. Toomey reported that thirteen-year-old "Samira" remained institutionalized as late as 2004.
38. Gledhill, "Muslims Give Adoption Warning."
39. Williams, "Bosnia's Orphans of Rape."
40. Willsher, "The Baby Born of Inhumanity."
41. Banks and Murray, "Ethnicity and Reports of the 1992–1995 Bosnian Conflict." As Dubravka Zarkov documents, this was very much the case in the Yugoslav press in all ethnic communities as well: "Both the images in the press and the violent strategies of the war were vested with a very specific power: the power to produce ethnicity." See Zarkov, *The Body of War*, 2.
42. Kent, *Framing War and Genocide*, 352.
43. Maas, *Love Thy Neighbor*, 69.
44. Allen et al., "War, Ethnicity and the Media," 59.
45. Reljić, "The News Media and the Transformation of Ethnopolitical Conflicts," 3.
46. International Federation of Journalists and the Center for War, Peace and the News Media, *Reporting Diversity*, quoted in Reljić, "The News Media and the Transformation of Ethnopolitical Conflicts," 4.
47. On the origins of the term *ethnic cleansing* see Kent, *Framing War and Genocide*, 149.
48. Bringa, *Being Muslim the Bosnian Way*.
49. For example, Bosniak Fikret Abdić led 25,000 Muslim refugees in an uprising against the Izetbegović government between 1994 and 1995. See Lischer, *Dangerous Sanctuaries*.
50. Korać, "Understanding Ethnic–National Identity and Its Meaning," 138.
51. See Morokvasic-Müller, "From Pillars of Yugoslavism to Targets of Violence." Children resulting from such "boundary-enforcing" rapes would not necessarily have been constructed as "of the enemy" in the sense that the media narrative suggested.
52. Hansen, "Gender, Nation, Rape."
53. Price, "Finding the Man in the Soldier–Rapist"; Baaz and Stern, "Why Do Soldiers Rape?"
54. Rodgers, "Bosnia, Gender and the Ethics of Intervention in Civil Wars."
55. "Three Serbs on Trial over Gang-Rape Camps."
56. Mann, "A Different Voice at the Table."
57. Kaufman and Williams, "Who Belongs?" 417; Bringa, *Being Muslim the Bosnian Way*.
58. Mann, "A Different Voice at the Table."
59. Joachim, "Shaping the Human Rights Agenda," 156; Neier, *War Crimes*.
60. Slapšak, "The Use of Women and the Role of Women in the Yugoslav War"; Zarkov, *The Body of War*.
61. Weitsman, "Children Born of War and the Politics of Identity," 121–122.

62. Kaufman and Williams, "Who Belongs?" 426.

63. A female camp attendant involved in detentions of Bosniaks was described by a survivor in an interview: "She said she was from the 'White Eagles' and that things were going to change for us. The girl told us to take down the babies' pants to see if they had been circumcised. The men started talking about making us pregnant. That night the rapes began." See Fisk, "Bosnia War Crimes."

64. See Ramet, *Women and Society in Yugoslavia and the Yugoslav Successor States.*

65. Skjelsbæk, "Victim and Survivor."

66. Barton, "The Bosnia Rape Baby Who Puts the World to Shame."

67. Branson, "A Generation of Children of Hate."

68. Herter, "The Disquieting Face of Wartime Atrocities."

69. Folnegovic-Smalc, "Psychiatric Aspects of the Rapes in the War Against the Republics of Croatia and Bosnia-Herzegovina," 177.

70. Copelon, "Surfacing Gender," 203.

71. Pine and Mertus, *Meeting the Health Needs of Victims of Sexual Violence in the Balkans.*

72. Goldstein, *Recognizing Forced Impregnation as a War Crime*, 14–15.

73. Copelon, "Surfacing Gender," 203.

74. Goldstein, *Recognizing Forced Impregnation as a War Crime*, 15.

75. Fisher, "Occupation of the Womb."

76. Allen, *Rape Warfare*, 103–132.

77. Ibid., 132.

78. Ibid.

79. Wing and Merchan, "Rape, Ethnicity and Culture," 20.

80. Goldstein, *Recognizing Forced Impregnation as a War Crime*, 17–18.

81. In fact, not all the children were abandoned by their mothers or the Bosniak community, although many were. The focus of feminist writing is on the archetypal raped woman who hates her child, not on those who choose to raise their children. This is in keeping with the mainstream notion in Western abortion rights discourse that a raped woman never wants to raise her child. On abortion discourse, see Condit, *Decoding Abortion Rhetoric.*

82. Allen, *Rape Warfare*, 99.

83. Drakulić, *S*, 129.

84. Drakulić, "Women Hide Behind a Wall of Silence," 4.

85. See *A Penguin Reader's Guide to S.*, p. 8.

86. See "Don't Abort, Pope Tells Rape Victims." Note that the pope did not say "human" beings.

87. "Handle with Care."

88. Effertson, "Children of Rape."

89. "Handle with Care."

90. Toomey, "Cradle of Inhumanity."

91. Holt and Hughes, "Bosnia's Rape Babies."

92. For example, the Bosnian and Korean case studies include only interviews with the rape survivors. Care was taken to protect the anonymity of the women interviewed in the Bosnian case. However, the Rwandan case includes images of a six-year-old child

who as of the time of the filming was unaware of her origins and could not have given informed consent to be publicly identified in an international documentary as a child born of genocidal rape. The child's mother is quoted in the film: "I would have liked to get rid of it, but I didn't do it. Even after she was born, I wasn't happy. . . . I kept thinking that she wouldn't be normal, that she would be a child of the enemy." Similarly, the narratives collected by Jonathan Torgovnik of children born to Rwandan rape survivors include pictures of the children but only narratives of and consent by their mothers. Indeed, some of these narratives would hardly be conducive to promoting a culture of protection around the children. See Torgovnik, *Intended Consequences.*

93. Smillie and Minear, *The Charity of Nations,* 182.

5. "PROTECTING CHILDREN IN WAR," FORGETTING CHILDREN
    OF WAR: HUMANITARIAN TRIAGE DURING THE WAR IN
    EX-YUGOSLAVIA

1. Rieff, *A Bed for the Night.*
2. Stoddard, *Humanitarian Alert.*
3. Buchanan-Smith and Randel, "Financing International Humanitarian Action."
4. Weiss, *Military–Civilian Interactions,* 79.
5. Weiss and Collins, *Humanitarian Challenges and Intervention,* 92.
6. Fagen, "Protecting Refugee Women and Children."
7. Mertus, *War's Offensive on Women,* 20.
8. Weiss and Collins, *Humanitarian Challenges and Intervention,* 205.
9. Minear, *The Humanitarian Enterprise.*
10. Weiss and Collins, *Humanitarian Challenges and Intervention.*
11. Paul, *Protection in Practice.*
12. Smillie and Minear, *The Charity of Nations,* 11.
13. Stoddard, *Humanitarian Alert,* vx.
14. Smillie and Minear, *The Charity of Nations,* 11.
15. Stoddard, *Humanitarian Alert,* 4.
16. Cooley and Ron, "The NGO Scramble."
17. It is like an NGO in that it is independent of government influence and is composed of a board of private citizens; but unlike other NGOs it operates under a mandate from governments, being the designated guardian of the Geneva Conventions. It is also funded by donations from governments, although it claims that it never allows governments to tell it what to do with the money.
18. Cockburn, *The Space Between Us,* 174.
19. During the war, Medica Zenica specialized in services for rape survivors; since then, it has increasingly turned its attention to domestic violence and trafficking.
20. Mertus, *War's Offensive on Women.*
21. For a detailed discussion of *zakat,* see Benthall and Bellion-Jourdan, *The Charitable Crescent.*
22. Burr and Collins, *Alms for Jihad,* 1.
23. Kroessin, "Islamic Charities and the War on Terror." If anything, terrorist lists have made it harder for Islamic NGOs to appeal to Western donors for grants, making it

likelier that they will accept funding from questionable sources in order to continue their work. This dynamic has also made it harder for NGOs in general to work in certain areas with Muslim-majority populations. The irony is that Islamic NGOs are often safer in some regions than Western (Christian or secular) aid organizations because they are seen as more legitimate. They have greater access to civilians, so their lack of access to main sources of funding means that Muslim populations in places such as Chechnya may receive much less aid overall than in areas where Western groups have a strong presence.

24. MacFarquharn, "As Muslim Group Goes on Trial, Other Charities Watch Warily."

25. However, Islamic Relief targets its programs primarily to emergencies where Muslims are at risk (e.g., Bosnia, Afghanistan, Chechen refugees in Ingushetia). This practice is characteristic of many Muslim aid agencies that favor channeling aid specifically to members of the Muslim *ummah*. (This doesn't always mean *all* Muslims either. The wealthiest donors in the Muslim world are Saudi Arabia and the United Arab Emirates, which are Sunni governments; the majority of aid from these donors to Iraq after the 2003 invasion went not to help all Muslim Iraqis but specifically to Islamic NGOs operating in the Sunni Triangle.) See Benthall, *Humanitarianism, Islam and September 11*.

26. Burr and Collins, *Alms for Jihad*, 144.

27. Ibid., 134.

28. Kohlmann, *Al-Qaida's Jihad in Europe*.

29. Benthall and Bellion-Jourdan, *The Charitable Crescent*.

30. Weiss, "Humanitarian Principles and Politics."

31. Wolfson and Wright, *A UNHCR Handbook for the Military on Humanitarian Operations*, 7.

32. Some have criticized the humanitarian international for failing to meet this criterion in allocating an unprecedented amount of aid to Bosnia in 1991–1995 while underserving African populations such as those recovering from the 1994 genocide in Rwanda.

33. Weiss, "Humanitarian Principles and Politics."

34. Anderson, *Do No Harm*.

35. Johnson, "Wars for Cities and Noncombatant Immunity in the Bosnian Conflict."

36. Quoted in Rieff, *A Bed for the Night*, 144.

37. Disaster Management Training Programme, *Humanitarian Principles and Operational Dilemmas in War Zones*.

38. Cutts, "The Humanitarian Operation in Bosnia 1992–1995."

39. Carpenter, *Innocent Women and Children*.

40. UNICEF, *Children and Women in Bosnia and Herzegovina*.

41. UNICEF, *Principles and Guidelines for the Ethical Reporting on Children and Young People Under 18 Years Old*.

42. Mazowiecki, *Situation of Human Rights in the Territory of the Former Yugoslavia*.

43. UNHCR, *Report on Situation of Women and Children in Bosnia-Herzegovina and Croatia*.

44. DCI, UNICEF, and UNHCR, *Report of the Joint Mission to the Republics of UNICEF, UNHCR and DCI to Ex-Yugoslavia*, 7.

45. Pine and Mertus, *Meeting the Health Needs of Victims of Sexual Violence in the Balkans.*

46. ICRC, *Protection of the Civilian Population in Periods of Armed Conflict,* 12.

47. Williamson, "Bosnia's Orphans of Rape."

48. Mazowiecki, "Situation of Human Rights in the Territory of the Former Yugoslavia," para. 93.

49. Williamson, "Bosnia's Orphans of Rape," 10.

50. The sentiment had merit, but such vague guidelines do not appear to have been sufficient (or sufficiently implemented) to offset the specific protection problems that children born of rape subsequently faced in postwar Bosnia. By 2004, when I arrived in the field, no international organization or government agency working in Bosnia appeared to have followed up or monitored the situation of these children or evaluated the local response to determine whether it was adequate and in what ways international actors could provide support.

51. World Council of Churches, *Rape of Women in War,* 11.

52. Effertson, "Children of Rape."

53. For example, UNHCR's 1994 field manual for the care of refugee children states, "It is UNHCR's policy that children in a emergency context are not available for adoption." See UNHCR, *Refugee Children,* 130.

54. Although the Bosnian government preferred this solution, it was not shared by all women's and children's advocates in the region. One local employee of Catholic Relief Services I spoke with after the war told me, "I think [foreign adoption] would be the perfect thing to do for those children. I think they will always have difficulties here in Bosnia because every time they hear about the war they will remind themselves that they are a result of the war and not a married couple. So I think if the future is better for the child abroad, if the family is really capable to support and raise the child."

55. See Mazowiecki, *Situation of Human Rights in the Territory of the Former Yugoslavia,* para. 94; and Pine and Mertus, *Meeting the Health Needs of Victims of Sexual Violence in the Balkans,* 9.

56. For an excellent analysis of this debate, see Stanley, "Reporting of Mass Rape in the Balkans."

57. "The Babies of Bosnia."

58. DCI, UNICEF, and UNHCR, *Report of the Joint Mission to the Republics of UNICEF, UNHCR and DCI to Ex-Yugoslavia,* 15–16. See also Pine and Mertus, *Meeting the Health Needs of Victims of Sexual Violence in the Balkans,* 3.

59. DCI, UNICEF, and UNHCR, *Report of the Joint Mission to the Republics of UNICEF, UNHCR and DCI to Ex-Yugoslavia,* 7.

60. For example, Medica worked closely with traumatized mothers to help them accept and raise their babies, using naming ceremonies and counseling to combat the stigma. In many cases this worked, but the assumption that mothers could be convinced with help to care for their babies also could backfire. One Medica client who had been encouraged to sleep with her baby got up in the middle of the night, left the facility, and threw her child into the river.

61. Personal interview, Islamic Riyaset, Sarajevo, August 2004.

62. Benthall, *Humanitarianism, Islam and September 11,* 102.

63. Islamic Relief, *Islamic Relief in Bosnia-Herzegovina*. These programs are similar to Western adopt-a-child programs such as Childreach, only Islamic NGOs send the stipend directly to a child through his or her parents rather than pooling the stipends to build community projects such as wells.

64. The Islamic and secular Western NGOs' perspectives converged completely in one regard: the antipathy to foreign adoption. When I queried an Islamic aid organization in Bosnia about this policy option, I received responses such as, "There were many foreigners that were trying to adopt. When talking about Muslims, never can a family adopt a child, can be that child's master. Always the biological parents have more right to him."

65. "Al Sajh D'adulhaqq, Ali D'ajulhagg, alIma alakbar, Hukmu at fail n'nisa I al-mugetestibati fi l-Busneti wa l-Harsaki" ("Regulations Relating to the Children of Raped Women of BiH"), Cairo, 1994, III, 175–186, cited in Omerdić, "The Ryaset of Islamic Community of Bosnia and Herzegovina, Councilor." Document on file with author.

66. As I describe in chapter 6, their perception of themselves is not necessarily matched by an equal acceptance within Bosnian civil society.

67. In a training session I attended at Medica Zenica before participating in the UNICEF survey, I was informed that the Medica clients who had had the easiest time accepting their babies were those who were religious.

68. Merry, *Human Rights and Gender Violence*.

69. Benthall, *Humanitarianism, Islam and September 11*, 103.

70. That the child is a product of rape does not go out on the profile sent to prospective donors, however.

71. Personal interview, Islamic Relief, Sarajevo, May 2006.

72. UNHCR, *Sexual Violence Against Refugees*.

73. Ward, *If Not Now, When?*

74. UNHCR, *Prevention and Response to Sexual and Gender-Based Violence in Refugee Situations*.

75. Lindsey, *Women Facing War*.

76. See http://www.amnesty.org/en/library/info/AFR54/084/2004; Amnesty International, *Darfur*.

77. See http://www.svri.org/.

6. "Forced to Bear Children of the Enemy": Surfacing Gender and Submerging Child Rights in International Law

1. Schabas, *An Introduction to the International Criminal Court*.

2. Pilch, "Sexual Violence, NGO, and the Evolution of International Humanitarian Law"; Chappell, "Contesting Women's Rights."

3. In ICC jargon, "situations" are conflict zones in which it is alleged that crimes within the court's jurisdiction may have been committed. The court may investigate such "situations" without bringing a formal "case." The latter occurs when specific individuals are identified and charged with specific instances of atrocity within a wider situation.

4. Personal interview, ICC Gender and Children Unit, The Hague, 2007.

5. See Charlesworth and Chinkin, *The Boundaries of International Law*, 334.

6. Hagan, *Justice in the Balkans*; Hazan, *Justice in a Time of War*.

7. Bass, *Stay the Hand of Vengeance*.

8. Charlesworth and Chinkin, *The Boundaries of International Law*; Engle, "Feminism and Its Discontents," 778–816.

9. In particular, I focus here on the essays in Alexandra Stiglmayer's edited volume *Mass Rape: The War Against Women in Bosnia-Herzegovina*, Beverly Allen's influential *Rape Warfare*, legal briefs developed by the Women's Human Rights Clinic at City University of New York and by the Center for Reproductive Law and Policy, and assorted scholarly articles published in law journals during the period.

10. Niarchos writes, "The Trojan War, described in the Iliad, demonstrated that women could expect rape and enslavement from warfare. The Old Testament reported that Hebrew tribes invading Canaan seized the following spoils of war, in this order: 'sheep, cattle, asses, and thirty-two thousand girls who had had no intercourse with a man.' . . . Hugo Grotius, writing in the seventeenth century, described classical admonitions to respect the 'chastity of women and girls' as well as frequent violations of those admonitions; although Grotius frowned upon rape during warfare, he apparently found the practice of seizing women for purposes of marriage more acceptable." See Niarchos, "Women, War and Rape," 660.

11. Meron, "Rape as a Crime Under International Law."

12. Brownmiller, *Against Our Will*.

13. See *United States v. Goring*, 22 Trial of the Major War Criminals Before the International Military Tribunal 411, 475 (1948).

14. Copelon, "Surfacing Gender," 197.

15. Charlesworth and Chinkin, *The Boundaries of International Law*; Copelon, "Surfacing Gender."

16. Notably, the laws of war relate to how soldiers may treat members of the enemy population in situations of armed conflict. For the laws to come into play, an armed conflict must be occurring, and the rules are different for wars between countries than for civil wars.

17. Article 6(c) of the Nuremberg Charter defines crimes against humanity as "murder, extermination, enslavement, deportation, and other inhumane acts committed against any civilian population, before or during the war, or persecution on political, racial or religious grounds in execution of or in connection with any crime within the jurisdiction of the Tribunal, whether or not in violation of the domestic law of the country where perpetrated."

18. Koenig, "Women and Rape in Ethnic Conflict and War," 132.

19. Niarchos, "Women, War and Rape," 679.

20. Copelon, "Surfacing Gender," 207. Both these authors note that this lacuna is analogous to a similar problem in asylum law of the period, which did not recognize gender as a source of persecution.

21. Hagan, *Justice in the Balkans*, 200.

22. Grave breaches of the 1949 Geneva Conventions include "willful killing, torture or inhuman treatment, including biological experiments, willfully causing great suffering or serious injury to body or health, unlawful deportation or transfer or unlaw-

ful confinement of a protected person, compelling a protected person to serve in the forces of a hostile power, or willfully depriving a protected person of the right of fair and regular trial prescribed in the present Convention, taking of hostages and extensive destruction and appropriation of property, not justified by military necessity and carried out unlawfully and wantonly." See Fourth Geneva Convention, Article 147.

23. Niarchos, "Women, War and Rape," 678.
24. Green et al., "Affecting the Rules for the Prosecution of Rape and Other Gender-Based Violence," 186–187.
25. Blatt, "Recognizing Rape as a Form of Torture"; Copelon, "Surfacing Gender," 201; Green et al., "Affecting the Rules for the Prosecution of Rape and Other Gender-Based Violence," 186.
26. Koenig, "Women and Rape in Ethnic Conflict and War," 138.
27. Niarchos, "Women, War and Rape"; Green et al., "Affecting the Rules for the Prosecution of Rape and Other Gender-Based Violence." The legal definition of genocide is "any of the following acts committed with intent to destroy, in whole or in part, a national, ethnic, racial or religious group as such: a) killing members of the group; b) causing serious bodily or mental harm to members of the group; c) deliberately inflicting on the group conditions of life calculated to bring about its destruction in whole or in part; d) imposing measures intended to prevent births within the group; and e) forcibly transferring children from the group to another group. See Convention and Punishment of the Crime of Genocide, Article 2.
28. Brownmiller, "Making Female Bodies the Battlefield," 38.
29. Seifert, "War and Rape," 62.
30. MacKinnon, "Rape, Genocide, and Women's Human Rights," 187.
31. Ibid., 188.
32. Ibid., 191.
33. Allen, *Rape Warfare*.
34. Copelon, "Surfacing Gender," 198.
35. Goldstein, *Recognizing Forced Impregnation as a War Crime*, 15.
36. Fisher, "Occupation of the Womb," 99.
37. Goldstein, *Recognizing Forced Impregnation as a War Crime*, 22.
38. Copelon, "Surfacing Gender," 203; Goldstein, *Recognizing Forced Impregnation as a War Crime*, 16.
39. Fisher, "Occupation of the Womb," 102.
40. Goldstein, *Recognizing Forced Impregnation as a War Crime*, 15, 25.
41. Wing and Merchan, "Rape, Ethnicity and Culture"; MacKinnon, "Rape, Genocide, and Women's Human Rights"; Pilch, "Sexual Violence, NGOs, and the Evolution of International Humanitarian Law"; Goldstein, *Recognizing Forced Impregnation as a War Crime*.
42. Fisher, "Occupation of the Womb," 122–123; Goldstein, *Recognizing Forced Impregnation as a War Crime*, 23; MacKinnon, "Rape, Genocide, and Women's Human Rights," 188; Koenig, "Women and Rape in Ethnic Conflict and War," 137; Green et al., "Affecting the Rules for the Prosecution of Rape and Other Gender-Based Violence," 194.
43. Fisher, "Occupation of the Womb," 120.

44. Ibid., 120–121.

45. Green et al., "Affecting the Rules for the Prosecution of Rape and Other Gender-Based Violence," 194.

46. Niarchos, "Women, War and Rape," 657.

47. MacKinnon, "Rape, Genocide, and Women's Human Rights," 191.

48. Goldstein, *Recognizing Forced Impregnation as a War Crime*, 4.

49. Ibid., 17.

50. Several authors seemed to recognize this confusion and provided more careful analytical labels for the various elements of the crime. Under the auspices of the International Women's Human Rights Clinic of City University of New York, Jennifer Green and her colleagues jointly presented a proposal to the judges of the ICTY in which they distinguished between rape, forced impregnation, and forced maternity. See Green et al., "Affecting the Rules for the Prosecution of Rape and Other Gender-Based Violence," 186–187. However, beyond this one sentence the internal logic of the piece does not reflect the analytical or legal distinctions between these crimes.

51. Neier, *War Crimes*.

52. Such a conception was never on the agenda, despite the prolife claims of religious conservatives.

53. Genocide Convention, Article 2.

54. MacKinnon, "Rape, Genocide, and Women's Human Rights," 191.

55. Goldstein, *Recognizing Forced Impregnation as a War Crime*, 27.

56. Green et al., "Affecting the Rules for the Prosecution of Rape and Other Gender-Based Violence," 194.

57. Allen, *Rape Warfare*, 87.

58. Ibid., 88.

59. Ibid., 131.

60. Ibid., 131.

61. Fisher, "Occupation of the Womb," 99.

62. Horvath, "Children of the Rapes," 12.

63. Fisher, "Occupation of the Womb," 93.

64. Goldstein, *Recognizing Forced Impregnation as a War Crime*, 99.

65. Wing and Merchan, "Rape, Ethnicity and Culture," 20. To these authors' credit, they are careful to point out that they are describing the Bosnian Muslims' beliefs that the children are non-Muslim, not imposing their own construction of the child's identity. Their assumptions about the possibility of the children being considered Muslim turned out to be incorrect, as I demonstrate in chapter 5.

66. Fisher, "Occupation of the Womb," 121; Goldstein, *Recognizing Forced Impregnation as a War Crime*, 23–24.

67. Green et al., "Affecting the Rules for the Prosecution of Rape and Other Gender-Based Violence," 194.

68. Wing and Merchan, "Rape, Ethnicity and Culture," 19.

69. Boon, "Rape and Forced Pregnancy Under the ICC Statute," 660.

70. Dixon, "Rape as a Crime in International Law," 704–705.

71. Engle, "Feminism and Its Discontents," 781.

72. Hagan, *Justice in the Balkans*.
73. McHenry, "Justice for Foča."
74. Hagan, *Justice in the Balkans*, 179.
75. Drakulić, "Women Hide Behind a Wall of Silence," 60.
76. Hagan, *Justice in the Balkans*.
77. Dixon, "Rape as a Crime in International Law," 699.
78. Campbell, "Rape as a Crime Against Humanity," 507.
79. ICTY Transcript, May 2, 2000.
80. ICTY Transcript, May 29, 2000.
81. ICTY Transcript, May 27, 2000.
82. ICTY Transcript, September 20, 2000.
83. Zarkov, "War Rapes in Bosnia."
84. ICTY Transcript, March 20, 2000.
85. ICTY Transcript, May 2, 2000.
86. ICTY Transcript, June 12, 2002
87. ICTY Transcript, November 11, 2000.
88. ICTY Kunarac Appeals Judgment, February 22, 2001.
89. Campbell, "Rape as a Crime Against Humanity," 510.
90. See Letter to the Prosecutor submitted August 15, 2006, by the Women's Initiative for Gender Justice.
91. Schabas, *An Introduction to the International Criminal Court*, 55.
92. Preparatory committees (or prepcoms) are an early stage of multilateral treaty making. At prepcoms, international experts hash out preliminary concerns and create a draft document for delegates to consider at the final conference.
93. Quoted in Chappel, "Contesting Women's Rights," 29.
94. Goodhart, "Children Born of War and Human Rights." There is some legal precedent for such an approach: A French court found in favor of an adult child conceived by a French soldier's rape of an Algerian woman in the 1970s, when as an adult he sued the French government for reparations for the stigma he had experienced as a child.
95. van der Vyver, "Civil Society and the International Criminal Court"; Pilch, "Sexual Violence, NGO, and the Evolution of International Humanitarian Law"; Boon, "Rape and Forced Pregnancy Under the ICC Statute."
96. Engle, "Feminism and Its Discontents."
97. This stands in stark contrast to earlier feminist efforts to reframe gender crimes as crimes against women rather than their male-dominated communities. Even after the conference, some feminist writers remain uneasy with the way in which the concept of forced pregnancy reproduces traditional conceptions of women in their relationship to men, children, and groups. See Charlesworth and Chinkin, *The Boundaries of International Law*; Chappel, "Contesting Women's Rights."
98. Boon, "Rape and Forced Pregnancy Under the ICC Statute," 630.
99. Ibid., 657.
100. See Gallup data on American attitudes toward abortion at http://www.gallup.com/poll/22222/Religion-Politics-Inform-Americans-Views-Abortion.aspx.
101. Chappel, "Contesting Women's Rights," 28.

102. van der Vyver, "Civil Society and the International Criminal Court."
103. Slobodan Milošević's trial at the ICTY included sixty charges and went on for several years before the defense could present its case; numerous delays resulted in a trial that had not yet concluded by the time of his death.
104. Personal interview, Office of the Prosecutor, The Hague, July 2007. For example, the Darfur investigation has included a focus on mass rape but not on forced pregnancy, despite the many reports of "Janjaweed babies" resulting from the rapes and the testimonies of victims that their captors told them they were being raped to produce "light-skinned babies."
105. Meron, "Rape as a Crime Under International Law."
106. Blatt, "Recognizing Rape as a Form of Torture."
107. Seifert, "War and Rape."
108. Grossman, "A Question of Silence."
109. Fisher, "Occupation of the Womb"; International Criminal Tribunal for Rwanda, *The Prosecutor v. Jean-Paul Akayesu.*
110. Mertus, *War's Offensive on Women.*
111. Gardam and Jarvis, *Women, Armed Conflict and International Law*; Charlesworth and Chinkin, *The Boundaries of International Law.*
112. DeLaet, "Theorizing Justice for Children Born of War."

7. "These Children (Who Are Part of the Genocide), They Have No Problems": Thinking About Children Born of War and Rights in Postwar Bosnia-Herzegovina

1. Over the course of our several weeks together Jasna had become less of a standard interpreter and more of a co-researcher, a development I initially resisted for methodological reasons but came to embrace as I began to understand how much of my access and rapport with locals depended on her active collaboration in the conversations.
2. As Joel Oestreich writes, "To help children achieve their right to immunization [for example] differs from simply providing immunization by placing it in a political context where children and their mothers become empowered to understand the need for such services and to demand them from the primary obligation holder, the government." See Oestreich, *Power and Principle*, 37.
3. Donnelly, *Universal Human Rights in Theory and Practice.*
4. For example, states would be prohibited from torturing or arbitrarily imprisoning people; correspondingly, they would be required to provide such things as education, shelter, and sufficient food to the population. Although this distinction is often expressed as "negative" rights and "positive" rights, Jack Donnelly points out that even a negative right such as "don't torture" requires positive action on the part of the state, such as appropriate training of police. See Donnelly, *Universal Human Rights in Theory and Practice.*
5. See Bob, *Rights on the Rise.* For an example, Hopgood documents how Amnesty International's concept of human rights gradually expanded over the several decades it has been active. See Hopgood, *Keepers of the Flame.*
6. Donnelly, *Universal Human Rights in Theory and Practice.*

7. Okin, *Is Multiculturalism Bad for Women?*
8. Brysk, *Human Rights and Private Wrongs.*
9. Oestreich, *Power and Principle.*
10. "Consensus" at multilateral conferences is achieved not when all agree but when no one objects. See Merry, *Human Rights and Gender Violence*, 42. If states choose, they may add reservations to a treaty upon signing.
11. After 9/11, when the U.S. government determined that harsh interrogations of terror suspects were needed to ensure national security, the Bush administration undertook a series of efforts to limit the definition of torture under this legislation.
12. Risse et al., *The Power of Human Rights.*
13. Simmons, *Mobilizing for Human Rights.*
14. See Office of the High Commissioner for Human Rights, *Status of Ratifications of the Principal Human Rights Treaties.*
15. Holt and Hughes, "Bosnia's Rape Babies."
16. Bose, *Bosnia After Dayton.*
17. Hayden, *Blueprints for a House Divided*, 126.
18. According to Bose, most significant executive powers in the Federation are held at the canton level, including the police forces, land and housing policy, education, regulating business, communication, and taxation. See Bose, *Bosnia After Dayton.*
19. Bose, *Bosnia After Dayton*, 78.
20. Ibid., 70.
21. Stefansson, "Urban Exile," 59.
22. Coles, "Ambivalent Builders," 267.
23. As will be discussed later in this chapter, such ethnic stratification not only affects children directly but also has an important impact on the space available to make sense of or articulate identities based on multiplicity, such as those brought into relief by the acknowledgement of children born of war rape.
24. Toomey, "Cradle of Inhumanity," 6.
25. This is quite consistent with a large literature on shifts in gender relations during periods characterized by changing configurations in the relationship between militaries and the state. For example, see Enloe, *The Morning After*, and Meintjes et al., *The Aftermath.*
26. Rees, "International Intervention in Bosnia-Herzegovina," 54.
27. Cynthia Cockburn details how even seemingly gender-sensitive international planners could overlook women's capacities to assist with postwar reconstruction because of their gendered assumptions about the appropriate division of labor. See Cockburn, "Women's Organization in the Rebuilding of Bosnia-Herzegovina," 68–84. This resulted in inefficient programs and in the further disempowerment of women's groups.
28. In Bosnia, as in many postwar contexts, the priority was to channel former combatants (primarily men) into employment, which exacerbated discrimination and wage discrimination against women without an attendant consideration of how to offset the subsequent hardship faced by widows and caretakers of traumatized war veterans. However, Walsh points out that women have a significant advantage in employment with international organizations. See Walsh, "Women's Organizations in Post-Conflict Bosnia and Herzegovina," 61.

29. Personal interview, Office of the High Commissioner for Human Rights, Sarajevo, April 2004.

30. Bose, *Bosnia After Dayton*, 6.

31. Carlane, The "International" and the "Local."

32. Coles, "Ambivalent Builders," 256.

33. Vandenberg, "Peacekeeping, Alphabet Soup, and Violence Against Women in the Balkans," 158–159.

34. Coles suggests that it may "sabotage attempts at state-building through state-displacement: how important is the 'state' if the very purveyors of the idea of viable state institutions act in ways that minimize or displace its authority?" See Coles, "Ambivalent Builders," 269.

35. Stefansson, "Urban Exile," 73–74.

36. The tension between Western and Islamic approaches to postwar programming have also mediated the space in which human rights claims, and child rights in particular, can be articulated in postwar society. These dynamics interplay with changing conceptions of national identity and with the activities of the Bosnian civil sector, each of which is explored later in this chapter.

37. Anderson, *Imagined Communities*.

38. In reality, as some realist scholars suggest, this period is generally only a resting period between wars, and as feminist analysts point out, "the post-war" moment often entails shifts in, rather than an end to, violence against women. See Enloe, *The Morning After*.

39. Oberschall, "The Manipulation of Ethnicity."

40. Actually, Milošević appealed skillfully to both communist and nationalist factions in Serbia, and a number of other Serbian politicians were more vehemently militaristic than Milošević. Vujačić, "Institutional Origins of Contemporary Serb Nationalism"; Ron, *Frontiers and Ghettos*.

41. Neuffer, *The Key to My Neighbor's House*.

42. Duijzings, "Commemorating Srebrenica."

43. MacDonald, *Balkan Holocausts*, 7.

44. For example, Izetbegović "argued that in the future of Yugoslavia, Slobodan Milosevic would speak for Serbs and Franjo Tudjman for the Croats, rallying Bosniaks with the slogan, 'Who will speak for you? Alija Izetbegović!'" See Burr and Collins, *Alms for Jihad*, 132. Elissa Helms suggests that the postwar Bosniak narrative of a purely multiethnic prewar society undone by violent Serb and Croat nationalisms is only a partial truth and should be understood instead as "a claim to moral superiority." See Helms, *Gendered Visions of the Bosnian Future*, 64.

45. For a description of this process, see Ignatieff, *The Warrior's Honor*.

46. See Stefansson, "Urban Exile," 59–78.

47. Bringa, *Being Muslim the Bosnian Way*.

48. Helms, *Gendered Visions of the Bosnian Future*, 66.

49. Markotich and Moy, *Political Attitudes in Serbia*.

50. A great deal has been written on the ways in which gender discourse is manipulated during conflicts. For example, see Yuval-Davis, *Gender and Nation*; Peterson, "Gendered Nationalisms."

51. True, "National Selves and Feminine Others."

52. Mežnarić, "Gender as an Ethno-Marker"; Mostov, "Our Women/Their Women."

53. Mertus, "Women in the Service of National Identity."

54. Nikolić-Ristanović, "War, Nationalism and Mothers in the Former Yugoslavia," 234–239. For example, the leader of the Serb Orthodox Church, Patriarch Pavle, accused women without children of sinning against the Serbian nation.

55. Korać, "Women Organizing Against Ethnic Nationalism and War in the Post-Yugoslav States," 25–36; Mladjenović, "Feminist Politics in the Anti-War Movement in Belgrade," 157–166.

56. For descriptions of these and other feminine archetypes manipulated during armed conflicts, see Kesić, "Women and Gender Imagery in Bosnia," 187–202.

57. For a more detailed analysis, see Helms, *Gendered Visions of the Bosnian Future*.

58. In addition to the soldiers who took part in rapes, there were also cases of ethnic Serb soldiers who refused orders to rape and paid for it with their lives. For heart-breaking examples, see Askin, *War Crimes Against Women*, 271.

59. Carpenter, *Innocent Women and Children*.

60. Brysk, "Children Across Borders," 155.

61. Balorda, *War Babies and Identity*.

62. On the complexity of historical memory among Bosnians and its relationship to postwar identities, see Duijzings, "Commemorating Srebrenica."

63. Consider the following anecdote: "In a school in Belgrade, the teacher asked the children to write something on how they feel about who they are. The [refugee] boy wrote: 'I am nobody.' When asked why he felt this way, he replied: 'Because my father is from Croatia, my mother is from Serbia. Where am I from?'" See Korać, "Understanding Ethnic–National Identity and Its Meaning," 133.

64. Latić, "Bezbojni," quoted in Helms, "'Politics Is a Whore,'" 98.

65. Mustafa Spahić wrote a treatise in 1994 in which he denigrated mixed marriages as a threat to Islam, calling children and friendships formed through them as a worse "evil" even than the war rapes and babies conceived as a result. See Helms, *Gendered Visions of the Bosnian Future*, 98.

66. Ibid., 87.

67. Correspondingly, ethnic Serb women raped by Muslim men were given attention in the Serb media if impregnated. According to Dubravka Zarkov, "The story about forced pregnancies pointed back to the Serb men as the victim . . . hated by the world and deprived of his [pure Serb] offspring." Zarkov, "War Rapes in Bosnia," quoted in Helms, *Gendered Visions of the Bosnian Future*, 72.

68. Although my field data come entirely from the Federation, it can be hypothesized that the reverse would be the case in the RS. There, discussion of children born of rape would be centered on female Serb victims raped by Bosniaks or Croats. This was the pattern discovered by the UNICEF research team upon speaking to women's groups in Banja Luka.

69. On Germany, see Grossman, "A Question of Silence," 33–52; on Bangladesh, see D'Costa, "Marginalized Identity."

70. Daniel-Wrabetz, "Children Born of War Rape in Bosnia-Herzegovina and the Convention on the Rights of the Child."

71. Ibid., 25.

72. Bougarel, "Death and the Nationalist."

73. For example, a prominent representative of the Ryaset of the Islamic Community in Bosnia and Herzegovina cited approvingly a 1994 fatwa from a religious scholar in Cairo arguing, "If a mother rejects her illegitimate baby, and leaves it to the mercy of others, it is a great sin. That is why a great and grave responsibility falls to her." Quoted in Omerdić, "The Position of the Islamic Community on the Care for Children of Raped Mothers," 430.

74. Helms, *Gendered Visions of the Bosnian Future*, 98.

75. Nothing underscores this more than attending a memorial service for the Srebrenica victims, now an annual event in Potocari. I traveled there in 2007 with a group of academics visiting Sarajevo for the seventh biennial conference of the International Association of Genocide Scholars. Our tour guide and organizer from University of Sarajevo spent much of the bus ride describing the massacre in graphic detail, and about every other sentence of the narrative was about not the actions of the Bosnian Serb Army but rather than inefficacy of the Dutch peacekeepers who stood by while the town fell.

76. Pupavac, "Misanthropy Without Borders."

77. Walsh, "Women's Organizations in Post-Conflict Bosnia and Herzegovina," 176.

78. International Council of Voluntary Associations, *Directory of Humanitarian and Development Organizations in BiH*, 154.

79. Helms, "Women as Agents of Ethnic Reconciliation?"

80. Walsh, "Women's Organizations in Post-Conflict Bosnia and Herzegovina," 167.

81. On the tension between these types of women's groups during the war, see Boric, "Against the War" and Cockburn, *The Space Between Us.*

82. Stover and Shigekane explore these tradeoffs in their analysis of the politics of exhumations. See Stover and Shigekane, "Exhumation of Mass Graves."

83. See Senjak, *When Somebody Says Rape as if Calls My Name*; Pojskić, "Research."

84. Daniel, *No Man's Child.*

85. This probably also explains the underrepresentation of adopted or institutionalized children in the data collected for this study.

86. For example, a representative from a women's organization described a child who was being stigmatized by his maternal grandparents and whose mother had come to the women's organization for therapy. The NGO, whose focus is on women's health, provided psychosocial assistance to the mother but was not in a position to intervene with the extended family or seek a means of assisting the child himself.

87. Bonnet, "The Silence of Croatia's Children," 15.

88. Weber, *International Relations Theory*; Weldes, "Going Cultural"; Sylvester, *Feminist International Relations.*

89. Not, as my informant cited in the Preface told me, at a riverside with a distraught war baby.

90. However, Gegić did arrange various gifts for Alen, including a television, a computer, and a vacation to the sea.

91. Gegić told me that he channeled much of the proceeds to Alen for school supplies, a computer, an Internet connection, trips to the sea, and other necessities.

92. As an example of the former, the Bosnian paper *Oslobodenje* editorialized in a review of the film, "War criminal Ratko Mladić and Radovan Karadžić are still free. . . . In addition to genocide, they are responsible for the rapes of 22,000 women in BiH, and it seems nobody has an interest to arrest them. That is a shame for Europe." See "Zlatni Medvjed za Grbavicu," *Oslobodenje*, February 12, 2006. On file with author.

93. Although the lead cinema company in Banja Luka originally agreed to air the film, the owner eventually backed down to pressure from public opinion in the Republika Srpska. The *LA Times* reported on the Republika Srpska's response to the film in April 2006. The article includes quotes from hate mail sent to the director and lead actress, Mirjana Karanovic: "Whore, you think that Serbian heroes would have raped those hideous Muslim women? They are repulsive. They stink." "Serbia's Shame, on Film."

94. Stache, "Bosnian Actors Celebrate Golden Bear for 'Grbavica.'"

95. Žbanić, public remarks at International Association of Genocide Scholars Conference, July 2007, Sarajevo.

96. Ibid.

97. Helms, "'Politics Is a Whore,'" 241.

98. Merry, *Human Rights and Gender Violence*, 5.

99. Brysk, "Children Across Borders," 155.

100. Daniel, *No Man's Child*.

101. "We need to treat whole families," one informant told me. "We must find ways to help the victims reintegrate into society. This is not a women's issue, this is a social issue, it is the responsibility of others to accept these women and face this issue."

102. Goodhart, "Children Born of War and Human Rights."

8. "A Very Complicated Issue": Agenda Setting and Agenda Vetting in Transnational Advocacy Networks

1. Bob, *The International Struggle for New Human Rights*.

2. Donnelly, *Universal Human Rights in Theory and Practice*; Nelson and Dorsey, *New Rights Advocacy*.

3. See Provencher, *War Babies*; Grieg, *The War Children of the World*; War and Children Identity Project Web site.

4. Minutes, expert meeting on "Consolidating the Evidence Base of Children Born of War," Central Archive for Empirical Social Research at the University of Cologne, December 7–8, 2006.

5. For example, one issue raised in the context of the Bosnia-Herzegovina study was that the term *war babies* does not retain the same meaning when translated from English into Bosnian.

6. Some practitioners also expressed concern about lumping together children born of genocidal rape, children born of forced marriages in captivity, and children born of consensual but exploitive relationships. One focus group participant remarked, "There's a lot of complexities to [forced marriage], and to define the children as being born out of that is in some ways denying the complexity of the relationship that that extended unit has in terms of their connections to the origins of the child."

7. The working group that culminated in the edited volume *Born of War* eventually adopted the term *children born of war*, largely as a way of speaking to humanitarian practitioners on this point while retaining a frame broad enough to include many children, not just those born to sexual violence survivors. See Carpenter, "Gender, Ethnicity and Children's Human Rights," 16.

8. This reflects a broader debate within the children and armed conflict network, occurring as early as the original Machel report about the value of thematic categories and victim categories.

9. Oestreich, *Power and Principle.*

10. Bob, *The Marketing of Rebellion.*

11. Cobb and Ross, *Cultural Strategies of Agenda Denial.*

12. Clifford Bob's gatekeeper model stresses the importance of organizational culture and mandate in engendering sympathy for some causes (or some frames) but not others. See Bob, *The Marketing of Rebellion.* However, Finnemore and Barnett demonstrate how international organizations also redefine their mandates when faced with internal support for a new position. See Barnett and Finnemore, *Rules for the World.*

13. Carpenter, "Setting the Advocacy Agenda."

14. Jones and Baumgartner, *The Politics of Attention.*

15. For example, although "women and children" is often treated as a single constituency in advocacy discourse, hyperlink analysis of the organizations addressing women and armed conflict overlap with organizations addressing children and armed conflict by only 60 percent, suggesting that these are distinct, though highly interdependent, advocacy communities. See Carpenter, "Setting the Advocacy Agenda."

16. Mische, "Cross-Talk in Movements," 261.

17. Tarrow, *The New Transnational Activism.*

18. Ibid., 165.

19. Mische, "Cross-Talk in Movements."

20. University of Alberta. *Phase I: Impact Report.* Edmonton: Children and War Project, University of Alberta, 2004. On file with author.

21. Clifford Bob helpfully distinguishes between champions of a specific human rights and human rights claimants. Claimants are the specific people whose situation would be bettered through the enjoyment of a particular right. Champions are third parties interested in promoting claimants' causes for altruistic reasons. See Bob, *The International Struggle for New Human Rights.* Although champions may have better resources, mobility, or access to international organizations and powerful NGOs than rights claimants, they may lack (or be perceived to lack) credibility in accurately representing the rights of the aggrieved. See also Nelson and Dorsey, *New Rights Advocacy,* 93.

22. Merry, *Human Rights and Gender Violence.*

23. Hertel, *Unexpected Power.*

24. See Carpenter, *Innocent Women and Children.*

25. Allen, *Rape Warfare.* Such arguments are made through the lens of women's human rights, rather than child rights, and demonstrate that the two are not always unproblematically interchangeable, as is sometimes assumed in human rights discourse.

26. Beigbeder, *New Challenges for UNICEF.*
27. Oestreich, *Power and Principle.*
28. See Black, *Children First*, 183.
29. Oestreich, *Power and Principle.*
30. The relationship between the two projects was detailed in a memorandum of understanding negotiated between UNICEF and me, dated July 2, 2004.
31. At the same time, Matthes was insistent that the research not be undertaken "for its own sake." Rather, it must be "a fact-finding mission to determine whether there are intervention needs or not." He insisted that the study be organized around examining what role UNICEF could play in providing services to these children and their families.
32. Carpenter, *Children Born of Wartime Rape in Bosnia-Herzegovina.*
33. This decision was extremely significant insofar as "U.N. policy is driven by the issuance of certain reports and studies that are, in turn, adopted as Security Council resolutions." See Raven-Roberts, "Gender-Mainstreaming in United Nations Peacekeeping Operations," 46.
34. Black, *Children First.*
35. Joel Oestreich's analysis of UNICEF suggests that like many other international organizations beholden to governments, it is sensitive to which issues are too politically hot to approach. See Oestreich, *Power and Principle.*
36. Interestingly, this particular official made his case both by affirming child rights and excoriating women's groups who had contributed to the report: "It is the obligation of our society to ensure that these children are not discriminated against and that is why we are being very careful about drawing attention to them. Women do not traditionally talk about rape here, and those that do are using rape for political manipulation." Quoted in Holt and Hughes, "Bosnia's Rape Babies."
37. Members of the advisory committee did not feel that their concerns made a difference, however. In follow-up interviews with each participating organization, I heard a number of complaints, including that UNICEF took too long in paying them for their time, that it had overly complicated procedures, that they never saw the finalized version of the report after giving their feedback, and that the involvement of the advisory committee was just for show. One member of the team told me cynically, "All the comments that they gave at the advisory board meeting were not really used for anything. It was just like fulfilling a quota or something, you know, have the people get together, give their opinions, then that's that. It was like an international project where you get the locals in to say, 'We have the locals in the project,' so it would seem more objective. But their experiences were not really used." However, another member of the committee said that compared with many international organizations, which would do surveys with NGOs but never involve them as partners at all, they considered their experience with UNICEF to be an improvement over business as usual.
38. Translation of Institute for Research of Crimes Against Humanity and International Law, comments on draft report, June 2005. On file with author.
39. In his 2005 report to the secretary-general, Prince Zeid al-Hussein of Jordan specifically referred to "children fathered and abandoned by peacekeeping personnel" as

a category in need of assistance in their own right, and by April 2005 the idea was circulating at UN headquarters that the organization might owe reparations, including child support, to the women and particular attention to children stigmatized or abandoned as a result.

40. UNICEF, *Children Born of Sexual Violence in Conflict Zones*, 1.

41. For example, participants at a 2004 academic workshop on children born of war discussed the risks of associating the right of children too closely with those of their mothers. According to the proceedings, "There are many categories of mothers: those who want to keep babies and do, those who abort, those who kill their babies, those who abandon, those forced to abort or forced to abandon. War babies are thought of in relation to mothers but they have their own rights as well: the concepts of justice will be different for them." *Human Rights of Children Born of Wartime Rape and Sexual Exploitation*, proceedings of an interdisciplinary workshop, Pittsburgh, 2004. On file with author.

42. One study in Uganda found that demobilized girl soldiers carrying children conceived by sexual slavery while in captivity gave the babies names such as "A bad thing happened to me." See Apio, "Challenges of Integrating Children Born in Armed Conflict."

43. Black, *Children First*, 183.

44. For example, after I gave a briefing at UNICEF in the spring of 2005, staffers there objected to the language on my project Web site, which described the babies as "produced from conflict" rather than "born to mothers who have been victims of sexual violence."

45. Carpenter, "Studying Issue Non-Adoption in Transnational Advocacy Networks."

46. Bob, *The International Struggle for New Human Rights*.

47. Oestreich, *Power and Principle*.

48. Boyden, "Childhood and the Policy Makers."

49. Machel, *Impact of Armed Conflict on Children*, 1.

50. Nordstrom, "Girls and War Zones."

9. THE SOCIAL CONSTRUCTION OF CHILDREN'S HUMAN RIGHTS

1. Elshtain, *Women and War*.

2. Brocklehurst, *Who's Afraid of Children?* 171, 173.

3. Brysk, *Human Rights and Private Wrongs*, 32.

4. Mathias et al., *Identities, Borders and Orders*.

5. Burman, "Local, Global or Globalized?"

6. Freeman, "The Future of Children's Rights."

7. Pupavac, "Misanthropy Without Borders."

8. Goodhart, "Children Born of War and Human Rights."

9. Rimmer, "Orphans or Veterans?"

10. The War and Children Identity Project, *Our Goals*.

11. Personal conversation, Betty Bigombe, Peace Research Institute of Oslo, June 2006.

12. For example a new norm on dual nationality would constitute a significant reversal of earlier international norms enshrined in bilateral treaties, and a concerted ad-

vocacy movement would probably be needed to bring about such change. See Ko-slowski, "Demographic Boundary Maintenance in World Politics."

13.   Elna Johnsen, 2006, at a meeting in Cologne.

14.   Ryan Badol, 2003, quoted in Provencher, *War Babies*.

15.   Alen Muhić, Goražde, 2004.

APPENDIX

With the exception of those who have waived confidentiality, informants quoted in this study are not identified by name or by organization in the text. However, the civil society organizations whose staff provided the insights, opinions, or facts directly referenced in this book are listed here.

Amici dei Bambini
Association for Concentration Camp Survivors
Catholic Relief Services (CRS)
Center for Torture Victims
Committee for Aid and Relief Everywhere (CARE)
Defense for Children International
End Child Prostitution and Trafficking (ECPAT)
Human Rights Center, University of Sarajevo
Human Rights Watch (HRW)
Institute for Research on Crimes Against Humanity and Genocide
International Children's Institute
International Committee of the Red Cross (ICRC)
International Criminal Court (ICC)
International Criminal Tribunal for the Former Yugoslavia (ICTY)
International Rescue Committee
Islamic Community of Bosnia-Herzegovina
Islamic Relief Worldwide
Kosevo Hospital

Krousar Thmey
Medica Zenica
Médecins Sans Frontières (MSF)
Red Crescent of the United Arab Emirates (UAE)
Save the Children USA
Society for Threatened Peoples of Bosnia-Herzegovina
SOS Kinderdorf
State Commission for the Collection of Facts on War Crimes
United Nations Children's Emergency Fund (UNICEF)
United Nations Department of Economic and Social Affairs (UNDESA)
United Nations Development Fund for Women (UNIFEM)
United Nations High Commissioner for Human Rights (UNHCHR)
United Nations High Commissioner for Refugees (UNHCR)
United Nations Office for the Coordination of Humanitarian Affairs (OCHA)
United Nations Office of the High Representative in Bosnia-Herzegovina (OHR)
United Nations Office of the Special Representative to the Secretary-General for Children and Armed Conflict (OSRSG)
Vive Žene
War and Children Identity Project (WCIP)
Washington Network on Children and Armed Conflict
Watchlist for Children and Armed Conflict
Women for Women International
Women's Commission for Refugee Women and Children
Women's Initiative for Gender Justice
World Health Organization (WHO)
World Vision
Žene Ženema

REFERENCES

Aafjes, Astrid and Ann Tierney Goldstein. *Gender violence: The hidden war crime.* Washington, D.C.: Women, Law and Development International, 1998.

Aaldrich, G. H. and T. A. Baarda. *Final report of the Conference on the Rights of Children in Armed Conflict held in Amsterdam, the Netherlands, on 20–21 June.* Amsterdam: International Dialogues Foundation, 1994.

Ajanovic, Irfan. *I begged them to kill me: Crime against the women of Bosnia-Herzegovina.* Sarajevo: Center for Investigation and Documentation of the Association of Former Prison Camp Inmates of Bosnia-Herzegovina CID, 2000.

Allen, Beverly. *Rape warfare: The hidden genocide in Bosnia-Herzegovina.* Minneapolis: University of Minnesota Press, 1996.

Allen, Tim, Kate Hudson, and Jean Seaton. *War, ethnicity and the media.* London: South Bank University, 1996.

Amnesty International. *Bosnia-Herzegovina: Rape and sexual abuse by armed forces.* New York: Author, 1993.

——. *Darfur : Rape as a weapon of war—Sexual violence and its consequences.* New York: Author, 2004.

Anderson, Benedict. *Imagined communities: Reflections on the origins and spread of nationalism.* London: Verso, 1983.

Anderson, Mary. *Do no harm: How aid can support peace—or war.* Boulder, Colo.: Lynne Reinner, 1996.

Andrić-Ružičić, Duska. War rape and the political manipulation of survivors. In *Feminists under fire: Exchanges across war zones,* ed. Wenona Giles, Malathi de Alwis, Edith Kelin, and Neluka Silva, 103–114. Toronto: Between the Lines, 2003.

Apio, Eunice. *Challenges of integrating children born in armed conflict: A study of children born of the Lord's Resistance Army, Gulu Municipality, 1990–2003.* M.A. thesis, Makere University, 2002.

Armakolas, Ioannis. Identity and conflict in globalizing times: Experiencing the global in areas ravaged by conflict and the case of the Bosnian Serb. In *Globalization and national identities: Crisis or opportunity?*, ed. Paul T. Kennedy and Catherine J. Danks, 46–63. London: Palgrave Macmillan, 2001.

Askin, Kelly Dawn. *War crimes against women: Prosecution in international war crimes tribunals.* The Hague: M. Nijhoff, 1997.

Auerbach, Yehudith and Yaeli Bloch-Elkon. Media framing and foreign policy: The elite press vis-à-vis US policy in Bosnia. *Journal of Peace Research* 42, no. 1 (2005): 83–99.

Baaz, Maria Erikkson and Maria Stern. Why do soldiers rape? *International Studies Quarterly* 53, no. 2 (2009): 495–518.

The babies of Bosnia. *The Guardian*, January 8, 1993.

Baines, Erin. Body politics and the Rwandan crisis. *Third World Quarterly* 24, no. 3 (2003): 479–493.

Baldi, Guilia. *Sierra Leone war babies: International invisibility, country-level response.* Paper presented at the International Studies Association workshop, "War Babies," Montreal, Canada, March 16, 2004.

—— and Megan MacKenzie. Silent identities. In *Born of war: Protecting children of sexual violence survivors in conflict zones*, ed. Charli Carpenter, 78–93. Bloomfield, Conn.: Kumarian, 2007.

Balorda, Jasna. *War babies and identity.* Paper presented at the University of Pittsburgh Workshop on the Human Rights of Children Born of War, Pittsburgh, November 13, 2004.

Banks, Marcus and Monica Wolfe Murray. Ethnicity and reports of the 1992–1995 Bosnian conflict. In *The media of conflict*, ed. Tim Allen and Jean Seaton, 147–161. London: Zed, 1999.

Barnett, Michael and Robert Duvall. Power and global governance. In *Power and global governance*, ed. Michael Barnett and Robert Duvall, 1–32. Cambridge: Cambridge University Press, 2005.

—— and Martha Finnemore. *Rules for the world.* Ithaca, N.Y.: Cornell University Press, 2004.

Barton, Fiona. The Bosnia rape baby who puts the world to shame. *Mail on Sunday* (London), May 1, 1994, p. 16.

Bass, Gary. *Stay the hand of vengeance.* Princeton, N.J.: Princeton University Press, 2000.

Beah, Ishmael. *A long way gone: Memoirs of a boy soldier.* New York: Farrar, Straus and Giroux, 2007.

Bećirbašić, Belma and Dzenana Secic. *Invisible casualties of war.* London: Institute for War and Peace Reporting, 2002. http://www.iwpr.net/index.pl?archive/bcr3/bcr3_200211_383_4_eng.txt.

Beigbeder, Yves. *New challenges for UNICEF: Children, women and human rights.* New York: Palgrave Macmillan, 2002.

Bell, Pamela. The ethics of conducting psychiatric research in war-torn contexts. In *Researching violently divided societies*, ed. Marie Smyth and Gillian Robinson, 184–192. Tokyo: United Nations University Press, 2001.

Benhadj, Rachid. *Mirka* [Film]. Paris: D.D. Productions, 2000.

Bennett, Allison. *The reintegration of child ex-combatants in Sierra Leone with particular focus on the needs of females*, 2002. http://www.essex.ac.uk/armedcon/story_id/000025.doc.

Benthall, Jonathan. *Humanitarianism, Islam and September 11*. London: Overseas Development Institute, 2003.

—— and Jerome Bellion-Jourdan. *The charitable crescent: The politics of aid in the Muslim world*. London: I.B. Tauris, 2003.

Black, Maggie. *Children first: The story of UNICEF, past and present*. London: Oxford University Press, 1996.

Blatt, Deborah. Recognizing rape as a form of torture. *New York University Review of Law and Social Change* 19 (1992): 821.

Bob, Clifford, ed. *The international struggle for new human rights*. Philadelphia: University of Pennsylvania Press, 2009.

——. *The marketing of rebellion: Insurgents, the media and international activism*. Cambridge, Mass.: Cambridge University Press, 2005.

Bonnet, Catherine. The silence of Croatia's children. *International Children's Rights Monitor* 10, no. 3 (1993): 15.

——. Le viol des femmes survivantes du génocide au Rwanda. In *Rwanda : Un génocide du XXième siècle*, ed. R. Verdier, E. Decaux, and J.-P. Chretien, 17–29. Paris: L'Harmattan, 1995.

Boon, Kristen. Rape and forced pregnancy under the ICC Statute. *Columbia Human Rights Law Review* 32 (2001): 625–656.

Boric, Rada. Against the war: Women organizing across the national divide in the countries of the former Yugoslavia. In *Gender and catastrophe*, ed. Ronit Lentin, 36–49. London: Zed, 1997.

Bose, Sumantra. *Bosnia after Dayton : Nationalist partition and international intervention*. Oxford: Oxford University Press, 2002.

Bougarel, Xavier. Death and the nationalist: Martyrdom, war memory and veteran identity among Bosnian Muslims. In *The new Bosnian mosaic: Identities, memories and moral claims in a post-war society*, ed. Xavier Bougarel, Elissa Helms, and Ger Duijzings, 167–192. London: Ashgate, 2007.

Bouris, Erica. 2007. *Complex political victims*. Bloomington, Conn.: Kumarian.

Boyden, Jo. Childhood and the policy makers: A comparative perspective on the globalization of childhood. In *Constructing and reconstructing childhood*, ed. Allison James and Alan Prout, 187–210. London: Falmer, 1997.

Branson, Louise. A generation of children of hate. *The Toronto Star*, January 29, 1993.

Bringa, Tone. *Being Muslim the Bosnian way: Identity and community in a central Bosnian village*. Princeton, N.J.: Princeton University Press, 1995.

Brocklehurst, Helen. *Who's afraid of children? Children, conflict and international relations*. London: Ashgate, 2006.

Brownmiller, Susan. *Against our will: Men, women and rape.* New York: Bantam, 1975.

——. Making female bodies the battlefield. In *Mass rape: The war against women in Bosnia-Herzegovina*, ed. Alexandra Stiglmayer, 180. Lincoln: University of Nebraska Press, 1994.

Brysk, Alison. Children across borders: Patrimony, property or persons? In *People out of place: Globalization, human rights, and the citizenship gap*, ed. Alison Brysk and Gershon Shafir, 153–176. New York: Routledge, 2004.

——. *Human rights and private wrongs: Constructing global civil society.* New York: Routledge, 2005.

Buchanan-Smith, Margie and Judith Randel. *Financing international humanitarian action: A review of key trends.* Humanitarian Policy Group briefing no. 4. London: Overseas Development Institute, 2002.

Bunch, Charlotte and Niamh Reilly. *Demanding accountability: The global campaign and Vienna Tribunal for Women's Human Rights.* New York: United Nations Development Fund for Women, 1994.

Burman, Erica. Local, global or globalized? Child development and international child rights legislation. *Childhood* 3 (1996): 45–66.

Burr, Millard J. and Robert Collins. *Alms for jihad: Charity and terrorism in the Islamic world.* Cambridge: Cambridge University Press, 2006.

Busby, Joshua. *Listen! Pay attention! Transnational social movements, communicative action and global governance.* Paper prepared for the Critical Perspectives on Global Governance Conference, Amerang, Germany, November 1–4, 2002.

Campbell, Kirsten. Rape as a crime against humanity: Trauma, law and justice in the ICTY. *Journal of Human Rights* 2, no. 3 (2003): 507–515.

Canadian International Development Agency. *From words to action: Final conference report of the International Conference on War-Affected Children.* Quebec: Author, 2000. http://www.acdi-cida.gc.ca/inet/images.nsf/vluimages/childprotection/$file/warreportaug2001.pdf.

Carlane, John. The "international" and the "local": Globalisation, capitalism and the bureaucratisation of post-conflict regeneration of war-torn societies. Paper presented at "Critical Citizenship: The Role of Non-Governmental Organizations in Civil Society," San Diego, Calif., May 20, 2000.

Carpenter, Charli, ed. *Born of war: Protecting children of sexual violence survivors in conflict zones.* Bloomington, Conn.: Kumarian, 2007.

——. *Children born of wartime rape in Bosnia-Herzegovina: A preliminary study.* Internal UNICEF report, 2005.

——. Gatekeepers and global governance. In *Who governs the globe?*, ed. Martha Finnemore, Deborah Avant, and Susan Sell. Cambridge: Cambridge University Press, forthcoming.

——. Gender, ethnicity and children's human rights: Theorizing babies born of wartime rape and sexual exploitation. In *Born of war: Protecting children of sexual violence survivors in conflict zones*, ed Charli Carpenter, 1–20. Bloomfield, Conn.: Kumarian, 2007.

——. *Innocent women and children: Gender, norms and the protection of civilians.* London: Ashgate, 2006.

——. Setting the advocacy agenda: Theorizing issue emergence and non-emergence in transnational advocacy networks. *International Studies Quarterly* 511 (2007): 199–120.

——. Studying issue nonadoption in transnational advocacy networks. *International Organization* 61, no. 3 (2007): 643–667.

——. Surfacing children: Limitations of genocidal rape discourse. *Human Rights Quarterly* 22, no. 2 (2000): 428–477.

Carver, Terrell. Gender and international relations. *International Studies Review* 5, no. 2 (2003): 287–302.

Center for Defense Information Web site. http://www.cdi.org/program/index.cfm?pro gramid=21 (accessed February 1, 2008).

Center for Reproductive Law and Policy. *Meeting the health needs of sexual violence survivors in the Balkans.* New York: Author, 1994.

Chairs of the Experts Meeting of the International Conference on War-Affected Children. *Caught in the crossfire no more: A framework for commitment to war-affected children.* NGO draft outcome document summary of the International Conference on War-Affected Children, Winnipeg, Canada, September 10–17, 2000.

Chappel, Louise. Contesting women's rights: Charting the emergence of a transnational conservative counter-network. *Global Society* 20, no. 4 (2006): 491–520.

Charlesworth, Hilary and Christine Chinkin. *The boundaries of international law: A feminist analysis.* Manchester: Juris, 2000.

Checkel, Jeffrey. The constructivist turn in IR theory. *World Politics* 50 (1998): 324–348.

Chowdry, Mustafa. War babies. In *Banglapedia: National encyclopedia of Bangladesh,* 2004. http://banglapedia.search.com.bd/HT/W_0021.htm (accessed May 23, 2004).

Cobb, Roger and Marc Howard Ross. *Cultural strategies of agenda denial.* Lawrence: University of Kansas Press, 1997.

Cockburn, Cynthia. *The space between us: Negotiating gender and national identities in conflict.* London: Zed, 1998.

——. Women's organization in the rebuilding of Bosnia-Herzegovina. In *The postwar moment: Militaries, masculinities and international peacekeeping,* ed. Cynthia Cockburn and Dubravka Zarkov, 68–84. London: Zed, 2002.

Cohen, Bernard. *The press and foreign policy.* Princeton, N.J.: Princeton University Press, 1963.

Cohen, Cynthia Price. The United Nations Convention on the Rights of the Child: A feminist landmark. *William and Mary Journal of Women and Law* 3 (1997): 29–78.

Coles, Kimberly. Ambivalent builders: Europeanization, the production of difference and internationals in Bosnia-Herzegovina. In *The new Bosnian mosaic: Identities, memories and moral claims in a post-war society,* ed. Xavier Bougarel, Elissa Helms, and Ger Duijzings, 255–272. London: Ashgate, 2007.

Condit, Celeste Michelle. *Decoding abortion rhetoric: Communicating social change.* Chicago: University of Illinois Press, 1990.

Cooley, Alexander and James Ron. The NGO scramble: Organizational insecurity and the political economy of transnational action. *International Security* 27, no. 2 (2002): 5–39.

Copelon, Rhonda. Surfacing gender. In *Mass rape: The war against women in Bosnia-Herzegovina,* ed. Alexandra Stiglmayer, 197–218. Lincoln: University of Nebraska, 1994.

Costello, D. Girl tells of mass rapes in Bosnia. *QNP*, August 8, 1992.

Cox, Robert. *Production, power, and world order: Social forces in the making of history.* New York: Columbia University Press, 1989.

Cutts, Mark. *The humanitarian operation in Bosnia 1992–1995: Dilemmas of negotiating humanitarian access.* Working paper #8, United Nations High Commissioner for Refugees, 1999. http://www.unhcr.org/research/RESEARCH/3ae6a0c58.pdf.

Dale, Stephen. *McLuhan's children: The Greenpeace message and the media.* Toronto: Between the Lines, 1996.

Daniel, Joana. *No man's child: The war-rape orphans.* M.A. thesis, Boltzmann Institute of Human Rights, 2003.

Daniel-Wrabetz, Joana. Children born of war rape in Bosnia-Herzegovina and the Convention on the Rights of the Child. In *Born of war: Protecting children of sexual violence survivors in conflict zones*, ed. Charli Carpenter, 21–39. Bloomfield, Conn.: Kumarian, 2007.

David, Henry, Zdenek Dytrych, and Zdenek Matejcek. Born unwanted: Observations from the Prague study. *American Psychologist* 58, no. 3 (2003): 224–229.

DCI, UNICEF, and UNHCR. *Report of the Joint Mission to the Republics of UNICEF, UNHCR and DCI to Ex-Yugoslavia March 14–26, 1993.* On file at Defense for Children International, Geneva.

D'Costa, Bina. *The gendered construction of nationalism: From partition to creation.* Ph.D. dissertation, Australia National University, Canberra, 2003.

——. Marginalized identity: New frontiers of research in IR? In *Feminist methodologies for international relations*, ed. Brooke A. Ackerly, Maria Stern, and Jacqui True, 129–152. New York: Cambridge University Press, 2006.

Dearing, James W. and Everett M. Rogers. *Agenda-setting.* Thousand Oaks, Calif.: Sage, 1996.

DeLaet, Debra. Theorizing justice for children born of war. In *Born of war: Protecting children of sexual violence survivors in conflict zones*, ed. Charli Carpenter, 128–148. Bloomfield, Conn.: Kumarian, 2007.

Disaster Management Training Programme. *Humanitarian principles and operational dilemmas in war zones.* Madison: University of Wisconsin, 1993.

Dixon, Rosalind. Rape as a crime in international law: Where to from here? *European Journal of International Law* 13, no. 3 (2002): 697–719.

Donnelly, Jack. *Universal human rights in theory and practice.* Ithaca, N.Y.: Cornell University Press, 2003.

—— and Rhoda Howard. Assessing national human rights performance: A theoretical framework. *Human Rights Quarterly* 10 (1988): 214–248.

Don't abort, pope tells rape victims. *Houston Chronicle News*, February 27, 1993.

Drakulić, Slavenka. *S.: A novel about the Balkans.* London: Penguin, 2001.

——. Women hide behind a wall of silence. *The Nation*, March 1, 1993, pp. 268–272.

Duijzings, Ger. Commemorating Srebrenica: Histories of violence and the politics of memory in eastern Bosnia. In *The new Bosnian mosaic: Identities, memories and moral claims in a post-war society*, ed. Xavier Bougarel, Elissa Helms, and Ger Duijzigs, 141–166. London: Ashgate, 2007.

Effertson, Laura. Children of rape: The war produces a new generation of victims. *Maclean's*, May 24, 1993.

Elshtain, Jean-Bethke. *Women and war*. 2nd ed. Chicago: University of Chicago Press, 1995.

Engle, Karen. Feminism and its discontents: Criminalizing wartime rape in Bosnia and Herzegovina. *The American Journal of International Law* 99, no. 4 (2005): 778–816.

Enloe, Cynthia. *Maneuvers: The international politics of militarizing women's lives*. Berkeley: University of California Press, 2000.

——. *The morning after: Sexual politics at the end of the Cold War*. Berkeley: University of California Press, 1993.

Ericsson, Kjersti and Eva Simonsen, eds. *Children of World War II: The hidden enemy legacy*. Oxford: Berg, 2005.

Evans, Kathy. Legacy of war: Kuwait's littlest victims. *Calgary Herald*, July 29, 1993.

Fagen, Patricia Weiss. Protecting refugee women and children. *International Migration* 41, no. 1 (2003): 75–86.

Fearon, James and Alexander Wendt. Rationalism v. constructivism: A skeptical view. In *Handbook of international relations*, ed. Walter Carlsnaes, Thomas Risse, and Beth A. Simmons, 52–72. London: Sage, 2002.

Finnemore, Martha. *National interests in international society*. New York: Cornell University Press, 1996.

——, Deborah Avant, and Susan Sell. *Who governs the globe?* Working paper on file with author, 2008.

—— and Kathryn Sikkink. International norm dynamics and political change. *International Organization* 52, no. 4 (1998): 894.

——. Taking stock: The constructivist research program in international relations and comparative politics. *Annual Review of Politics Science* 4, no. 1 (2001): 391–416.

Fisher, Siobhan. Occupation of the womb: Forced impregnation as genocide. *Duke Law Journal* 46, no. 73 (1996): 93–110.

Fisk, Robert. Bosnia war crimes: The rapes went on day and night. *The Independent*, February 8, 1993.

Foeken, Ingrid. Confusing realities and lessons learned in wartime: Supporting women's projects in the former Yugoslavia. In *Assault on the soul: Women in the former Yugoslavia*, ed. S. Sharratt and E. Kaschak, 91–107. New York: Haworth, 1999.

Folnegovic-Smalc, Vera. Psychiatric aspects of the rapes in the war against the republics of Croatia and Bosnia-Herzegovina. In *Mass rape*, ed. Alexandra Stiglmayer, 174–179. Lincoln: University of Nebraska Press, 1994.

Freeman, Michael. The future of children's rights. *Children and Society* 14, no 4 (2000): 277–293.

Gaer, F. D. Reality check: Human rights NGOs confront governments at the UN. In *NGOs, the UN, and global governance*, ed. T. G. Weiss and L. Gordenker, 51–66. Boulder, Colo.: Lynne Rienner, 1996.

Gardam, Judith and Michelle Jarvis. *Women, armed conflict and international law*. The Hague: Kluwer Law Academic, 2001.

Gledhill, Ruth. Muslims give adoption warning. *London Times*, January 5, 1993.

Goldberg, Elissa and Don Hubert. Case study: The Security Council and the protection of civilians. In *Human security and the new diplomacy*, ed. Rob Mcrae and Don Hubert, 223–230. Montreal: McGill–Queen's University Press, 2001.

Goldstein, Anne Tierney. *Recognizing forced impregnation as a war crime*. New York: Center for Reproductive Law and Policy, 1993.

Goodhart, Michael. Children born of war and human rights: Philosophical reflections. In *Born of war: Protecting children of sexual violence survivors in conflict zones*, ed. Charli Carpenter, 192–193. Bloomfield, Conn.: Kumarian, 2007.

Granjon, P. and P. Deloche. Rape as a weapon of war. *Refugees Magazine*, August 1993.

Grant, Linda. Anyone here been raped and speak English? *The Guardian*, August 2, 1993.

Green, Jennifer, Rhonda Copelon, Patrick Cotter, and Beth Stephens . Affecting the rules for the prosecution of rape and other gender-based violence before the International Criminal Tribunal for the former Yugoslavia: A feminist proposal and critique. *Hastings Women's Law Journal* 5 (1994): 171.

Grieg, Kai. *The war children of the world*. Bergen, Norway: War and Children Identity Project, 2001.

Grossman, Atina. A question of silence: The rape of German women by occupation soldiers. In *West Germany under construction: Politics, society, and culture in the Adenauer era*, ed. Robert G. Moeller, 33–51. Ann Arbor: University of Michigan Press, 1997.

Gutman, Roy. Mass rape: Muslims recall Serb attacks. *Newsday*, August 23, 1992.

Hagan, John. *Justice in the Balkans*. Chicago: University of Chicago Press, 2003.

Handle with care. *The Independent* (London), January 4, 2003.

Handwerker, W. Penn. *Births and power: Social change and the politics of reproduction*. Boulder, Colo.: Westview, 1990.

Hansen, Lene. Gender, nation, rape: Bosnia and the construction of security. *International Feminist Journal of Politics* 3, no. 1 (2001): 55–75.

Harding, Luke. The other prisoners. *The Guardian*, May 20, 2004.

Harris, Ruth. The child of the barbarian: Rape, race and nationalism in France during the First World War. *Past & Present* 141 (1993): 170–206.

Hawkins, Darren. Human rights norms and networks in authoritarian Chile. In *Restructuring world politics*, ed. Sanjeev Khagram, James Riker, and Kathryn Sikkink, 47–70. Minneapolis: University of Minnesota Press, 2002.

Hayden, Robert. *Blueprints for a house divided: The constitutional logic of the Yugoslav conflicts*. Ann Arbor: University of Michigan Press, 1999.

Hazan, Pierre. *Justice in a time of war*. College Station: Texas A&M University Press, 2004.

Helms, Elissa. *Gendered visions of the Bosnian future: Women's activism and representation in post-war Bosnia-Herzegovina*. Ph.D. dissertation, University of Pittsburgh, 2003a.

——. "Politics is a whore": Women, morality and victimhood in post-war Bosnia-Herzegovina. In *The new Bosnian mosaic: Identities, memories and moral claims in a post-war society*, ed. Xavier Bougarel, Elissa Helms, and Ger Duijzigs, 235–254. London: Ashgate, 2007.

——. Women as agents of ethnic reconciliation? Women's NGOs and international intervention in postwar Bosnia-Herzegovina. *Women's Studies International Forum* 26, no. 1 (2003b): 15–33.

Helsinki Watch. *War crimes in Bosnia-Herzegovina.* New York: Human Rights Watch, 1992.

Hertel, Shareen. *Unexpected power: Conflict and change among transnational activists.* Ithaca, N.Y.: Cornell University Press, 2006.

Herter, Philip. The disquieting face of wartime atrocities. *St. Petersburg Times,* February 20, 2000.

Hess, Rachel. *Babies of girl soldiers.* Working paper submitted to the International Studies Association Workshop on War Babies, Montreal, Canada, March 15–19, 2004.

Holmes, Melissa, Heidi A. Resnick, Dean G. Kirkpatrick, and Connie L. Best. Rape-related pregnancy: Estimates and descriptive characteristics from a national sample of women. *American Journal of Obstetrics and Gynecology* 175, no. 2 (1996): 320–325.

Holt, Kate and Sarah Hughes. Bosnia's rape babies: Abandoned by their families, forgotten by the state. *The Independent,* December 13, 2005.

Hopf, Ted. The promise of constructivism in international relations theory. *International Security* 23 (1998): 171–200.

Hopgood, Stephen. *Keepers of the flame: Understanding Amnesty International.* Ithaca, N.Y.: Cornell University Press, 2006.

Horvath, Danielle. Children of the rapes. *World Press Review,* June 1993.

Human Rights Watch. *Shattered lives: Sexual violence during the Rwandan genocide and its aftermath.* New York: Author, 1996.

——. *The war within the war: Sexual violence against women and girls in eastern Congo.* New York: Author, 2002.

ICRC. *Principles of conduct for the International Red Cross and Red Crescent Movement and NGOs in disaster response programmes.* Geneva: Author, 1992.

——. *Protection of the civilian population in periods of armed conflict.* Geneva: Author, 1995.

Ignatieff, Michael. *The warrior's honor: Ethnic war and the modern conscience.* New York: Owl Books, 1998.

International Campaign Against Honor Killings Web site. http://www.stophonourkillings.com/ (accessed February 11, 2009).

International Council of Voluntary Associations. *Directory of humanitarian and development organizations in BiH.* Geneva: Author, 2003/2004.

International Criminal Court. Child soldier charges in the first International Criminal Court case [press release]. The Hague: Author, 2006. http://www.icc-cpi.int/Menus/ICC/Structure+of+the+Court/Office+of+the+Prosecutor/Reports+and+Statements/Press+Releases/Press+Releases+2006/.

International Criminal Tribunal for Rwanda. *The Prosecutor* v. *Jean-Paul Akayesu* (trial judgment), ICTR-96-4-T, September 2, 1998. http://www.unhcr.org/refworld/docid/40278fbb4.html.

International Federation of Journalists and the Center for War, Peace and the News Media. *Reporting diversity: A training and resource manual for journalists on covering minorities, inter-ethnic relations and other diversity issues.* Brussels: Author, 1997.

International Planned Parenthood Foundation. Country profiles: Bosnia-Herzegovina. *International Planned Parenthood Foundation Country Profiles.* http://ippfnet.ippf.org/pub/IPPF_Regions/IPPF_CountryProfile.asp.

Islamic Relief. *Islamic relief in Bosnia-Herzegovina*. Internal document on file with author, 2004.

James, Allison and Alan Prout. *Constructing reconstructing childhood: Contemporary issues in the sociological study of childhood*. Philadelphia: The Farmer Press, 1997.

Jarratt, Melynda. By virtue of his service. In *Voices of the left behind*, ed. Olga Rains, Lloyd Rains, and Melynda Jarratt, 169–182. New Brunswick, N.J.: Project Roots, 2004.

Jenson, Jane. Changing discourse, changing agendas: Political rights and reproductive politics in France. In *The women's movement of the United States and Western Europe*, ed. Mary F. Katzenstein and Carol McClurg Mueller, 64–88. Philadelphia: Temple University Press, 1987.

Joachim, Jutta. *Agenda-setting, the UN and NGOS: Gender violence and reproductive rights*. Washington, D.C.: Georgetown University Press, 2005.

——. Framing issues and seizing opportunities: The U.N., NGOs and women's rights. *International Studies Quarterly* 47 (2003): 247–274.

——. Shaping the human rights agenda: The case of violence against women. In *Gender politics in global governance*, ed. Mary Meyer and Elisabeth Prugl, 142–160. Lanham, Md.: Rowman and Littlefield, 1998.

Johnson, James Turner. Wars for cities and noncombatant immunity in the Bosnian conflict. In *Religion and justice in the war over Bosnia*, ed. G. Scott Davis, 63–90. New York: Routledge, 1996.

Jones, Bryan and Frank Baumgartner. *The politics of attention: How government prioritizes problems*. Chicago: University of Chicago Press, 2005.

Jordan, Michael. Born of rape. *Miami Herald*, July 1, 1995.

Joyce, T., R. Kaestner, and S. Korenman. The effect of pregnancy intention on child development. *Demography* 37, no. 1 (2000): 83–94.

Kaplan, Robert. *Balkan ghosts*. New York: St. Martin's Press, 1993.

Katzenstein, Peter, ed. *The culture of national security*. New York: Columbia University Press, 1996.

Kaufman, Joyce and Kristen Williams. Who belongs? Women, marriage and citizenship. *International Feminist Journal of Politics* 6, no. 3 (2004): 416–435.

Keck, Margaret and Kathryn Sikkink. *Activists beyond borders: Advocacy networks in international politics*. Ithaca, N.Y.: Cornell University Press, 1998.

Kent, Gregory. *Framing war and genocide: British policy and news media reaction to the war in Bosnia*. London: Hampton, 2005.

Kesić, Obrad. Women and gender imagery in Bosnia: Amazons, sluts, victims, witches and wombs. In *Women and society in Yugoslavia and the Yugoslav successor states*, ed. Sabrina Ramet, 187–202. University Park: Pennsylvania State Press, 1999.

Khagram, Sanjeev, James Riker, and Kathryn Sikkink, eds. *Restructuring world politics: Transnational social movements, networks and norms*. Minneapolis: University of Minnesota Press, 2002.

Klotz, Audie. *Norms in international relations: The struggle against apartheid*. New York: Cornell University Press, 1996.

Koenig, Dorean Marguerite. Women and rape in ethnic conflict and war. *Hastings Women's Law Journal* 5, no. 2 (1994): 129–140.

Kohlmann, Evan. *Al-Qaida's jihad in Europe: The Afghan–Bosnian network*. Oxford: Berg, 2004.

Koonz, Claudia. *Mothers in the fatherland: Women, the family, and Nazi politics*. New York: St. Martin's Press, 1987.

Korać, Maja. Understanding ethnic–national identity and its meaning. *Women's International Studies Forum* 191, no. 1/2 (1996): 138.

——. Women organizing against ethnic nationalism and war in the post-Yugoslav states. In *Feminists under fire: Exchanges across war zones*, ed. Wenona Giles, Malathi de Alwis, Edith Klein, and Neluka Silva, 25–36. Toronto: Between the Lines, 2003.

Korbin, Jill. "Good mothers," "babykillers," and fatal child maltreatment. In *Small wars: The cultural politics of childhood*, ed. Nancy Scheper-Hughes and Caroly Sargent, 253–276. Berkeley: University of California Press, 1998.

Koslowski, Rey. Demographic boundary maintenance in world politics: Of international norms on dual nationality. In *Identities, borders and orders*, ed. Mathis Albert, David Jacobson, and Yosef Lapid, 203–224. Minneapolis: University of Minnesota Press, 2001.

Kowert, Paul and Jeffrey Legro. Norms, identity and their limits: A theoretical reprise. In *The culture of national security*, ed. Peter Katzenstein, 451–497. New York: Columbia University Press, 1996.

Krasner, Stephen D., ed. *International regimes*. Ithaca, N.Y.: Cornell University Press, 1983.

Kratochwil, Friedrich. Politics, norms, and peaceful change. *Review of International Studies* 24, no. 5 (1998): 193–218.

Kroessin, Mohammed R. Islamic charities and the war on terror: Dispelling the myths. *Humanitarian Exchange Magazine* 38, June 2007.

Kuwait's adoptions rise as Iraqis' children born. *Reuters*, March 14, 1992.

Lake, David and Wendy Wong. *The politics of networks: Interests, power and human rights norms*. Working paper, University of California San Diego, 2005.

Lathrop, Anthony. Pregnancy resulting from rape. *Journal of Obstetric, Gynecologic and Neonatal Nursing* 27 (1998): 25–31.

Latić, Džemaludin. Bezbojni. *Ljiljan* 89, no. 40, June 10, 1994.

LeBlanc, Lawrence. *The Convention on the Rights of the Child: UN lawmaking on human rights*. Lincoln: University of Nebraska Press, 1995.

Lewis, George and Jonathan Lewis. The dog in the night-time: Negative evidence in social research. *British Journal of Sociology* 31 (1980): 544–558.

Lindsey, Charlotte. *Women facing war*. Geneva: ICRC, 2001.

Lindsey, Rose. From atrocity to data: Historiographies of rape in former Yugoslavia and the gendering of genocide. *Patterns of Prejudice* 36, no. 4 (2002): 59–78.

Lischer, Sarah Kenyon. *Dangerous sanctuaries: Refugee camps, civil war and the dilemmas of humanitarian aid*. Ithaca, N.Y.: Cornell University Press, 2005.

Lorch, Donatella. Rwanda: Rape, used as weapons, creates "genocide orphans." *Ottawa Citizen*, May 20, 1995.

Lumsdaine, David. *Moral vision in world politics: The foreign aid regime 1949–1989*. Princeton, N.J.: Princeton University Press, 1993.

Maas, Peter. *Love thy neighbor: A story of war.* London: Macmillan, 1996.

MacDonald, David. *Balkan holocausts: Serbian and Croatian victim-centered propaganda and the war in Yugoslavia.* Manchester: Manchester University Press, 2002.

MacFarquharn, Neil. As Muslim group goes on trial, other charities watch warily. *The New York Times,* July 17, 2007.

Machel, Graça. *Impact of armed conflict on children.* New York: United Nations, 1996.

——. *The impact of armed conflict on children: A critical review of progress made and obstacles encountered in increasing protection for war-affected children.* Report presented at the International Conference on War-Affected Children, Winnipeg, Canada, September 10–17, 2000.

MacKinnon, Catharine. Crimes of war, crimes of peace. In *On human rights: The Oxford amnesty lectures,* ed. Stephen Shute and Susan Hurley, 83–110. New York: Basic Books, 1993.

——. Rape, genocide, and women's human rights. In *Mass rape: The war against women in Bosnia-Herzegovina,* ed. Alexandra Stiglmayer, 183–196. Lincoln: University of Nebraska Press, 1994.

Mann, Judy. A different voice at the table. *Washington Post,* January 6, 1993.

Markotich, Stan and Patricia Moy. *Political attitudes in Serbia.* RFE/Rl research report, April 15, 1994.

Matheson, Isabel. Darfur war breeds "dirty babies." *BBC Online,* December 15, 2004. http://news.bbc.co.uk/2/hi/africa/4099601.stm.

Mathias, Albert, David Jacobsen, and Yosef Lapid. *Identities, borders and orders: Rethinking international relations theory.* Minneapolis: University of Minnesota Press, 2001.

Mazowiecki, Tadeuz. *Situation of human rights in the territory of the former Yugoslavia.* Report submitted to the Commission of Human Rights pursuant to Commission Resolution 1992/S-1/1 of 14 August 1992, February 23, 1993.

Mazurana, Dyan and Khristopher Carlson. War slavery: The role of children and youth in fighting forces in sustaining armed conflicts and war economies in Africa. In *Conflict, gender, and development,* ed. Dubravka Zarkov, 205–235. New Delhi: Zubaan, 2008.

—— and Susan McKay. *Girls in fighting forces in northern Uganda, Sierra Leone and Mozambique: Policy and program recommendations.* Copenhagen: Save the Children Denmark, 2003a. http://www.redbarnet.dk/Files/Filer/Krig_Flugt/CIDA_June_03_policypaper.doc.

——. *Where are the girls?* Montreal: Centre for Rights and Democracy, 2003b.

McCombs, Maxwell E. and Donald L. Shaw. The agenda-setting function of mass media. *The Public Opinion Quarterly* 36, no. 2 (1972): 176–187.

McEvoy-Levy, Siobhán. Human rights culture and children born of wartime rape. In *Born of war: Protecting children of sexual violence survivors in conflict zones,* ed. Charli Carpenter, 149–179. Bloomfield, Conn.: Kumarian, 2007.

——. Silenced voices?: Youth and peer relationships in armed conflict and its aftermath. In *A world turned upside down: Social ecological approaches to children in armed conflict,* ed. Neil Boothby, Alison Strang, and Michael Wessells, 133–154. San Francisco: Kumarian, 2006.

McGoldrick, Annabel and Jake Lynch. What is peace journalism? *Activate,* Winter 2001, pp. 4–9.

McHenry, James. Justice for Foča: The International Criminal Tribunal for Yugoslavia's prosecution of rape and enslavement as crimes against humanity. *Tulsa Journal of Comparative and International Law* 10 (2002): 183.

McKelvey, Robert. *The dust of life: America's children abandoned in Vietnam.* Seattle: University of Washington Press, 1999.

McKinley, James C. Legacy of Rwanda violence: The thousands born of rape. *New York Times*, September 23, 1996.

Meintjes, Sheila, Anu Pillary, and Meredith Turshen. *The aftermath: Women in post-conflict transformation.* London: Zed, 2002.

Meron, Theodor. Rape as a crime under international law. *American Journal of International Law* 87, no. 3 (1993): 424–428.

Merry, Sally Engle. *Human rights and gender violence: Translating international law into local justice.* Chicago: University of Chicago Press, 2006.

Mertus, Julie. *War's offensive on women: The humanitarian challenge in Bosnia, Kosovo, and Afghanistan.* Bloomfield, Conn.: Kumarian, 2000.

——. Women in the service of national identity. *Hastings Women's Law Journal* 5, no. 1 (1994): 5–23.

Mežnarić, Silva. Gender as an ethno-marker: Rape, war and identity politics in the former Yugoslavia. In *Identity, politics and women: Cultural reassertions and feminisms in international perspective*, ed. Valentine Moghandam, 76–97. Boulder, Colo.: Westview, 1994.

Mills, Jean and Richard Mills, eds. *Childhood studies: A reader in perspectives of childhood.* New York: Routledge, 2000.

Minear, Larry. *The humanitarian enterprise.* Bloomfield, Conn.: Kumarian, 2002.

——, Jeffrey Clark, Roberta Cohen, Dennis Gallagher, Iain Guest, and Thomas G. Weiss. *Humanitarian action in the former Yugoslavia: The U.N.'S role 1991–1994.* Providence, R.I.: Thomas Watson Institute for International Studies, 1994.

——, Colin Scott, and Thomas Weiss. *The news media, civil war and humanitarian action.* Boulder, Colo.: Lynne Reinner, 1996.

Mische, Ann. Cross-talk in movements: Reconceiving the culture–network link. In *Social movements and networks: Relational approaches to collective action*, ed. Mario Diani and Doug Mcadam, 258–280. New York: Oxford University Press, 2003.

Mladjenović, Lepa. Feminist politics in the anti-war movement in Belgrade. In *Feminists under fire: Exchanges across war zones*, ed. Wenona Giles, Malathi de Alwis, Edith Klein, and Neluka Silva, 157–166. Toronto: Between the Lines, 2003.

Mookherjee, Nayanika. Ethical issues concerning representation of narratives of sexual violence of 1971. In *"A lot of history": Sexual violence, public memories and the Bangladesh liberation war of 1971.* Doctoral thesis in social anthropology, Soas, University of London, 2003. http://www.drishtipat.org/1971/docs/war_nayanika.pdf.

Morokvasic-Müller, Mirjana. From pillars of Yugoslavism to targets of violence: Interethnic marriages in the former Yugoslavia and thereafter. In *Sites of violence: Gender and conflict zones*, ed. Wenona Giles and Jennifer Hyndman, 134–151. Berkeley: University of California Press, 2004.

Mostov, Julie. Our women/their women: Symbolic boundaries, territorial markers and violence in the Balkans. *Peace and Change* 20, no. 4 (1995): 515–529.

Neier, Aryeh. *War crimes: Brutality, genocide, terror and the struggle for justice*. London: Crown, 1998.

Nelson, Paul and Ellen Dorsey. *New rights advocacy: Changing strategies of development and human rights NGOs*. Washington, D.C.: Georgetown University Press, 2008.

Neuffer, Elizabeth. *The key to my neighbor's house: Seeking justice in Bosnia and Rwanda*. New York: Picador, 2001.

Niarchos, Catherine. Women, war and rape: Challenges facing the International Tribunal for the Former Yugoslavia. *Human Rights Quarterly* 17, no. 4 (1995): 348–349.

Nikolić-Ristanović, Vesna. War, nationalism and mothers in the former Yugoslavia. In *The women and war reader*, ed. Jennifer Turpin, 234–239. New York: New York University Press, 1998.

——. *Women, violence and war: Wartime victimization of refugees in the Balkans*. Budapest: Central European University Press, 2000.

Nisbet, Matthew. Evaluating the impact of *The day after tomorrow*: Can a blockbuster film shape the public's understanding of a science controversy? *The Skeptical Inquirer*, June 16, 2004. http://www.csicop.org/scienceandmedia/blockbuster (accessed August 11, 2007).

Nordstrom, Carolyn. Girls and war zones: Troubling questions. In *Engendering forced migration*, ed. Doreen Indra, 63–82. New York: Bergahn, 1999.

Nowrojee, Bianifer. *Shattered lives: Sexual violence during the Rwandan genocide and its aftermath*. New York: Human Rights Watch, 1996.

Oberschall, Anthony. The manipulation of ethnicity: From ethnic cooperation to violence and war in Yugoslavia. *Ethnic and Racial Studies* 23, no. 7 (2000): 982–1001.

Oestreich, Joel. *Power and principle: Human rights programming in international organizations*. Washington, D.C.: Georgetown University Press, 2007.

——. UNICEF and the implementation of the Convention on the Rights of the Child. *Global Governance* 4 (1998): 183–198.

Office of the High Commissioner for Human Rights. *Status of ratifications of the principal human rights treaties*, June 9, 2004. http://www2.ohchr.org/english/bodies/docs/status.pdf (accessed September 8, 2009).

Office of the Special Representative of the Secretary-General for Children and Armed Conflict Web site. http://www.un.org/special-rep/children-armed-conflict/ (accessed May 22, 2005).

Okin, Susan. *Is multiculturalism bad for women?* Princeton, N.J.: Princeton University Press, 1999.

Omerdić, Muharem. The position of the Islamic community on the care for children of raped mothers. In *The plucked buds*, ed. Mirsad Tokača, 428–432. Sarajevo: Commission for Gathering Facts on War Crimes in Bosnia and Herzegovina, 2001.

Pan, Esther. *Liberia : Child soldiers*. New York: Council on Foreign Relations, 2003.

Paul, Diane. *Protection in practice: Field-level strategies for protecting civilians from deliberate harm*. Relief and Rehabilitation Network paper 30. London: Overseas Development Institute, 1999.

A Penguin reader's guide to S.: A novel about the Balkans. New York: Penguin, 1999.

Peterson, V. Spike. Gendered nationalisms: Reproducing "us" versus "them." In *The women and war reader*, ed. Jennifer Turpin, 41–49. New York: New York University Press, 1998.

Pettman, Jan Jindy. *Worlding women: A feminist international politics*. Sydney: Allen & Unwin, 1996.

Pilch, Frances. Sexual violence, NGOs, and the evolution of international humanitarian law. *International Peacekeeping* 10, no. 1 (2003): 90–102.

Pine, Rachel and Julie Mertus. *Meeting the health needs of victims of sexual violence in the Balkans*. New York: Center for Reproductive Law and Policy, 1994.

Plattner, Denise. Protection of children in international humanitarian law. *International Review of the Red Cross* 240 (1995): 140–152.

Pojskić, Mirha. *Research: Dominant gynecological and psychological consequences of rape*. Unpublished report available from Medica Women's Therapy Center, Zenica, BiH, 1995.

Polgreen, Lydia. Darfur's babies of rape are on trial from birth. *New York Times*, February 11, 2005.

Powell, Siam. East Timor's children of the enemy. *The Weekend Australian*, March 10, 2001.

Price, Lisa. Finding the man in the soldier–rapist. *Women's International Studies Forum* 24, no. 2 (2001): 211–227.

Price, Richard. *The chemical weapons taboo*. Ithaca, N.Y.: Cornell University Press, 1997.

——. Reversing the gun sights: Transnational civil society targets land mines. *International Organization* 52 (1998): 613–644.

—— and Nina Tannenwald. Norms and deterrence: The nuclear and chemical weapons taboos. In *The culture of national security: Norms and identity in world politics*, ed. Peter J. Katzenstein, 114–143. New York: Columbia University Press, 1996.

Provencher, Raymonde. *War babies*. Montreal: Macumba Productions, 2002.

Pupavac, Vanessa. *Children's rights and the new culture of paternalism*. Sheffield: Sheffield Hallam University Learning Centre, 2002.

——. Misanthropy without borders: The international child rights regime. *Disasters* 25, no. 2 (2001): 95–112.

Raghavan, Sudarsan. Rape victims, babies face future labeled as outcasts. *Miami Herald*, December 7, 2004. http://www.peacewomen.org/news/Sudan/Dec04/outcasts.html.

Rains, Olga, Lloyd Rains, and Melynda Jarratt. *Voices of the left behind*. New Brunswick, N.J.: Project Roots, 2004.

Ramet, Sabrina, ed. *Women and society in Yugoslavia and the Yugoslav successor states*. University Park: Pennsylvania State Press, 1999.

Ramos, Howard. *Setting the human security agenda: News media coverage of international human rights*. Working paper, Canadian Consortium on Human Security, 2005.

Raven-Roberts, Angela. Gender-mainstreaming in United Nations peacekeeping operations: Talking the talk, tripping over the walk. In *Gender, conflict and peacekeeping*, ed. Dyan Mazurana, Angela Raven-Roberts, and Jane Parpart, 43–64. Lanham, Md.: Rowman and Littlefield, 2005.

Rees, Madeleine. International intervention in Bosnia-Herzegovina: The cost of ignoring gender. In *The postwar moment: Militaries, masculinities and international peacekeeping*, ed. Cynthia Cockburn and Dubravka Zarkov, 51–67. London: Lawrence and Wishart, 2002.

Rehn, Elizabeth and Ellen Johnson Sirleaf. *Women, war and peace*. New York: UNIFEM, 2002.

Reinharz, Shulamit. *Feminist methods in social research*. Oxford: Oxford University Press, 1992.

Reljić, Dušan. The news media and the transformation of ethnopolitical conflicts. In *Berghof handbook for conflict transformation*, ed. Martina Fischer, 1–17. Berlin: Berghof Research Center for Constructive Conflict Management, 2004.

Reproductive Health for Refugees Consortium. *Conference proceedings: Findings on reproductive health of refugees and displaced populations*. New York: Author, 2000. Available online at http://www.rhrc.org/resources/general_reports/conoo/conood.html.

Rieff, David. *A bed for the night: Humanitarianism in crisis*. New York: Simon & Schuster, 2002.

Rimmer, Susan Harris. Orphans or veterans? Justice for children born of war in East Timor. In *Born of war: Protecting children of sexual violence survivors in conflict zones*, ed. Charli Carpenter, 53–77. Bloomington, Conn.: Kumarian, 2007.

Risse, Thomas, Stephen Ropp, and Kathryn Sikkink, eds. *The power of human rights: International norms and domestic change*. Cambridge: Cambridge University Press, 1999.

Robertson, Chris and Una McCauly. The return and reintegration of child soldiers in the Sudan. *Forced Migration Review*, September 2004, pp. 30–32.

Robinson, Bridget. Putting Bosnia in its place: Critical geopolitics and the representation of Bosnia in the British print media. *Geopolitics* 9, no. 2 (2004): 379.

Rodgers, C. S., A. J. Lang, E. W. Twamley, and M. J. Stein. Sexual trauma and pregnancy: A conceptual framework. *Journal of Women's Health* 12, no. 10 (2003): 961–970.

Rodgers, Jane. Bosnia, gender and the ethics of intervention in civil wars. *Civil Wars* 1, no. 1 (1998): 103–116.

Ron, James. *Frontiers and ghettos: State violence in Serbia and Israel*. Berkeley: University of California Press, 2003.

——, Howard Ramos, and Kathleen Rodgers. Transnational information politics: NGO human rights reporting, 1986–2000. *International Studies Quarterly* 49 (2005): 557–587.

Rozario, Santi. Disasters and Bangladeshi women. In *Gender and catastrophe*, ed. Ronit Lentin, 255–268. London: Zed, 1997.

Sadkovich, James. *The US media and Yugoslavia 1991–1995*. London: Praeger, 1998.

Salzman, Paul. Rape camps as a means of ethnic cleansing. *Human Rights Quarterly* 20, no. 2 (1998): 348–378.

Schabas, William. *An introduction to the International Criminal Court*. Cambridge: Cambridge University Press, 2004.

Scheper-Hughes, Nancy and Carolyn Fishel Sargent. *Small wars: The cultural politics of childhood*. Berkeley: University of California Press, 1998.

Seaton, Jean. The new ethnic wars and the media. In *The media of conflict*, ed. Tim Allen and Jean Seaton, 43–63. London: Zed, 1999.

Seifert, Ruth. War and rape: A preliminary analysis. In *Mass rape: The war against women in Bosnia-Herzegovina*, ed. Alexandra Stiglmayer, 54–72. Lincoln: University of Nebraska Press, 1994.

Senjak, Marijana. *When somebody says the word "rape" it is as if somebody is calling my name: Ten years later*. Proceedings of a workshop at the International Trauma Study Program at New York University. On file with author. 2002.

Serbia's shame, on film. *LA Times*, April 14, 2006.

Shanks, Leslie and Michael J. Schull. Rape in war: The humanitarian response. *CMAJ*, October 31, 2000, p. 163.

Sideris, Tina. Rape in war and peace: Social context, gender, power and identity. In *The aftermath: Women in post-conflict transformation*, ed. Sheila Meintjes, Anu Pillay, and Meredeth Turshen, 142–157. London: Zed, 2001.

Simmons, Beth. *Mobilizing for human rights: International law in domestic politics*. Cambridge: Cambridge University Press, 2009.

Simon, Thomas W. United Nations Convention on the Wrongs to the Child. *The International Journal of Children's Rights* 8, no. 1 (2000): 1–13.

Skjelsbæk, Inger. Sexual violence in the conflicts in ex-Yugoslavia. In *War discourse and women's discourse: Essays and case-studies from Yugoslavia and Russia*, ed. Svetlana Slapsak, 117–146. Ljubljana, Slovenia: Ish-Fakulteta Za Podiplomski Humanissticni Studij, Topos, 2000.

——. Victim and survivor: Narrated social identities of women who experienced rape during the war in Bosnia-Herzegovina. *Feminism and Psychology* 16, no. 4 (2006): 374–403.

Slapšak, Svetlana. The use of women and the role of women in the Yugoslav war. In *Gender, peace and conflict*, ed. Inger Skjelsbæk and Dan Smith, 161–183. London: Sage, 2001.

Smillie, Ian and Larry Minear. *The charity of nations: Humanitarian action in a changing world*. Bloomfield, Conn.: Kumarian, 2004.

Smith, Helena. Rape victims' babies pay the price of war. *The Observer*, April 16, 2000.

Stache, Soeren. Bosnian actors celebrate Golden Bear for "Grbavica." *Deutsche-Press Agentur*, February 19, 2006. http://movies.monstersandcritics.com/news/article_1131143 .php/Bosnia_actors_celebrate_Golden_Bear_for_Grbavica.

Stanley, Penny. Reporting of mass rape in the Balkans: Plus ça change, plus c'est la même chose? From Bosnia to Kosovo. *Civil Wars* 2, no. 2 (1999): 74–110.

Steans, Jill. *International relations: Perspectives and themes*. London: Longman, 1996.

Stefansson, Anders. Urban exile: Locals, newcomers and the cultural transformation of Sarajevo. In *The new Bosnian mosaic: Identities, memories and moral claims in a post-war society*, ed. Xavier Bougarel, Elissa Helms, and Ger Duijzings, 59–80. London: Ashgate, 2007.

Stephens, Sharon. *Children and the politics of culture*. Princeton, N.J.: Princeton University Press, 1995.

Stiglmayer, Alexandra, ed. *Mass rape: The war against women in Bosnia-Herzegovina*. Lincoln: University of Nebraska Press, 1994.

Stoddard, Abby. *Humanitarian alert: NGO information and its impact on US foreign policy*. Bloomfield, Conn.: Kumarian, 2006.

Stover, Eric and Rachel Shigekane. Exhumation of mass graves: Balancing legal and humanitarian needs. In *My neighbor, my enemy: Justice and community in the aftermath of atrocity*, ed. Eric Stover and Harvey Weinstein, 85–103. Cambridge: Cambridge University Press, 2004.

Sullivan, Stacy. Born under a bad sign. *Newsweek*, September 23, 1996.

Swiss, Shana and Joan Giller. Rape as a crime of war: A medical perspective. *Journal of the American Medical Association* 270, no. 5 (1993): 612–615.

Sylvester, Christine. *Feminist international relations*. Cambridge: Cambridge University Press, 2002.

Tamayo, Juan. Abandoned babies conceived by rape are war's new casualty. *Times-Picayune*, January 28, 1993, p. A-18.

Tarrow, Sidney. *The new transnational activism*. London: Cambridge University Press, 2005.

Thomas, Daniel. Boomerangs and superpower: International norms, transnational networks and US foreign policy. *Cambridge Review of International Affairs* 15 (2002): 25–43.

Three Serbs on trial over gang-rape camps. *The Toronto Star*, March 21, 2000.

Tickner, J. Ann. *Gendering world politics*. New York: Columbia University Press, 2001.

Toomey, Christine. Cradle of inhumanity. *Sunday Times*, November 12, 2003.

Torgovnik, Jonathan. *Intended consequences: Rwandan children born of rape*. New York: Aperture Foundation, 2009.

Trinder, Liz, Julie Feast, and David Howe. *The adoption reunion handbook*. West Sussex: John Riley and Sons, 2004.

True, Jacqui. National selves and feminine others. *Fletcher Forum of World Affairs* 17, no. 2 (1993): 75–89.

UNHCR. *Prevention and response to sexual and gender-based violence in refugee situations: Inter-agency lessons learned*. Geneva: Author, 2001.

——. *Protecting refugees: Questions and answers*. Brochure. Geneva: Author, 2002.

——. *Refugee children: Guidelines on protection and care*. UNHCR Refworld, 1994. http://www.unhcr.org/cgi-bin/texis/vtx/refworld/rwmain?docid=3ae6b3470.

——. *Report on situation of women and children in Bosnia-Herzegovina and Croatia*. Geneva: Author, 1993.

——. *Sexual violence against refugees: Guidelines on protection*. Geneva: Author, 1995.

UNICEF. *Children born of sexual violence in conflict zones: Considerations for UNICEF response*. Outcome document of a meeting held November 23, 2005. On file with author.

——. *Children and women in Bosnia and Herzegovina : A situation analysis*. New York: Author, 1994.

——. *Filling knowledge gaps: A research agenda on the impact of armed conflict on children*. Florence: Innocenti Institute , June 2–4, 2001.

——. *Principles and guidelines for the ethical reporting on children and young people under 18 years old*. New York: UNICEF Press Office, 2002.

United Nations. *Universal Declaration of Human Rights*, 2009, Article 25, no. 2. http://www.un.org/Overview/rights.html.

United Nations Secretary-General. *Women, peace and security*. Study for the secretary-general pursuant to Security Council Resolution 1325. New York: United Nations, 2002. UN Doc. S/2002/1154.

United Nations Security Council. *Cross-cutting report on children and armed conflict*. New York: United Nations, 2008.

——. *Final report of the commission of experts established pursuant to Security Council Resolution 780*. New York: United Nations, 1994. UN Doc. Gen/1994/674.

United States v. Goring, 22, Trial of the Major War Criminals Before the International Military Tribunal 411, 475 (1948).

University of Alberta. *Phase I: Impact report*. Edmonton: Children and War Project, University of Alberta, 2004.

van der Vyver, Johan. Civil society and the International Criminal Court. *Journal of Human Rights* 2, no. 3 (2003): 425–439.

Vandenberg, Martina. Peacekeeping, alphabet soup, and violence against women in the Balkans. In *Gender, conflict and peacekeeping*, ed. Dyan Mazurana, Angela Raven-Roberts, and Jane Parpart, 150–167. Lanham, Conn.: Rowman and Littlefield, 2006.

Vranic, Seada. *Breaking the wall of silence: The voices of raped Bosnia*. Zagreb: Anti Barbarus, 1996.

Vujačić, Veljko. Institutional origins of contemporary Serb nationalism. *East European Constitutional Review* 5, no. 4 (1996): 51–61.

Walker, Matt. Insult to injury. *New Scientist*, June 21, 2001, pp. 10–11. http://www.newscientist.com/article/dn907-insult-to-injury.html.

Walsh, Martha. Women's organizations in post-conflict Bosnia and Herzegovina. In *Women and civil war*, ed. Krishna Kumar, 165–183. London: Lynne Reinner, 2001.

The War and Children Identity Project. *Our goals*. http://www.warandchildren.org/our%20goals.html (accessed August 8, 2009).

The War and Children Identity Project. *Who are they*. http://www.warandchildren.org/who%20are%20they.html (accessed February 11, 2009).

Ward, Jeanne. *If not now, when? Addressing gender-based violence in refugee, internally displaced and post-conflict settings*. New York: Reproductive Health for Refugees Consortium, 2002.

Watson, Alison M. S. Children and international relations: A new site of knowledge? *Review of International Studies* 32 (2006): 237–250.

Wax, Emily. Rwandans struggle to love children of hate. *Washington Post*, March 29, 2004.

Weber, Cynthia. *International relations theory: A critical introduction*. London: Routledge, 2005.

Weiss, Thomas. Humanitarian principles and politics. *Ethics and International Affairs* 13 (1999): 1–22.

——. *Military-civilian interactions: Humanitarian crises and the responsibility to protect*. New York: Rowman and Littlefield, 2005.

—— and Cindy Collins. *Humanitarian challenges and intervention*. 2nd ed. Boulder, Colo.: Westview, 2000.

Weitsman, Patricia. Children born of war and the politics of identity. In *Born of war: Protecting children of sexual violence survivors in conflict zones*, ed. Charli Carpenter, 110–127. Bloomfield, Conn.: Kumarian, 2007.

——. *The discourse of rape in wartime: Sexual violence, war babies and identity*. Paper presented at the annual meeting of the International Studies Association, Portland, Oregon, February 26–March 1, 2003.

Weldes, Jutta. Going cultural. *Millennium: Journal of International Studies* 28, no. 1 (1999): 117–134.

Wendt, Alexander. What is IR for? Notes toward a post-critical view. In *Critical theory and world politics*, ed. Richard Wyn Jones, 205–224. Boulder, Colo.: Lynne Rienner, 2000.

Wessels, Michael. *Child soldiers: From violence to prevention*. Cambridge: Cambridge University Press, 2007.

Weston, Kath. *Gender in real time: Power and transience in a visual age*. London: Routledge, 2002.

White, Harrison C. *Identity and control*. Princeton, N.J.: Princeton University Press, 1992.

Whitney, Craig. Peacemaking's limit. *New York Times*, May 21, 1993.

Williams, Louise and Leonie Lamont. Rape used over and over as a systematic torture. *The Sydney Morning Herald*, September 11, 1999.

Williamson, Carol. Bosnia's orphans of rape: Innocent legacy of hatred. *LA Times*, July 24, 1993.

Williamson, Jan. *Bosnian children of war: The adoption question*. New York: International Social Service, 1993.

Willsher, Kim. The baby born of inhumanity. *QNP*, January 12, 1993.

——. The outcast. *QNP*, March 7, 1993.

Wilmer, Franke. *The social construction of man, the state and war: Identity, conflict and violence in the former Yugoslavia*. New York: Routledge, 2002.

Wing, Adrian and Sylke Merchan. Rape, ethnicity and culture. *Columbia Human Rights Law Review* 25, no. 1 (1993): 1–48.

Wolfson, Stephen and Neill Wright. *A UNHCR handbook for the military on humanitarian operations*. Geneva: UNHCR, 1994.

Wood, Elisabeth Jean. Variation in sexual violence during war. *Politics & Society* 34, no. 3 (2006): 307–342.

World Council of Churches. *Rape of women in war: A report of the Ecumenical Women's Team visit*. Geneva: Author, 1992.

World Health Organization. *Reproductive health during conflict and displacement: A guide for program managers*. Geneva: Author, 2000.

Yuval-Davis, Nira. *Gender and nation*. London: Sage, 1997.

Zalewski, Marysia and Jane Parpart. *The man question in international relations*. Boulder, Colo.: Westview, 1998.

Zarkov, Dubravka. *The body of war*. Durham, N.C.: Duke University Press, 2007.

——. War rapes in Bosnia: On masculinity, femininity, and the power of rape victim identity. *Tijschrift Voor Criminologie* 39, no. 2 (1997): 140–151.

INDEX

abandonment of children born of war rape; 4, 17, 18, 74, 88, 196, 230n41; adoption and, 131; in Bangladesh, 24, 144; in Bosnia, xiii, 1, 25, 29–34, 55, 64, 72, 73, 75, 77, 90, 91, 93, 116–17, 213n81; as evidence of "barbarity," 56, 60, 61, 62; as nonpriority of aid agencies, 81–82; UNHCR on, 89; UNICEF and, 182

abortion, 109, 117, 120–22, 213n81

abortion, abortions, of children born of war rape, 24, 26, 70, 143–144, 230n41; forced, 29, 203n56, 230n41; late-term, 22, 95, 149; papal opposition to, 74, 122

abortion, abortions, of children born of war rape in Bosnia-Herzogevina, 9, 25, 34–35, 115–17, 203n58, 205n81; Islamic NGOs and, 95; late-term, 149, 203n56; legality of, 22; numbers of, 199n44, 202–203n52; prevention of access to, 22, 108, 109–110, 120–21, 141, 199n46. *See also* forced pregnancy

abuse of children born of war rape, 3, 4, 34, 50; in Bosnia, xiv, 17, 25, 73, 87, 93; by mothers, 182, 186, 205n81; protection against, 18, 39, 40, 49, 131, 201n16; in Rwanda, 17, 26; in Uganda, 27–28. *See also* neglect of children born of war rape; sexual abuse

adolescence, 35–36

adoption of children born of war rape, 36, 70, 226n85; in Bangladesh, 31, 143; in Bosnia, xii, 37, 88, 94, 131, 149, 150, 182, 209n43, 210n1, 211n13, 216n54; Britain and, 31, 49, 63, 91, 209n44; changing laws for, 88; under CRC, 88–89; early as best, 35; facilitation of, 89; foreign or international, 31, 64, 74, 89, 91–92, 143, 144, 209n43, 211n13, 216n54, 217n64; immediate, 30; Muslims and, 64; overstated need for, 91–92; in UNHCR manual, 216n53; in war zone, xiii; by Westerners, 60, 217n63. *See also* Muhić, Alen

Royalties from the publication of this book will be used to support the education of Alen Muhić.

To assist efforts to support other survivors of sexual violence and their children in Bosnia-Herzegovina, readers are encouraged to donate to Medica Zenica:
Medica Zenica Women's Association
Krivače 40, 72000 Zenica Bosnia and Herzegovina
Tel/Fax =387 32 463 924
Email: medica1@bih.net.ba
Website: http://medicazenica.org

To support educational grants for children born of genocidal rape in Rwanda, readers are encouraged to donate to Foundation Rwanda:
Foundation Rwanda
241 Avenue of the Americas, Suite 14C
New York, NY 10014, USA
Email: info@foundationrwanda.org
Website: http://www.foundationrwanda.org/